HANDWRITTEN

HANDWRITTEN

EXPRESSIVE LETTERING IN THE DIGITAL AGE

HANDW

EXPRESSIVE

STEVEN HELLER & MIRKO ILIĆ

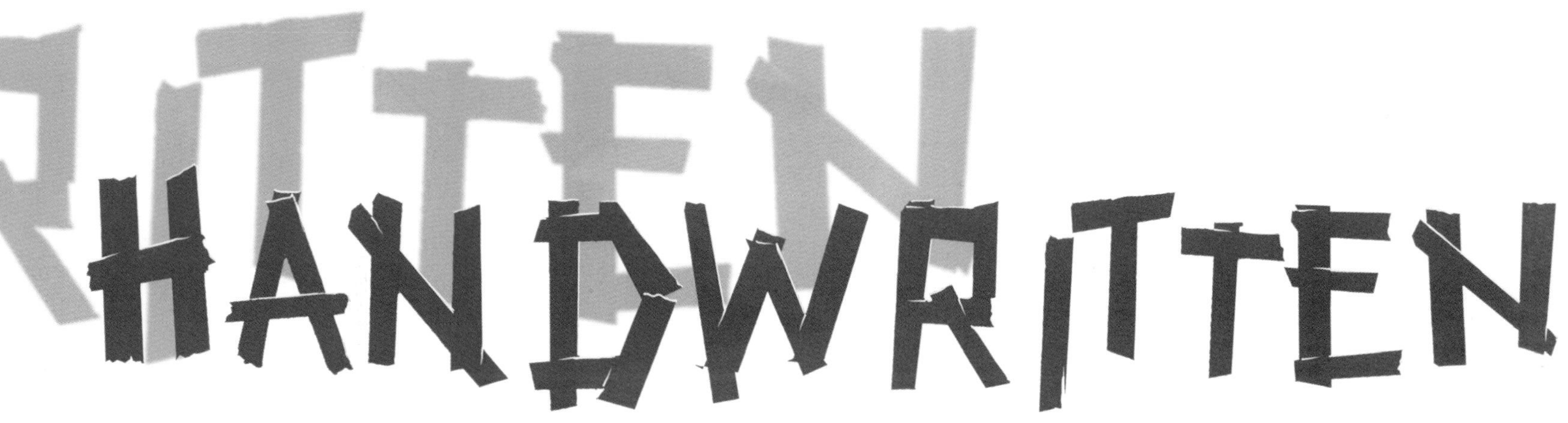

HANDWRITTEN

LETTERING IN THE DIGITAL AGE

This book is dedicated to
R. Crumb, master of hand-drawn letters.

With over 500 illustrations.

Acknowledgments

The authors are indebted to Simona Barta for her hard work and loyal support during the research and production of this book. Without her, there would be no book.

Our deep gratitude goes to our editors at Thames & Hudson, Lucas Dietrich and Catherine Hall: to Lucas for seeing the value in an anthology of this timely material and to Catherine for shepherding the project from conception to completion with skill and patience.

Thanks also to Luka Mjeda for photographing much of the material in the book. We are further indebted to various friends and colleagues who have aided and abetted us in obtaining the material herein: Laetitia Wolff, Steven Brower, Rob Treadway, Design Depo, Andrea Lopes, Dejan Krsić and Jasna Rackov.

And, last but not least, hats off to all the contributors to this book. Without their cooperation we would have had to handletter everything ourselves.

– SH and MI

First published in 2004 in hardcover in the United States of America by Thames & Hudson Inc., 500 Fifth Avenue, New York, New York 10110

thamesandhudsonusa.com

First paperback edition 2006

Library of Congress Catalog Card Number 2004102379

ISBN-13: 978-0-500-28595-4
ISBN-10: 0-500-28595-0

Printed and bound in China by C & C Offset

Chapter opener lettering by Ina Salz

pp 4–5: Drawings by R. Crumb
for the story *Frosty The Snowman and His Friends*, 1975.

table of contents

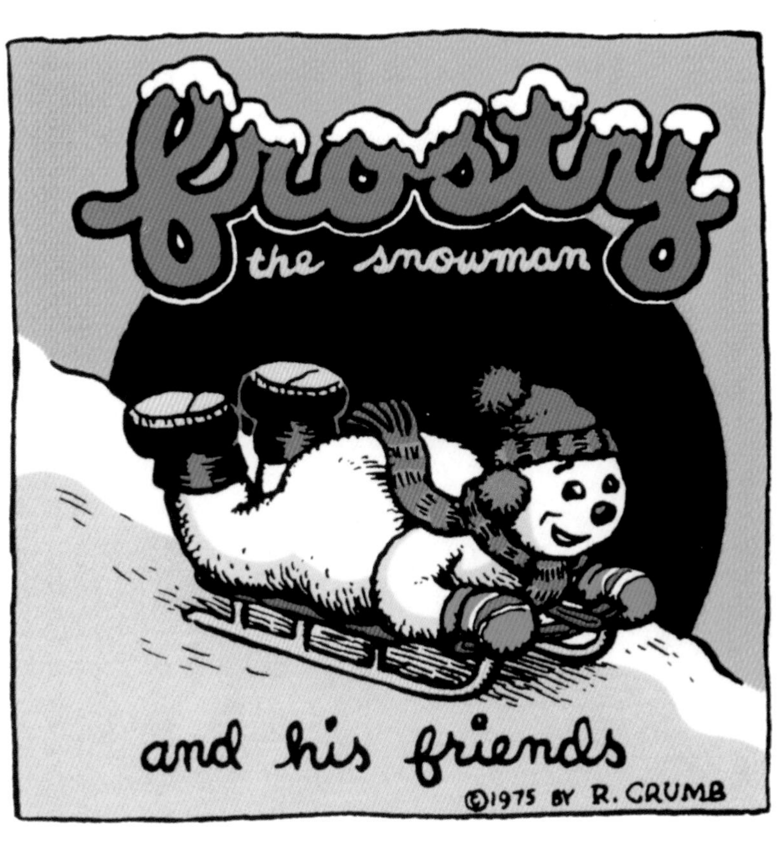

Long before the computer, artists and artisans used a very complex tool for making letterforms: their hands. At five digits per hand it was the first digital lettering tool, drawing, carving and engraving letterforms in all shapes and sizes. Even allowing for various technological flaws and idiosyncrasies, the hand has still enabled the creation of some of the most beautiful lettering ever devised, which underscores the paradox that after centuries of progress we have both gained and lost something with new technology. The computer has made arduous procedures unnecessary and has allowed for increased precision, yet it has also atrophied instincts needed to create beautiful and beautifully bawdy handlettering. Although drawing on screen is perhaps no less complicated than it is on paper by hand, the newer method eliminates that fortuitous edge unique to the older one.

The motto of *Handwritten* is 'the hand is mightier than the pixel', and the book chronicles a full-scale trend in handlettering throughout graphic design today. This may sound strange in an era consumed by new media, but it is arguably also a predictable reaction to the peculiarities of the digital revolution.

During the 1990s, veteran designers had to reconcile themselves to the consequences of new digital media and neophytes had to define the computer's effects. It became possible to conduct brazen typographic experiments that challenged legibility and readability. Old typefaces were remade to conform to new digital standards and novel ones exploited the surprising programmatic tics and quirks. The tenets of fine typography were abandoned for freedom of

sleight

expression. The 1990s saw fonts become popularized and type become almost as common in the public's consciousness as popular music. Any artist or designer with the software could produce and distribute unique alphabets and letterforms simply because the personal computer brought type into everyone's home. No longer was type the purview of skilled craftsmen alone, and this realization induced a major reaction: handlettering, of an expressively witty and artful, yet also artless, variety.

The forms surveyed here are nothing new in the history of modern graphic design; the hand has long been the tool of choice and, while not always the fastest or most precise, it is the most emotive. Going directly from hand to paper (or wood, stone, textile) is the most effective means of achieving unfettered communication. Nonetheless, styles change as technology advances, and the widespread introduction of type-setting machines (hot type and phototype) in the early-twentieth century altered the definition and increased the parameters of art and design. When Bauhaus typography master László Moholy-Nagy (1895–1946) pronounced a 'mechanical art for mechanical times', he was asserting that the modern era was no longer dictated by the past and that all aspects of art and design must be transformed to fit new paradigms.

Progress hit graphic design with a vengeance throughout the twentieth century when photography, photomontage and other mechanical techniques more or less replaced drawing and painting (unless it was surreal or abstract). Type became more geometric, its

# of hand

streamlined form connoting speed and motion and knocking staid calligraphic styles out of fashion. As typesetting evolved from hot metal to film, precision became the quintessential virtue, and the advent and adoption in the late 1940s of the grid as design's most necessary armature replaced rationalism with eclecticism. Only a few universal typefaces were sanctioned for use in this design scheme, which developed into a rigid style that was ripe for a counter-reaction in the 1960s and 1970s, characterized, in part, by a handlettering renaissance.

Typesetting is official; handlettering is informal. Typesetting is mechanical; handlettering is expressive. The hand made a comeback in the 1980s, as now, in profound and imaginative ways that drew on both the past and the present. Yet, for inspiration, designers do not return to medieval times when nobles made merry with sheep and scribes laboriously composed ornate manuscripts in cloistered towers far from the allure of barnyard sirens. Although it helps to know the long legacy of handlettering and to understand that it was integral to graphic design for centuries after the invention of moveable type, it does not matter today if designers reinvent the wheel since each person's hand tends to produce unique signatures.

Some historical rumination is useful to illustrate where handlettering came from and where it is going to. In the early-twentieth century, typographers and type designers produced precise lettering by hand because time, technology and economy demanded it. When photostats were too expensive, handlettering was the cheapest way to create a custom-made headline for a book jacket, poster or point-of-purchase display. Sho-Card lettering, the creation of handmade, one-of-a-kind advertisements in the early-twentieth century, demanded a decidedly high degree of lettering know-how; not just copying existing traditional alphabets but devising novel and novelty scripts, sans serifs and hybrids. To expertly handletter in the 'old days' was the equivalent of mastering QuarkXPress, Illustrator or PhotoShop today. A virtuoso of handlettering is William Addison Dwiggins (1880–1956); the book spines and title pages he created in the 1920s and 1930s were flawless specimens. What designer today wouldn't give their right arm (or right foot) to hand draw letters with such grace?

Dwiggins's work was more formal than informal because his books were designed to stand the test of time. However, other designers engaged in ad-hoc writing simply as a respite from the rigour of traditional typography and as a way of loosening up their work. Examples abound, and during the late 1930s it was fairly common for designers to use brush and pen scrawls as display lettering and personal signature. Paul Rand (1914–96), a modernist pioneer of mass-market advertising, frequently used a light-line, hand-drawn script instead of conventional type to give certain advertisements (notably those for New York's Orbachs department store) the informality necessary to intimately involve the audience. Handwriting became an antidote to the hard-sell Gothic type conventions that prevailed in most newspaper adverts. Rand's playful scrawls became

his signature style and were ultimately used on packages for IBM computer and typewriter products and various book covers and annual reports.

At the same time, Alex Steinweiss, the first graphic designer to create original artwork for 78rpm record covers and who later helped invent 33⅓ LP album packaging, developed Steinweiss Scrawl lettering to inject quirky character traits into his illustrative album designs. Steinweiss's curlicue script was licensed to the New York-based PhotoLettering Inc. and sold as a standard typeface to those looking for a more colloquial sensibility. Similarly, Alvin Lustig (1915–55), the modernist graphic, interior and product designer, used handwriting on book jackets to complement expressionistic collage and montage. Lustig sought to re-create the plasticity of such modern painters as Paul Klee (1879–1940) and Mark Rothko (1903–70) in commercial art rather than conform to rigid standards, and his informal hand script contributed to this fluidity. Concurrently, a fashion reigned (particularly in book-jacket design) for conventional calligraphy that Rand and Lustig argued was too decorous and stiff. Instead, they believed, handwriting was more natural and, therefore, consonant with the anti-ornamental tenets of Modernism.

There is no shortage of examples from the 1940s and 1950s of handlettering created for commercial purposes; but by the mid to late 1960s, it had become a socio-political statement. With the beginnings of the American Underground Press in the 1960s, the clarion of alternative cultures (anti-war, civil rights, sex, drugs and rock'n'roll), graphic styles radically changed from precisionist to ad hoc in reaction to the real and symbolic implications of professionalism. In the design language of the time, purposefully artless handlettering intensified the schism between alternative and mainstream methods (and was a subtle protest against the latter's authority). Words scrawled in an untutored way using a magic marker became headlines in underground papers and on posters that criticized the establishment's social, cultural and economic stance on war, race and gender. Posters produced by the 1968 French radical student design collective, Atelier Populaire, never contained standard type but instead such phrases as 'Fascist Vermin', 'Order Begins' and 'We Are the Power', violently inscribed by a designer's hand, underscored the polemic import of each message.

A more aesthetic side was practised by psychedelic poster artists who fashioned a meticulous hand-rendered lettering language based on the resurrection of old Victorian wood types and Art Nouveau metal types. In the United States, Victor Moscoso helped mastermind psychedelic alphabetics by using the negative spaces between letters (and not the letters themselves) to create vibrating sensations. Every detail was rendered by hand to maintain the total control necessary to achieve Moscoso's typographic optical illusions; moreover, there were no economical technologies available that could match his obsessive artistry – the computer had not yet been personalized.

As a radical lettering style psychedelic art did not last long, although handlettering continued to be popular throughout the 1970s and into the early 1980s. With the introduction in the 1980s of the Apple Macintosh as graphic design's primary design and typography tool, handlettering's role in the design world diminished. Type designers scurried to create typefaces for the new digital platforms, experimenting with bitmapped and high-resolution concoctions that led to a postmodern typographic style rooted in such new traits as degradation and distortion. Nonetheless, a unique phenomenon arose that married handlettering concepts with high-tech digital software. Designers in the 1990s, many of whom had never before designed a typeface, used the new programs to transform otherwise one-of-a-kind handlettered beauties *and* monstrosities into downloadable font packages available to anyone. Thus the age of ersatz handlettering began.

Handwritten does not cover the earlier periods of handlettering, but many of the designers and illustrators in the book pay homage to those times. Instead, this book focuses on the lettering produced in the late 1990s and early 2000s, which might be called 'the new scrawl': brush, ink, sewn, stencilled and carved work, delicate and indelicate, personal scribbling that sometimes flouts and other times simulates conventional letterforms. Since one of the consequences of computer-aided design is the standardization of formats proficiently used ad nauseam by anyone with a template, returning to hand work and play has enabled designers to imbue their work with greater distinction, leading to some outrageous and innovative work.

For handlettering, the variations are finite and the genres limited, so we have collected a solid representation of the best individual approaches, from untutored scrawls to sophisticated swashes in numerous media and for diverse purposes. We have also categorized them under headings starting with 'S' that suggest the means and methods of production. Some of the designers are fine typographers who use this form as a respite from the rigours of more conventional design, others are novices who do not possess the skill to do anything more finished. The paradox of this book is that by showing this as unconventional work it implies its own conventionality. The fate of most avant-gardes is acceptability. When and if every designer makes scrawls instead of using type, a natural reaction to conformity will ensue. But, for now, the strength of the hand is in its ability to render serendipitous results.

[pp 4–9] **R. Crumb created these unique, tongue-in-cheek drawings** and quirky variations on the lettering for a 1975 version of the classic Christmas tale *Frosty The Snowman and His Friends.*
Illustrator, letterer: R. Crumb Editor: Art Spielgelman Client: *Arcade* magazine

raw, splotchy, untidy

Websters defines scrawl as, 'To write, draw, or mark awkwardly, hastily, or carelessly; esp. to write with sprawling, poorly formed letters.' Furthermore, when written with verve and vibrato the word 'scrawl' is the perfect onomatopoeia; we can actually hear the awkward letter amalgamation and guttural intonation. It sounds like it looks and looks like it sounds. In the dictionary 'scrawl' follows 'scratch' (a mark, scrape or cut), which is another chapter found later in this book. However, here scrawl precedes scratch because today it is the more prevalent form of handlettering. Under the scrawl rubric are marks so rudimentary that anyone can make them – and everyone probably has – but in truth not everyone makes them with the same panache as the people featured on the following pages.

It requires artistry to concoct the perfect scrawl, and it demands a real artist to make it then work in a visual composition. A sophisticated hand and knowing eye are prerequisites – even the most raw, splotchy and untidy scrawls are often rendered with curious grace, flair and, yes, a degree of self-control. If this sounds like a meaninglessly complicated over-rationalization about marks that are meant to be resolutely irrational and anarchic, the fact is that scrawl is deliberately (often with considerable forethought) employed in graphic design as an emotive and expressionistic component. When outstandingly rendered, it can be more demonstrative than the boldest Gothic typeface in the largest point size.

Scrawls in contemporary design, created usually with brushes but also with pens, markers, crayons and grease pencils, are as much graphic conceit as philosophical statement. In the digital era, when perfection is only a keystroke away, to scrawl is the logical alternative – a slap in the (type)face – to official typography. Yet you need to be very conscientious to scrawl. Scrawling words on a layout may seem like it is diametrically opposed to placing proper Helvetica or Univers on a grid, but it is not so. In fact, such gridlocked design is so standardized as to be unrepentantly knee-jerk. Conversely, for scrawled lettering to succeed, it takes a modicum of trial and error and an acute sense of what works.

Scrawlers are not always untutored. While they may not be capable of drawing pristine alphabets (which requires a significant amount of learned skill), they are not merely brazen doodlers. However, not all scrawls are created equally. The reason some scrawls are more resonant than others depends on the renderer's, dare one say, magical ability to make random marks on paper come alive. The impromptu essence of a scrawl is doubtless further enhanced by some kind of genetic strand that allows the artist's hand to conjure beauty through improvisation. The best scrawling is a form of automatic writing in which serendipity is key, however, in the right hands not every scrawl is totally surprising. The signature scrawl of satiric cartoonist and author Ralph Steadman is formally predictable and yet never routine; it is a form of handwriting so violent that you can virtually see the artist's arms flailing around (with mouth foaming) as he writes. Each stroke has inherent properties that underwrite his overall graphic personality. He has proven that even the most aggressive scrawl can

be turned into a stunning composition that draws attention as it stimulates contemplation.

Despite its increased application in the digital era, scrawl is not a new phenomenon. Before the turn of the nineteenth century, lithography had made drawing letters directly onto the litho stone easier than typesetting them in wood or metal. While some of the era's most well-known posters and printed ephemera were run through presses more than once to imprint an extra layer of type, the master poster artists, including Henri de Toulouse-Lautrec, Jules Chéret and Alphonse Mucha, drew directly with grease crayon on the litho surface to avoid using type in favour of a totally integrated artistic composition. While some of their respective letterforms were precisely conceived and rendered to achieve a formal look, the majority was deliberately ad hoc. Chance reigned supreme – designers often had only one opportunity to make the perfect rendering – and thus scrawl was elevated to the status of high commercial art. Not all nineteenth-century scrawls were so artistically motivated, however; sometimes a scrawl was no more or less than convenience, the fastest means of inscribing a message – and the essence of the word itself.

Scrawl has three manifestations in design history. The first is in the presence of the artist's hand, integrating art, design and message into seamless compositions, as in the great advertising posters of the late-nineteenth century. The second is in the deliberate rejection of official type to convey emotion and expression in often dispassionate media, generally political manifestos. The third is simple economy: when designers could not afford to purchase costly hand-set or machine-set type they turned to scrawling. Most designers were skilled enough to flawlessly re-create (or simulate) actual typefaces because from the nineteenth to the mid-twentieth centuries they had been highly trained. Meanwhile, other artisans tossed formal concerns to the wind and made resolutely impromptu letterforms that did not resemble anything in the specimen books.

With the dawn of the Modern Movement and the introduction of a machine-age graphic style, typified by the rejection of such antiquated ornamental design conceits as Victorian Tuscans and countless other decorative typefaces, a preference grew (and an ideology prevailed) for a few austere geometric sans-serif faces. Well-ordered, precisely composed columns of bold type replaced the calligraphic sensibility so rooted in late-nineteenth-century commercial art. In place of antiquated fonts and stuffy calligraphy, which was abhorred, handwriting and especially scrawled writing was welcomed. Whereas calligraphy was mannered (even the curvaceous variety), the scrawl was more *au naturel* – unpretentious and immediate. 'I never did calligraphy,' stated the American Modernist pioneer Paul Rand, 'but handwriting is an entirely different kind of thing. It's part of the syndrome of Modernism. . . . It's part of that asceticism.'

The handwritten scrawl to which Rand refers is not just an emblem of Modernism, nor simply a symbol of asceticism. It is also a tool of postwar anti-Modernism and 1980s and 1990s Postmodernism, used to dirty the sanctified (and often monotonous) modernist grid.

During the 1950s, when clean and precise Helvetica and Univers ruled and when orthodox modernists followed strict templates to attain formal purity signifying a triumph of rationalism over emotionalism, the scrawl became something of a rebellious banner. While harmonious typefaces and crisp photographs were relied on by modernist graphic designers to communicate a universal design language, scrawl was occasionally introduced on posters, packages, book and record covers, where personal and emotive approaches worked best to convey the message. For example, Ben Shahn (1898–1969), the American painter, printmaker, book-cover and poster artist, preferred to draw his own letterforms that reflected the stark linearity of his art and increased the expressive power of his work. Likewise, Seymour Chwast and Milton Glaser, the co-founders in 1954 of Push Pin Studio, did their fair share of scrawling, combining lettering and illustration to produce a complete work of art.

Scrawled letters were used by tutored designers in the 1950s as a deliberate conceit, but by the psychedelic 1960s and through the punk 1970s, scrawl became the most expedient do-it-yourself tool. Standard typefaces were not cheap and drawing precise display letters was time consuming, which left handwriting as the viable economic alternative and one that came to define the graphic style of an eclectic era. For some psychedelic artists with design training, scrawl had a formal underpinning (the work of Pablo Picasso, Paul Klee and Marcel Duchamp), but for most it was a practical means of conveying a message, regardless of any aesthetic virtue.

Underground newspapers and hippie posters of the 1960s slapped willy-nilly onto the layout a veritably unedited mélange of disparate graphic elements. Owing to the immediacy and convenience of photolithography, handscrawling directly onto the layout board was so easy as to become a matter-of-fact method. Nonetheless, psychedelic artists' work was both ad hoc and studied: the classic rock posters were intensively handlettered to approximate or invent immutable letterforms that harked back to the ornamental days, but improvised scrawls printed in vibrant and vibrating colours were also prevalent when time or drugs ran out. In the early 1970s, underground sensibilities gave way to punk, a movement in which 'designers' were shamelessly anti-art in their introduction of cut-and-paste ransom-note lettering. Yet, these ransom-note letterers actually cared about the look of things; other punk artists did not care at all and simply scrawled their messages (headline and body texts) in magic marker in the roughest, ugliest and most irreverent ways. By so doing, they made a statement about the superficiality of the entire design process.

Symbolically, scrawl has had even more profound political applications beyond hippie and punk cultural anarchy. Putting aside graffiti, the most popular and historic of all scrawls, rough-hewn letters are generally found in many political – especially protest – missives. During the Vietnam war (running concurrently with the psychedelic era), quite a few posters were professionally produced, but the ones with the most immediacy, like Lorraine Schneider's classic placard showing a sickly flower with the slogan 'War Is Not Healthy for Children and Other Living Things' (1968) scrawled in coarse, broad strokes, were the most powerful of the era's iconography because they were heartfelt. Alsatian Tomi Ungerer's series of acerbic antiwar posters, including one with the word 'Eat' scrawled over a Vietnamese man who is physically forced to succumb to American might, was memorable because it was so graphically raw. The posters of Atelier Populaire, the graphics arm of the group that organized the 1968 French student and worker strike against the right-wing government of Charles de Gaulle, were the quintessence of ad-hoc lettering with bold but simple images and hand-scrawled letters that defined the aesthetic of rebellion. Influenced by Polish poster art of the 1950s and 1960s and its almost exclusive use of hand scrawls as a means to avoid censorship during the typesetting process, these polemic graphics were used in the service of the political moment. The design lessons learned from the 1968 strike, for example, were reapplied decades later by the graphics collective Grapus (comprised of Atelier Populaire members) for posters that addressed political and cultural concerns in post–de Gaulle France.

Many years later, during the 2003 Iraq war, scrawl was employed again, not as a conceit but as a necessity. Throughout the United States and Europe protesters took to the streets with official and handmade signs that were purely about function and not aesthetics. In Iraq itself, a nation where the print medium (and no less so the electronic media) was restricted to government supporters alone, the opposition had no choice but to scrawl. After the war, on a wall near an abandoned racetrack, photographers recorded a handwritten Arabic

message: 'Happy Birthday Saddam Hussein, you donkey'. Blocks away, another scrawl insults the two main Kurdish party leaders: 'Jalal [Talabani] and Massoud [Barzani] are pimping for the nasty Bush'.

Regardless of the political message, in the current design milieu most handwork is not as much about polemics as it is about a formalist response to digital perfection. With so many templates on the market designed to insure a pedestrian standard of competent design, the need to break free from the grid has driven some to seek sublime imperfection. As an alternative to mediocrity, flawed artistry is better than conformist predictability.

Scrawl emerges in a variety of sub-genres and mannerist categories. Joshua Berger's 'Scary Nightmare' lettering for a cover of *Plazm* magazine (see p. 15) represents the stalker's crayon scrawl, suggesting the presence of something ominous. Likewise, Jugoslav Vlahovíc's rendition of the word 'Gerila' (see p. 32) is the blood scrawl designed to provoke a sense of dread. Conversely, Maria Kalman's book *Hey Willy, See the Pyramids* (see p. 25) presents a swishy brush-stroke scrawl, meant as a lyrical rendering of pleasant words into soothing sounds. On a controversial note, the covers for 'Appetite' and 'Design Anarchy' (see p. 15), for the anti-branding magazine *Adbusters,* use handlettering as a code for anti-professionalism and rebellion against commercial culture. At the other end of the commercial spectrum, Doug Rucker and Kyle Friedel's 'Eat Mor Chikin' (see p. 46) on the Chick-fil-A billboard is a faux drippy scrawl that parodies graffiti. Then there are font designer Pepe Gimeno's grease-crayon markings that are the epitome of artlessness (see p. 29). Alternatively, Henry Steiner's 'Observatoire International des Prisons' (see p. 32), a poster cautioning against prisoner abuse, is a mannered signature scrawl that suits his comic impromptu drawing style. Similarly, another mannered method is Michal Batory's poster for the '20e Fête de la Musique' (see p. 38), a carefully jotted scrawl that clearly expresses a textual message and a decidedly spontaneous approach. Also, Daniel van der Velden's 'Loveletter' (see p. 28) is unadulterated handwriting, the truest of all the examples. Gary Panter's illustrations about the Branch Davidian Compound Site in Waco, Texas (see p. 25), with map and notes, are doodle scrawls raised to the level of art by the seamless way the art and letters are combined. The record sleeve for Lord High Fixers (see p. 52) by American Art Chantry demands an active response from the viewer.

Some scrawl, like Panter's 'Waiting for Waco', is a (seemingly) perfect extension of the creator's personality; other examples, like Justin Fines's magazine advertisement for Ecko (see p. 51), appear a little contrived though no less convincing as personal expression. Finally, David Shields and Mark Todd's type for *Cat Fish Hens* (see p. 23) is the vernacular scrawl, writing so endemic to everyday life that it is hard to distinguish it from more regimented design.

Anything is possible with scrawl. If it were prescribed, it would not be scrawl. One thing is common to all scrawl: resolute awkwardness. Nothing aligns and little is balanced. So, as purposeful (i.e. designed) as scrawl may be, it is the marriage of gawky and awkward, combined with rowdy and rough, that makes scrawl so compelling.

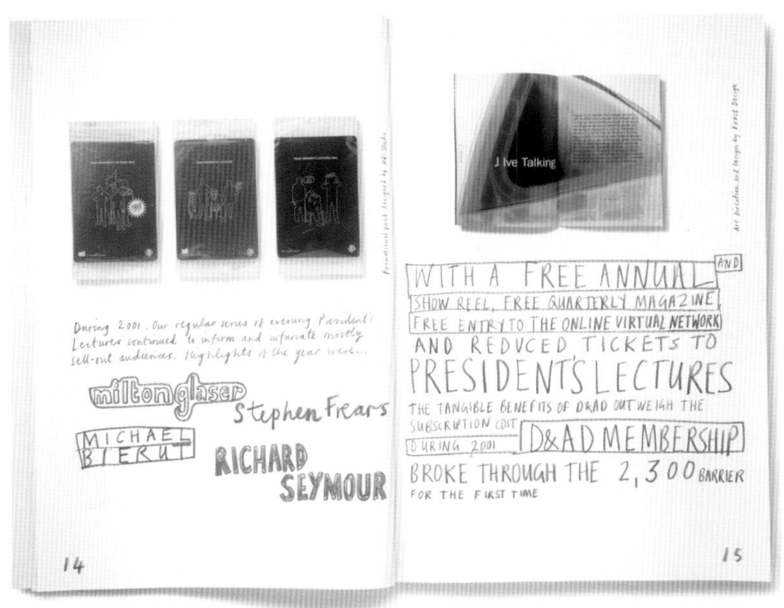

Scrawl is recognized as an acceptable typographic form when a leading design organization, in this case D&AD, uses it in its annual report. These scrawls are both demonstrative and subdued to contrast with the slick design work.
Designer: Vince Frost Letterer, illustrator: Marion Deuchars Client: D&AD

Hand scrawling is the main mission for *[Kak]*, a Russian graphic-design magazine. Each issue explores how many ways and on how many surfaces scrawl can communicate and add texture to the covers.
[right] 'Art of Illusion' and [below] 'American Design' Designer: Petr Bankov Letterer, illustrator: Vlad Vasilyev
Photographer: Andrey Gutnik [bottom right] 'Design of Periodical Editions' Designer, letterer: Petr Bankov
Photographer: Andrey Gutnik Client: *[KAK]*

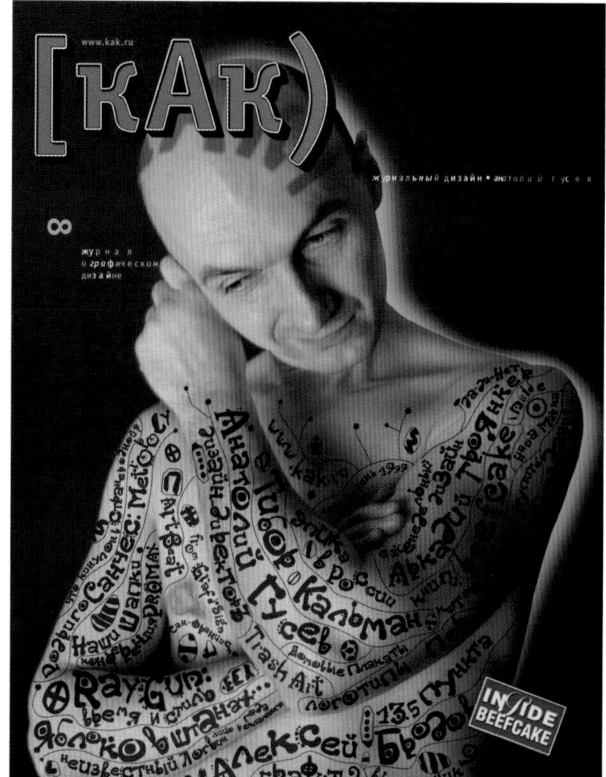

In a graffiti-like manner, *Adbusters* frequently uses marker scrawls to show its contempt for bourgeois design practices while still practising what it considers to be good design.
[left] 'Appetite' Designer: *Adbusters* Cake-maker: Dominique Jarry Photographer: Shannon Mendes
[bottom left] 'Design Anarchy' Designer, photographer: *Adbusters* Letterer: Mike Simons Client: *Adbusters*

Charles Manson's famous killing spree is brought to mind in the crayon lettering on this magazine cover for *Plazm*. Reminiscent of the Helter Skelter writing on the walls at the murder scenes, the filled letters are most eerie.
Art directors: Joshua Berger, Niko Courtelis, Pete McCracken, Enrique Mosqueda Designer: Niko Courtelis
Letterer: John McKenzie Client: *Plazm*

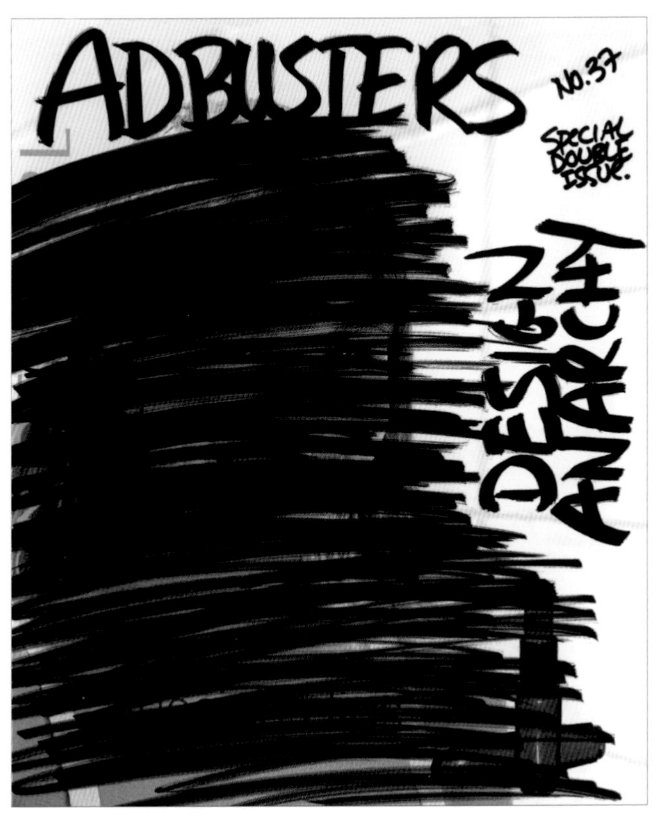

EL MUNDO
METROPOLI
metropoli
cine
para
niños
LAS PELÍCULAS INFANTILES
COPAN LA CARTELERA MADRILEÑA
DURANTE LAS NAVIDADES

EL MUNDO
METROPOLI
Nº 650 DEL 8 AL 14 DE NOVIEMBRE DE 2002
TIENDAS
QUE
VENDEN
DISEÑO
LA NUEVA TENDENCIA QUE SE EXTIENDE POR MADRID

16

EL MUNDO
METROPOLI
LA REVISTA DE MADRID. DEL 8 AL 14 DE MARZO DE 2002
CONCIERTO = THE
CRANBERRIES
(+) DOVER
(+) WEEZER
13-MARZO
PALACIO DE
VISTALEGRE
20 HORAS

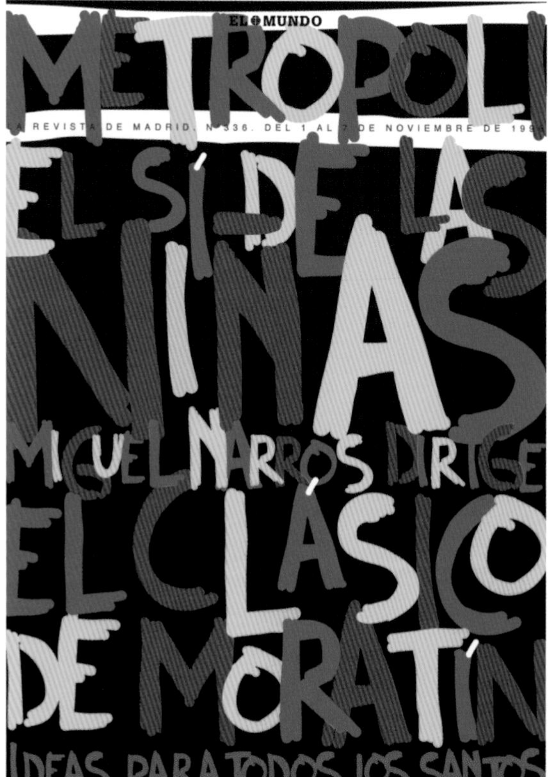
EL MUNDO
METROPOLI
LA REVISTA DE MADRID. Nº 336. DEL 1 AL 7 DE NOVIEMBRE
EL SÍ DE LAS
NIÑAS
MIGUEL NARROS DIRIGE
EL CLÁSICO
DE MORATÍN
IDEAS PARA TODOS LOS SANTOS

ABOVE **Following no particular rule of lettering**, typical brush scrawl nonetheless reveals a certain sophistication, as is apparent in the words and pictures on this cover for issue 89 of *Etapes*.
Art directors: Michel Chanaud, Patrick Morin Artist, letterer: Josef Flejsar Client: *Etapes*

TOP RIGHT **Void of artistic nuance**, this politically motivated writing on a wall is still an artist's commentary; pure type would not offer the same immediacy or emotion as scrawl on this magazine cover for *NY Arts*.
Letterer: Hlynur Hallsson Client: *NY Arts*

RIGHT **It is impossible to pigeonhole** Ed Fella's handlettering as pure scrawl because most of his letters are so artful; yet scrawl is definitely part of it, as seen in the middle line of this magazine cover for *2+3 D*.
Designers: Jacek Mrowczyk, Kuba Sowinski Letterer: Ed Fella
Client: Fundacja Rzecz Piekna WFP ASP, Krakow

OPPOSITE **Taking the art of hand scrawling to new levels**, *Metropoli* has produced covers that reveal a variety of individual signatures and aesthetic sensibilities.
[top left] 'Cine para Niños' Designer: Rodrigo Sanchez Letterer: Sofia Sanchez-Irazusta (age 7)
[top right] 'Tiendas Que Venden Diseño', [bottom left] 'Concierto=TheCranberries(+)Dover(+)Weezer',
[bottom right] 'El Si de las Niñas' Designer, letterer: Rodrigo Sanchez Client: Unidad Editorial S.A.

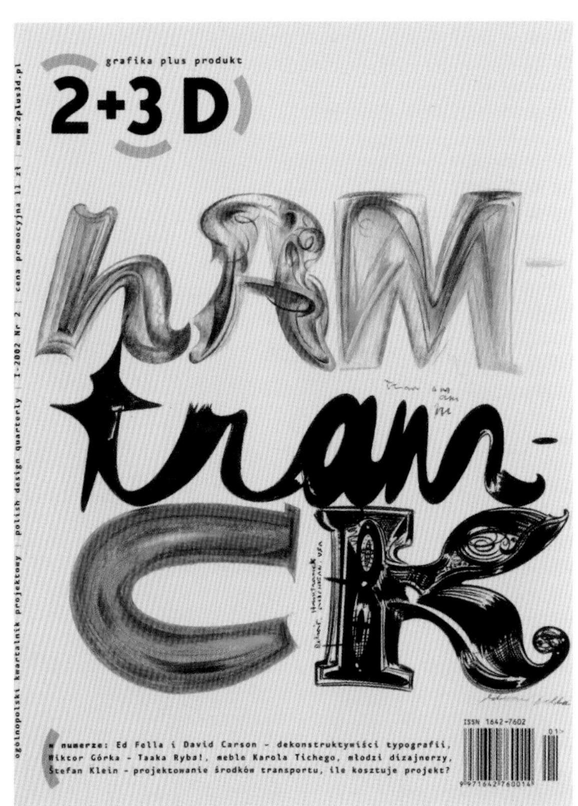

BLANCHE McCRARY BOYD

THE REVOLUTION OF LITTLE GIRLS

"A hilarious feminist road map…so funny that we laugh out loud."

—Michael Dorris, The New York Times Book Review

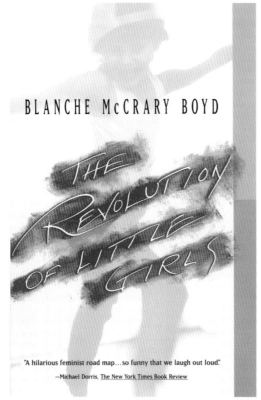

LEFT **Reversing out of a smudge of colour**, the scratched handwriting serves as an aggressive counterpoint to the faint background blur of a female figure on the book cover for *The Revolution of Little Girls*.
Designer, letterer: Susan Mitchell Photographer: Debra Lill Client: Vintage Books

BOTTOM LEFT **Derived from the Gothic, blood-and-gore school**, this mannered scrawl gives the distinct impression of serendipity but is actually quite meticulously and artfully rendered on the book cover for *Vampir z Gorjancev* (*Vampire from Gorjancev*).
Designer, letterer, illustrator: Kostja Gatnik Client: Mladinska Knjiga

BELOW **This terrifying scrawl has become a cliché** of the horror genre and, like every good cliché, creates the desired effect the minute it is seen on this book cover for *The Monster Show*.
Designer, letterer, illustrator: Charlotte Strick Photographer: unknown, publicity still from *The Devil Bat's Daughter* (1946) Client: Faber and Faber

Revised Edition
DAVID J. SKAL
A Cultural History of Horror
"Fascinating . . . lively and entertaining . . . To understand a culture, you must know what it fears."
—Stefan Dziemianowicz, THE WASHINGTON POST BOOK WORLD

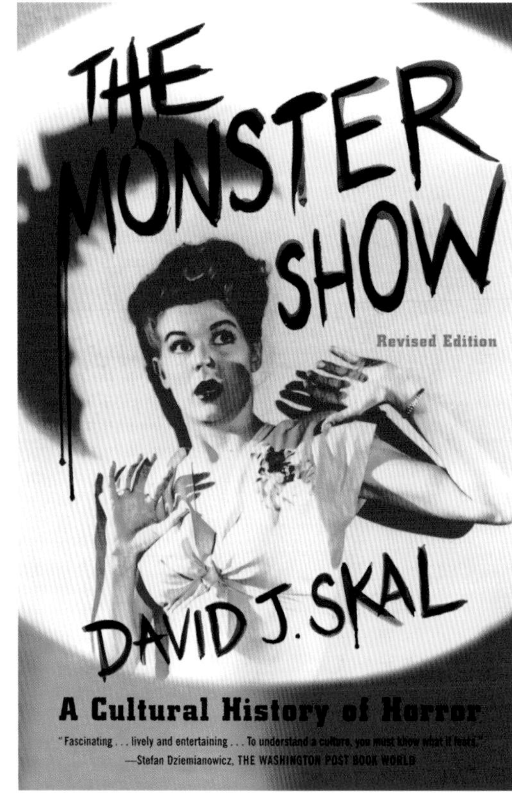

MATE
DOLENC

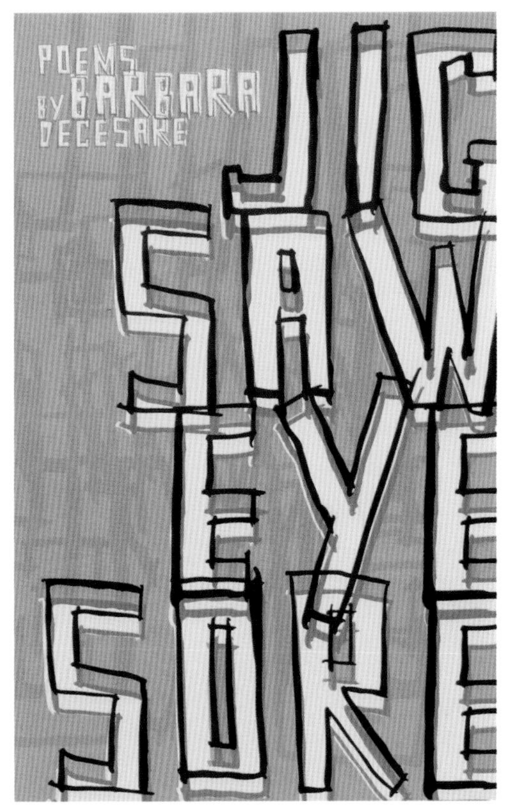

ABOVE **The eye is immediately drawn** to the red-and-blue, sketchy, scrawled title in the middle of the book cover for *Homo Zapiens*, and only after taking that in does it fall on the interesting carnal act below.
Designer, letterer, photographer: Darren Haggar Clients: Penguin USA, Paul Buckley

TOP RIGHT **The shaky, kinetic lettering** throws the eye into a spasm yet also has an almost hypnotic effect that works well with the rhythmic title on the book cover for *Jigsaweyesore*.
Designer: Joe Natoli Letterer: House Industries Photographer: Greg Ekey Client: AntiMan Press

RIGHT **The abstract representation of a rotating** bicycle wheel with the simply rendered title as the hub could be interpreted as a target with the hand-scrawled words as the bull's-eye on this book cover for *The Cyclist*.
Designer: Paul Sahre Letterer: Leanne Shapton Client: Simon & Schuster

THE DEFINITIVE EDITION OF BURROUGHS' SEMINAL FIRST NOVEL
BEFORE HIS 1959 BREAKTHROUGH, NAKED LUNCH, AN UNKNOWN WILLIAM S. BURROUGHS WROTE JUNK, HIS FIRST NOVEL. IT IS A CANDID EYE-WITNESS ACCOUNT OF TIMES AND PLACES THAT ARE NOW LONG GONE, AN UNVARNISHED FIELD REPORT FROM THE AMERICAN POST-WAR UNDERGROUND.
UNAFRAID TO PORTRAY HIMSELF IN 1953 AS A CONFIRMED MEMBER OF TWO SOCIALLY-DESPISED UNDERCLASSES (A NARCOTICS ADDICT AND A HOMOSEXUAL), BURROUGHS WAS WRITING AS A TRAINED ANTHROPOLOGIST WHEN HE UN-APOLOGETICALLY DESCRIBED A WAY OF LIFE – IN NEW YORK, NEW ORLEANS, AND MEXICO CITY – THAT BY THE 1940s WAS ALREADY DEMON-IZED BY THE ARTIFICIAL ANTI-DRUG HYSTERIA OF AN OPPORTUNISTIC BUREAUCRACY AND A CYNICAL, PROSTRATE MEDIA.
FOR THIS FIFTIETH-ANNIVERSARY EDITION, EMINENT BURROUGHS SCHOLAR OLIVER HARRIS HAS PAINSTAKINGLY RECREATED THE AUTHOR'S ORIGINAL TEXT, WORD BY WORD, FROM ARCHIVAL TYPESCRIPTS AND PLACES THE BOOK'S CONTENTS AGAINST A LIVELY HISTORICAL BACKGROUND IN A COMPREHENSIVE INTRODUCTION. HERE AS WELL, FOR THE FIRST TIME, ARE BURROUGHS' OWN UNPUBLISHED INTRODUCTION AND AN EN-TIRE OMITTED CHAPTER, ALONG WITH MANY "LOST" PASSAGES, AS WELL AS AUXILIARY TEXTS BY ALLEN GINSBERG AND OTHERS.
U.S. $14.00
CAN. $21.00
A PENGUIN BOOK | FICTION
ISBN 0-14-200316-6
JUNKY
WILLIAM S. BURROUGHS
EDITED WITH AN INTRODUCTION BY OLIVER HARRIS
JUNKY
WILLIAM S. BURROUGHS
50TH ANNIVERSARY DEFINITIVE EDITION

20

EVERYTHING IS ILLUMINATED
JONATHAN SAFRAN FOER
"A ZESTFULLY IMAGINED NOVEL OF WONDERS... HE WILL WIN YOUR ADMIRATION, AND HE WILL BREAK YOUR HEART" –JOYCE CAROL OATES
ISBN 0-618-17387-0
"DON'T JUST CHECK HIM OUT. READ HIM" — RUSSELL BANKS
"TO CALL IT THE BEST FIRST NOVEL I'VE EVER READ BELITTLES IT. IT IS ONE OF THE BEST NOVELS I'VE EVER BEEN FORTUNATE ENOUGH TO HOLD IN MY HANDS." — DALE PECK
JONATHAN SAFRAN FOER WAS BORN IN 1977 IN WASHINGTON, D.C. HE IS THE EDITOR OF THE ANTHOLOGY A CONVERGENCE OF BIRDS, AND HIS STORIES HAVE BEEN PUBLISHED IN THE PARIS REVIEW AND CONJUNCTIONS. THIS IS HIS FIRST NOVEL, PARTS OF WHICH APPEARED IN THE NEW YORKER. HE LIVES IN QUEENS, NEW YORK, AND IS AT WORK ON HIS SECOND NOVEL, WHICH TAKES PLACE IN A MUSEUM.
JACKET DESIGN: GRAY318
HOUGHTON MIFFLIN COMPANY
222 BERKELEY STREET
BOSTON, MASSACHUSETTS 02116
WWW.HOUGHTONMIFFLINBOOKS.COM

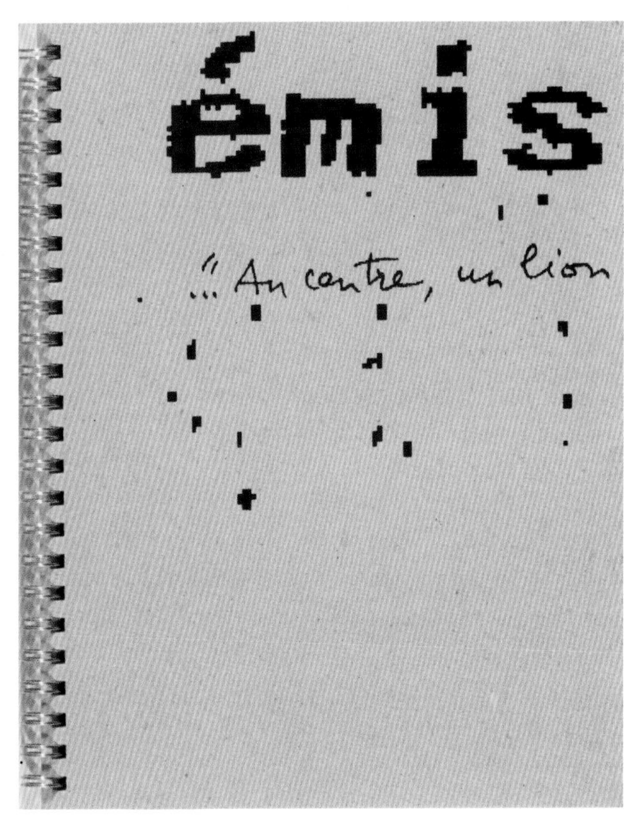

OPPOSITE, TOP **Handlettering was a cheap alternative to type** over fifty years ago; today it is often used on book covers, as here on *Junky*, as a stylistic conceit. William Burroughs's raw account calls for this approach.
Designer, letterer, illustrator: Neil Powell Clients: Penguin USA, Paul Buckley

OPPOSITE, BOTTOM **Sloppy handlettering on this book jacket acts as a virtual introduction**: *Everything is Illuminated* is about a Russian immigrant in the United States who scrawls out oddly transliterated letters.
Designer, letterer, illustrator: Jonathan Gray Client: Houghton Mifflin Books

THIS PAGE **A commentary on the bitmapped clichés** of the computer, the lettering, on the book cover and spread from *Emis*, is also a celebration of all sorts of traditional hand-wrought pen-and-ink renderings.
Letterer: Jean-Paul Bachollet Illustrator: Ronald Curchod Editor: Philippe Bissières Text: Brigitte David Client: *Emis*

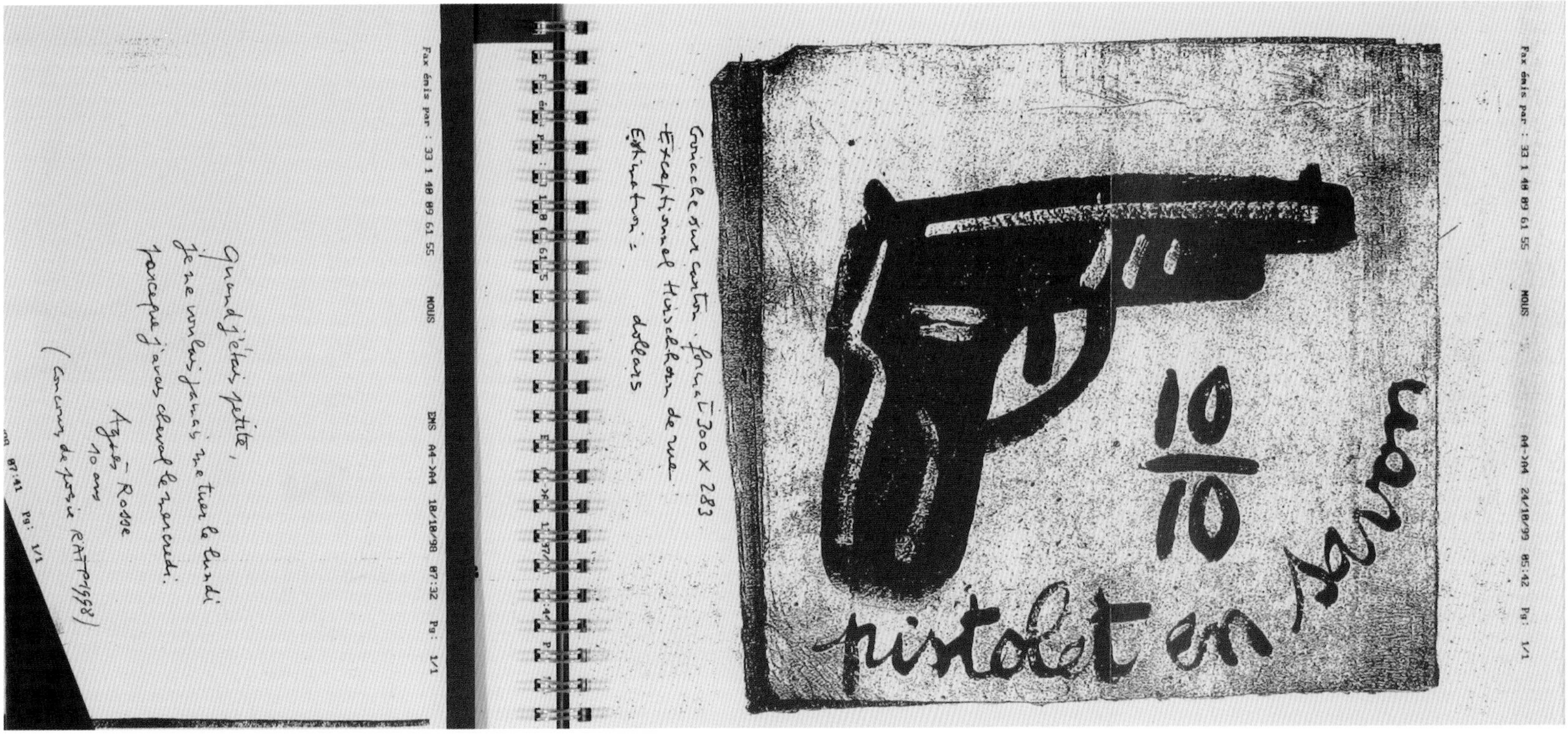

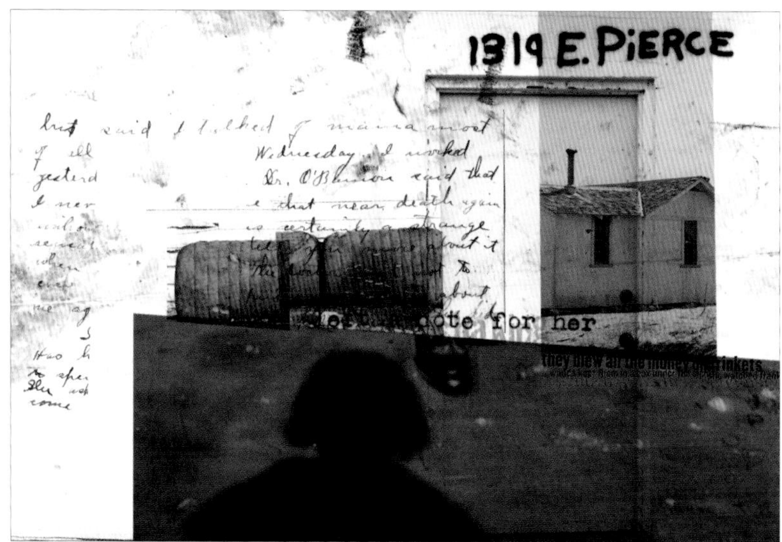

The inelegant scrawl highlights a patina that suggests the book, *Ashes Motors*, was pulled from behind an old box of soiled rags and leaky oil cans.
Designers, letterers, illustrators, photographers: Mark Todd, David Shields Client: White Gas

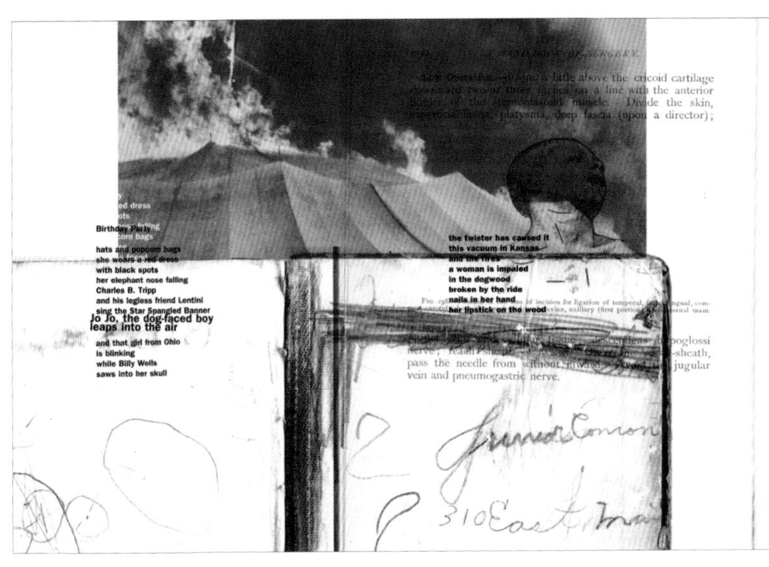

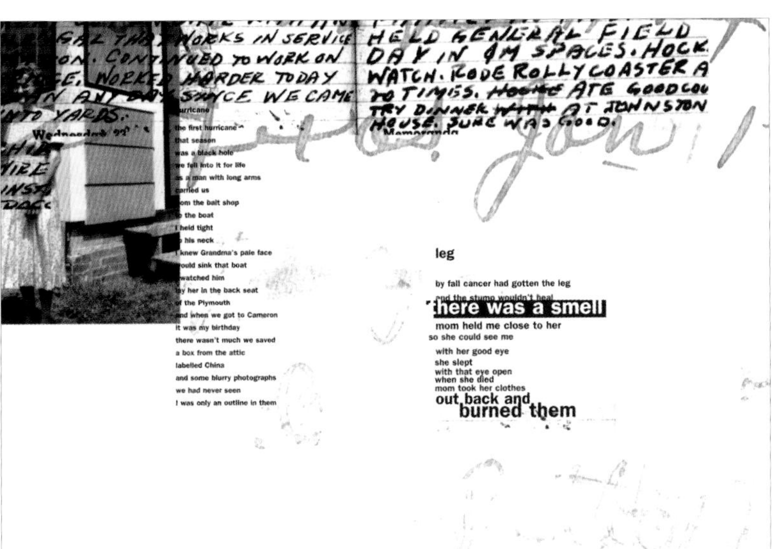

Artist and designer books that look and feel like vintage personal diaries, of which *Cat Fish Hens* is an example, are prevalent today, acting as a counterpoint to the ease of making books on the computer. Designers, letterers, illustrators, photographers: Mark Todd, David Shields Client: White Gas

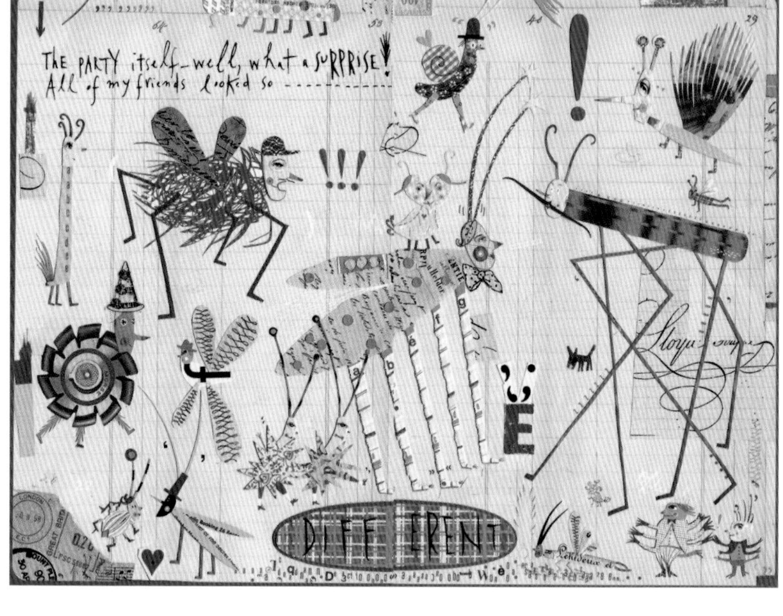

The free-form scrawls, printing and scripts have the same playful quality as the wildly kinetic images in the book *Dear Diary*.
Designer, letterer, illustrator: Sara Fanelli
Clients: Walker Books, Candlewick Press

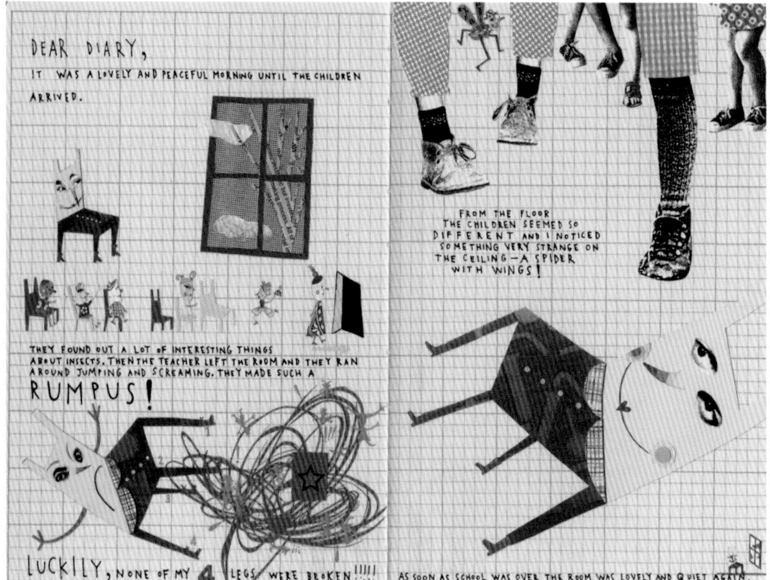

LEFT COLUMN **The writing in these visual essays** about the FBI siege of a religious cult's compound in Waco, Texas conveys the immediacy of being at the tragic event.
Designer, letterer, illustrator: Gary Panter Client: *The New Yorker*

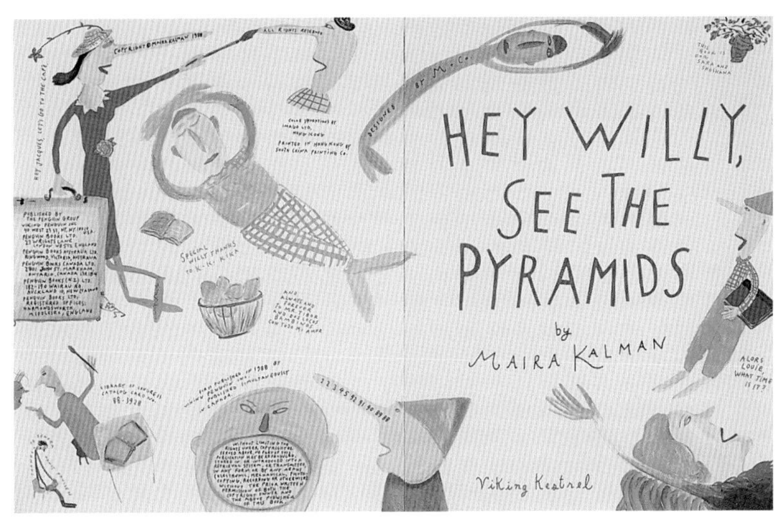

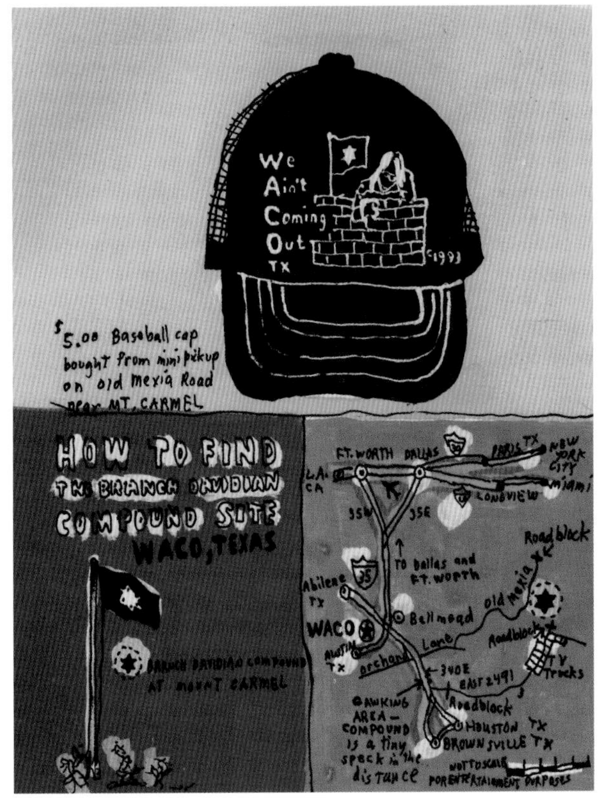

ABOVE **By combining type and handwriting**, Maria Kalman, in her book *Hey Willy, See the Pyramids*, distinguishes between two voices and adds an extra dimension that it is not possible to do with type alone.
Designer, letterer, illustrator: Maria Kalman Client: Viking

RIGHT **To read or not to read**, that is the question. Are these words, for the poster 'Central America and South America', considered as texture or data? The answer must be both because the map is formed by the names of the places that comprise it.
Designer, letterer, illustrator: Paula Scher, personal work

OPPOSITE, TOP LEFT **A sketch of words** drawn from actual commercial signs and messages, this improvisational scrawl for the poster 'Newspapers in Milan' looks like a page from a letterer's journal.
Designer, letterer, illustrator: Leanne Shapton, personal work

OPPOSITE, TOP RIGHT **Attention is drawn immediately** to the texture of these scrawls, but the words themselves are distinct and distinctive. The poster for The Barbican Lectures is designed to be read, not merely experienced.
Designer: C.D.T. London Letterer, illustrator: Marion Deuchars
Client: Barbican Art Centre

OPPOSITE, BOTTOM LEFT **To understand the message**, this poster, 'Materials + Science = Smart', must be read in a logical way. Nonetheless, each word and phrase jumps off the page at varying levels of intensity.
Art director: Michele Charier Letterer, illustrator: Brian Rea
Client: Herman Miller

OPPOSITE, BOTTOM RIGHT **Scrawls of typographic references** to the Red Cross in many languages are used to create a very rational design for this T-shirt. The words frame the negative space as the dominant graphic element.
Designer: Spild af Tid Aps Letterer: Jenz Koudahl
Clients: Baum und Pferdgarten, Danish Red Cross

IMPIEGATI
2668
1500
NUOVI CONCORSI
ASSISTENTI AMMINISTRATIVI
730
980
OFFERTE DI IMPEGIO DE'LL INDUSTRIA PRIVATA
IL POSTO

barbican
KARLHEINZ STOCKHAUSEN
JOHN PILGER - GERMAINE GREER
RALPH FIENNES - TOM STOPPARD
Wynton Marsalis - Adam Caruso
MARTIN PARR - HELMUT NEWTON
Andy Goldsworthy - YO-YO MA
Timberlake Wertenbaker - BIYI BANDELE
ROBERT ALTMAN - MICHAEL WOOD
talks

Flexing Back
MATERIALS + SCIENCE
clever
SIMPLE SOPHISTICATION
INTUITIVE
HONEST
REFRESHING
(PASSIVE) AND ACTIVE ADJUSTMENTS
Dynamic Innovation
SMART
A NEW LEVEL OF PERFORMANCE AND COMFORT THROUGH THE CLEVER USE OF MATERIALS, DESIGN, AND ENGINEERING.
POSTURE FIT SYSTEM
TOTAL BACK SOLUTION
VALUE
ANATOMY
SMART
WORK
APPEAL
Earth friendly
SOMETHING FOR EVERYONE
ONE-SIZE FITS ALL
SUSTAINABLE COMFORT
fresh
CURVY
FUN
Herman Miller

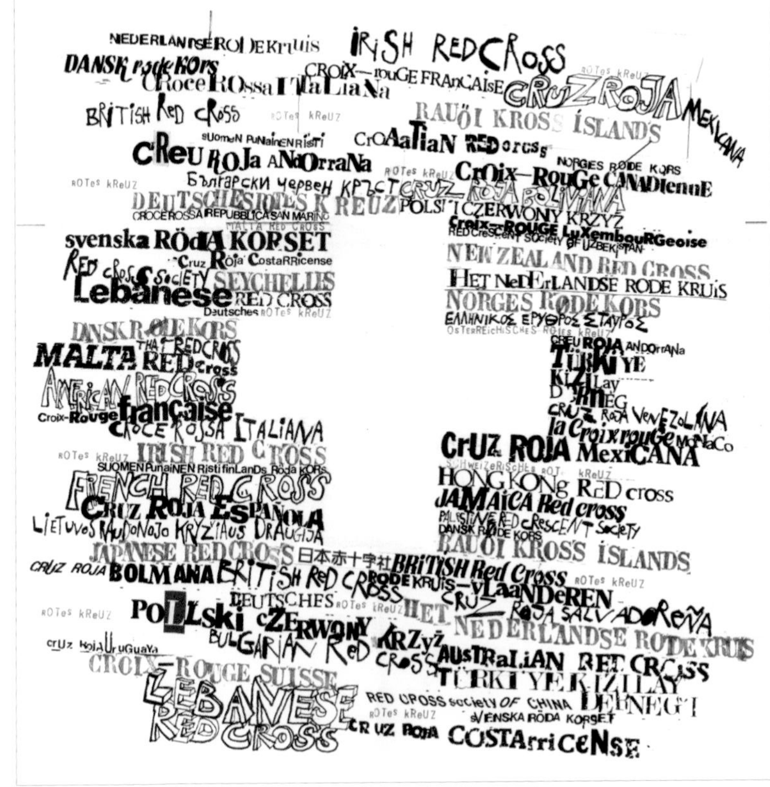
NEDERLANDSE RODE KRUIS
IRISH RED CROSS
DANSK RØDE KORS
CROIX-ROUGE FRANÇAISE
CROCE ROSSA ITALIANA
CRUZ ROJA MEXICANA
BRITISH RED CROSS
RAUÐI KROSS ÍSLANDS
CROATIAN RED CROSS
CRUZ ROJA ANDORRANA
NORGES RØDE KORS
CROIX-ROUGE CANADIENNE
svenska RÖDA KORSET
NEW ZEALAND RED CROSS
HET NEDERLANDSE RODE KRUIS
Lebanese RED CROSS
MALTA RED cross
AMERICAN RED CROSS
Croix-Rouge française
CROCE ROSSA ITALIANA
CRUZ ROJA MEXICANA
IRISH RED CROSS
FRENCH RED CROSS
HONG KONG RED CROSS
JAMAICA Red cross
CRUZ ROJA ESPAÑOLA
RAUÐI KROSS ÍSLANDS
JAPANESE RED CROSS
BRITISH Red Cross
POLSKI CZERWONY KRZYŻ
HET NEDERLANDSE RODE KRUIS
AUSTRALIAN RED CROSS
CROIX-ROUGE SUISSE
LEBANESE RED CROSS
RED CROSS society OF CHINA
CRUZ ROJA COSTARRICENSE

Dear,
This letter is to say that it is over between you and me. I'm so sorry I have to tell you this now. But don't take it personal. I hope we will stay friends.
For some time I have believed, like you, that we would stay together forever. This is over now Some things you shouldn't try to push. but just leave as they are...
As I find writing this letter very painful I won't make it too long. I don't have so much time either, because tonight (friday 25 february 2000) I'm going to the preview of a new show by Mattijs van den Bosch, Ronald Cornelissen, Gerrit-Jan Fukkink, Connie Groenewegen, Yvonne van der Griendt, Hine Kramer, Marc Nagtzaam, Désirée Palmen, Wouter van Riessen, Ben Schot and Thom Vink, 8 pm. I think it is at 1e Pijnackerstraat 100; I forgot the exact address, but I'll see.
Mattijs, Ronald, Gerrit-Jan, Connie, Yvonne, Hine, Marc, Désirée, Wouter, Ben and Thom are all great friends of mine. We will probably go out afterwards.
But this doesn't mean that I don't care about you
I have to go. I'm already late.

goodbye

ROOM invite 210x297 mm
recycled letter

1e Pijnackerstraat 100
NL 3035 GV Rotterdam
T/F 010 2651859
T/F 010 4773880
E roombase@luna.nl

friday / saturday / sunday
1 — 5 PM

ROOM organized by
roos campman / eric campman /
karin de jong / ewoud van rijn
ROEM organized by terry van druten
ROOM thanks to PWS Woningstichting

SIDE 2

ROOM

ROOM

I know this is a very bad moment

p.s. the show is on until april 2

ROOM invite 210x297 mm
recycled letter

1e Pijnackerstraat 100
NL 3035 GV Rotterdam
T/F 010 2651859
T/F 010 4773880
E roombase@luna.nl

ROEM — Marije Mooren
opening 25 2 2000 — 7 PM / 25 2 — 2 4 2000
friday / saturday 1 — 5 PM

Zwaanshals 317
NL 3036 KN Rotterdam
T 010 2763498
E roemroemroem@hotmail.com

O.K. BAD CHCE ABYM OPISAŁ TĘ OTO FOTOGRAFIE. WTEDY TO PODANO MI KOPIE JAKIEJŚ TAM FOTOGRAFII. PROCEDURA WYJASNIAJĄCA PROJEKTU ZAJEŁA TROCHĘ CZASU, JAKO ŻE NIE ŚPIE TERAZ NA SIANIE ALE ŻNIWA SIĘ ZBLIŻAJĄ I ŚPIE NA WIDŁACH, TAK NA IGŁACH ZDECYDOWANIE. JEŚLI CHODZI O MOJE TAK DLA PROPOZYCJI, CHOCIAŻ FOTO JAK FOTO JEDNO Z TYCH KLASYCZNYCH, ŁADNYCH MONA LISA TYP PRACY. CHOCIAŻ FOTOGRAFIA, CZY KAŻDY INNY WYCINEK Z RZECZYWISTOSCI NA CZYMŚ ZAWSZE POTRAFII SKUPIĆ UWAGĘ, I JEST JAK PRACA DOCHODZENIOWA DETEKTYWA, KTÓRY KAŻDEGO DNIA ODKRYWA COŚ NOWEGO, DOSTRZEGA CZY ŁĄCZY W ŁAŃCUCH MOŻLIWYCH ZWIĄZKÓW I WYDAŻEŃ, ZE WZGLĘDU NA TO I TAMTO TZN. OKOLICZNOŚCI TOWARZYSZĄCE OPISYWANEMU W TYM MIEJSCU ZDJĘCIU. NP. CZAS, PORA DNIA, KAWA DOBRA CZY OCHYDNA, FAJNE ŚNIADANIE CZY BRAK OBJADU, POGODA, RELACJA Z DZIEWCZYNĄ, SEN... ITP. MAJĄ KULMINACYJNY WPŁYW NA TO JAK WIDZE, BEZ WZGLĘDU NA TO CO WIDZE. OK. ALE ROBOTA MUSI BYĆ WYKONANA I DLATEGO PRÓBUJE SIĘ SKONCENTROWAĆ NA TYM CO WIDZE:
[CO TO ZA KABEL WISI? ZKĄD? DOKĄD PROWADZI?, CO ON TRZYMA W RĘKACH? CZY TO BANDAŻ NA GŁOWIE MURZYNA MONALISY. JAK SIĘ TAM ZNALAZŁ? DLACZEGO? CO TO ZA POMIESZCZENIE PO PRAWEJ. OCIENIONE. WYKLEJONE GAZETAMI. KULINARNE WYCINKI WYKLEJAJĄ ŚCIANE ZA SIEDZĄCYM. CZY JEST KUCHARZEM? CZY TEN BIAŁY BANDAŻ TO RODZAJ CZEPKA KUCHENNEGO. HMM. JAK MOZAIKA ZE WZORÓW CAŁOŚĆ. PUZZLE. KAŻDY Z ELEMENTÓW TO MOŻLIWE PYTANIE. TAJEMNICZY X. RĘKA W DRZWIACH W RUCHU ZASTYGŁA. DO KOGO NALEŻY BIAŁA PRZEPASKA NA PRZEGUBIE RĘKI Z PIĘŚCIĄ. KUCHARZE CZY BOJOWNICY MOŻLIWE ŻE JEDNO NIE WYKLUCZA DRUGIEGO. KIM JEST TAJEMNICZY Y ZA ŚCIANĄ WNĘKI? PRZY OPISYWANIU ZDJĘCIA OGRANICZAŁA MNIE TYLKO LINIA MARGINESU O 3CM.]

B.a.d Enterprises voor de Foto Biënnale Rotterdam

Ik beschrijf deze foto gemaakt uit een raket
ruimtelyke stuken meubels
een ruimtelijk evaluatie
de mensen die erop staan duiden een
~~plaats~~ ~~voor~~ tydelijk orde aan
het lykt ook wel op een bioscoop platje

blauwe ruimtelijke kleur
met materialistische stuken
oude wetse stoelen
strykplank
oude gordijn
het heeft te maken met een ontsnapping
herkenbare ruimte van mensen
soort ontsnappings ruimte
dierlyke voordracht van ruimte
menselyk voordracht van verdriet en geluk
De Ruimte heeft iets van een afstandelijk houding naar buiten en naar boven
het lykt ook wel op een dokters wachtruimte
een afkedachte parachute sprong

B.a.d Enterprises voor de Foto Biënnale Rotterdam

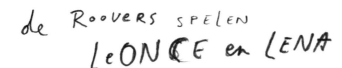

ABOVE **Scrawl is most effective** when located within a generous helping of negative space, as is portrayed elegantly in this poster entitled *Leonce en Lena*.
Designer, letterer, illustrator: Tom Hautekiet Client: Theater Company De Roovers

RIGHT **Had this kind of lettering** been produced by a school child it would have resulted in a failed grade. For this poster, 'The 5th Article of the Human Rights Declaration', the style is most appropriate.
Letterer: Pepe Gimeno Designers: Pepe Gimeno, Suso Pérez Client: Amnesty International

OPPOSITE, TOP **Curiously, resolutely informal handwriting** has become an advertising tool because it draws the eye away from more 'proper' typographies, as shown in this invitation entitled 'Loveletter'.
Designers, letterers: Maureen Mooren, Daniel van der Velden Client: ROOM

OPPOSITE, BOTTOM **It is difficult enough to read tightly lettered** personal correspondence let alone an advert in this style. Somehow, however, the reader is inclined to work at it in this poster called 'Can You Describe a Photograph?'.
Designer, letterer: B.a.d Enterprises Clients: Foto Biennale Rotterdam, Nederlands Foto Instituut

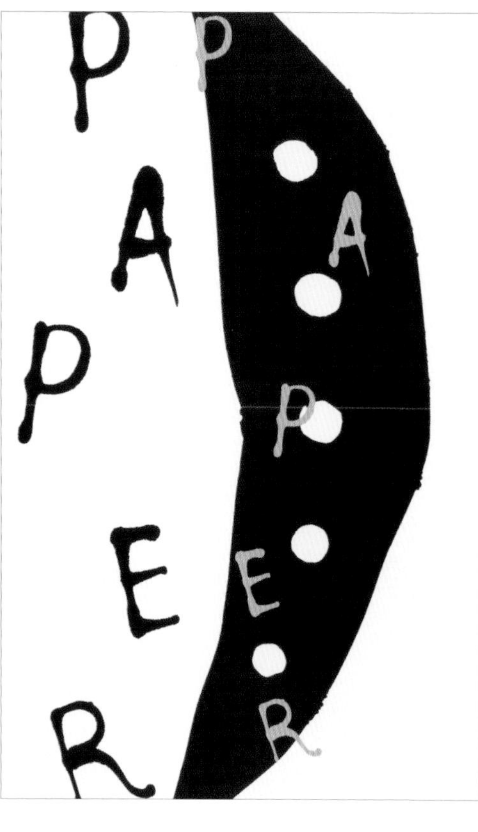

ABOVE **Simple scrawls and quirky shapes collide** to become a startling and enigmatic composition in this poster, 'April Wind Works No. 62', to promote a new type of paper.
Designer, letterer, illustrator: Shin Matsunaga Client: Cross Brand

ABOVE RIGHT **Composed of only a few wide brush strokes** and a delightful colour palette, these letters form a pleasing and readable pattern on the book cover for *Millennium.*
Creative director: Silas H. Rhodes Designer, letterer: George Tscherny Client: School of Visual Arts, New York

RIGHT **Carved out of the book cover material** in such a way, the scrawl appears both representational and abstract on *Design Exchange No. 13.*
Designer, letterer, photographer: Wang Xu Client: China Youth Press

The words seem to have been written by foot, and, as this poster entitled 'Danse 2000 Montpellier 20e Festival International' shows, it is not a bad job of prehensile movement.
Designer, letterer, illustrator: Beata Konarska Client: Galerie Anatome

RIGHT **A pyramid of harsh words** in bold brush scrawls gives weight to Amnesty International's optimistic message that a free man can triumph over tyranny in this poster for the Fiftieth Anniversary of the Universal Declaration of Human Rights.
Designer, letterer, illustrator: Woody Pirtle Client: Amnesty International

BELOW **Logos are supposed to be more finished** than this ersatz signature for Shirim, but the rules are fast changing as identities become too routine.
Designer, letterer: David Croy Client: Shirim

ABOVE **The Jackson Pollock drip method** worked for modern art and also has its place in modern and postmodern graphic design to create a certain mood, as shown on this logo for an LP record cover by Gerila.
Designer, letterer: Jugoslav Vlahovic Clients: Gerila, PGP RTS, Belgrade

RIGHT **While this poster conveys a serious message** about the treatment of prisoners, it does so with a clever doodle and collage that is underscored by a very quick scrawl as headline.
Art director, designer, illustrator: Henry Steiner Client: Amnesty International

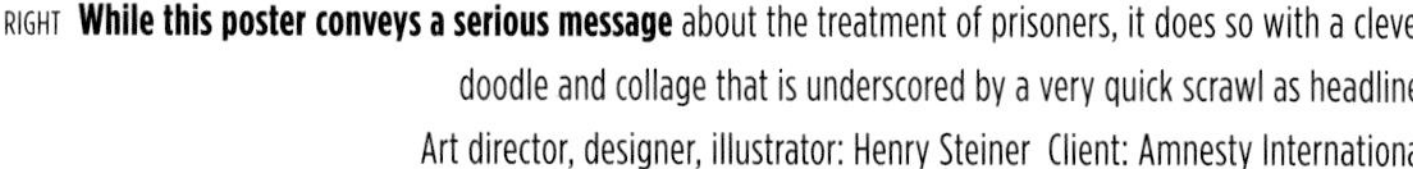

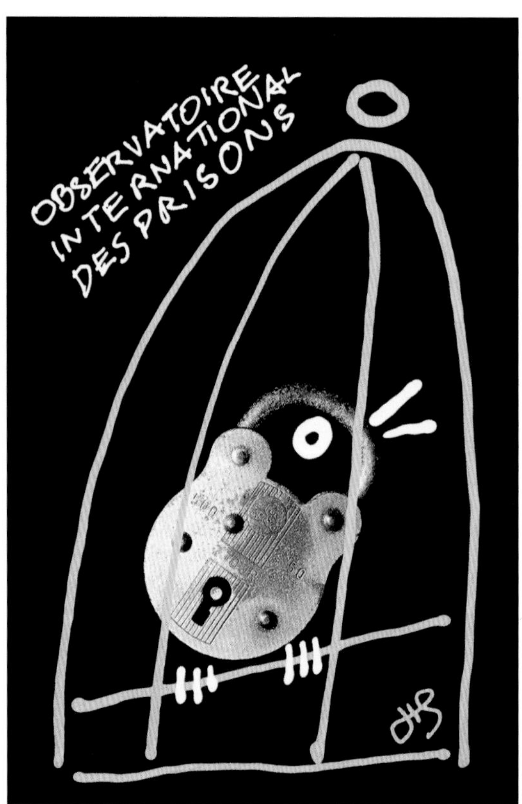

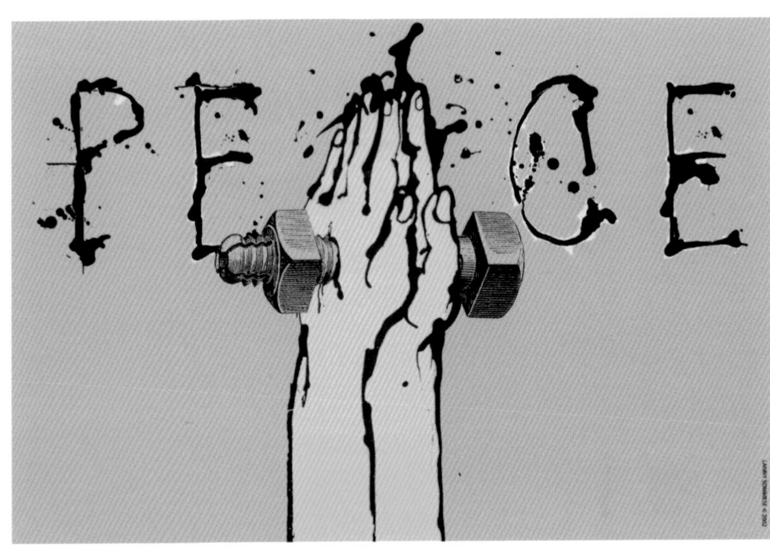

ABOVE **Ouch. This lettering is painfully at odds** with the meaning of the word it presents. Seeing 'peace' in such a violent scrawl on this poster begs the question, what kind of peace?
Art director, designer, illustrator: Lanny Sommese Client: Museum on the Seam, Israel

TOP LEFT **Ironically, everything about the political message** on this poster about Article X of the Declaration of Human Rights is communicated through a menacing hand.
Designer, letterer, illustrator: Oscar Mariné Client: Amnesty International

LEFT **Words communicate ideas**, and this assemblage of Martin Luther King's bons mots that form the civil rights leader's silhouette is a striking way of capturing the meaning and the man in a single image. It was used on the Martin Luther King Day gospel brunch invitation.
Designer: Digital Soup Letterer: PASH Client: I Have A Dream Foundation

LEFT **The brush lettering is inextricably part** of the startling graphic personality of this poster advertising the seventeenth Torino film festival.
Designer, letterer, illustrator: Ryszard Kajzer Client: Torino Film Festival

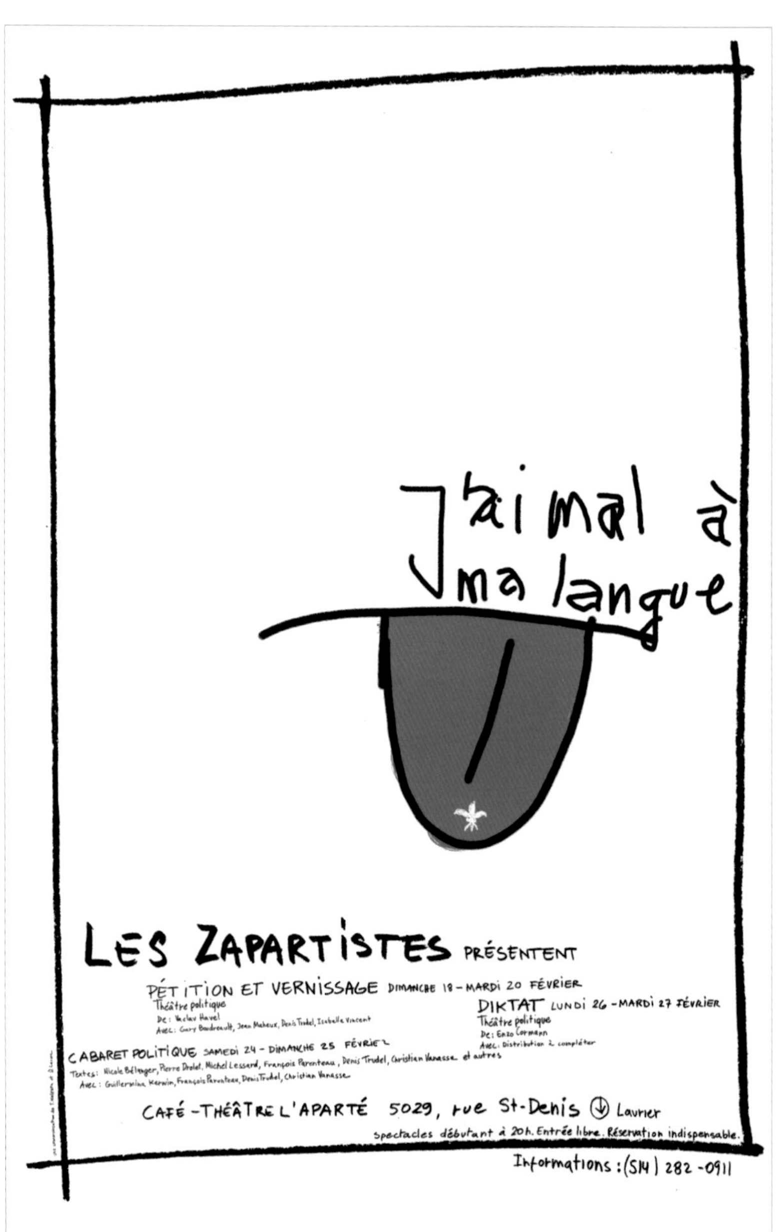

RIGHT **With such a simple drawing as this tongue**, it would be impractical to attempt any kind of standard typesetting; instead, ad-hoc writing is an eye-catching effect on the poster 'J'ai mal à ma langue'.
Designer, letterer, illustrator: Tomasz Walenta Client: Les Zapartistes

LEFT **Handlettering has been a symbol of protest** against the establishment, specifically the political left, ever since the Paris student uprising in 1968. The emotion is continued on this poster called 'L'Engagement politique social'.
Designer, letterer, illustrator: Nous Travaillons Ensemble Client: Chaumont Poster Festival

RIGHT **Not all scrawls are overtly political**, as this poster 'Rendez-vous des associations' indicates, but there is nonetheless an implied anti-bourgeois sensibility in the display of raw lettering.
Designer, letterer, illustrator: Nous Travaillons Ensemble Client: Aubervilliers

LE NOUVEAU SALON des CENT HOMMAGE A L'AFFICHISTE / ODE TO THE POSTER DESIGNER HENRI de TOULOUSE-LAUTREC POUR le CENTENAIRE de sa MORT, FOR THE CENTENARY OF HIS DEATH 1901-2001 • EXPOSITION INTERNATIONALE d'AFFICHES.
UN GESTE DE RESPECT ET DE GÉNÉROSITÉ DE CENT AFFICHISTES DU MONDE ENTIER
A GESTURE OF RESPECT AND GENEROSITY FROM A HUNDRED POSTER DESIGNERS ALL OVER THE WORLD

To honour the anniversary of the death of Henri de Toulouse-Lautrec, various artists produced their interpretation of the master's work, not least his handlettering. Shown here are posters [opposite] and the book, *Le Nouveau Salon des Cent* [right].

RIGHT Art director: Anthon Beeke
Designers: Anthon Beeke, Paulina Matusiak
OPPOSITE: TOP LEFT Designer, letterer, illustrator: George Tscherny
TOP RIGHT Designer, letterer, illustrator: Roger Pfund
BOTTOM LEFT Designer, letterer, illustrator: Heinz Edelmann
BOTTOM RIGHT Designer, letterer, illustrator: Pierre Bernard
Client: Editions Odyssée

exposition internationale d'affiches
HOMMAGE à TOULOUSE LAUTREC
Nouveau salon des cent

Nouveau
Salon
des 100
HOMMAGE à TL

Nouveau
Salon des
Cent
EXPOSITION INTERNATIONALE
d'Affiches
Hommage à
TLautrec

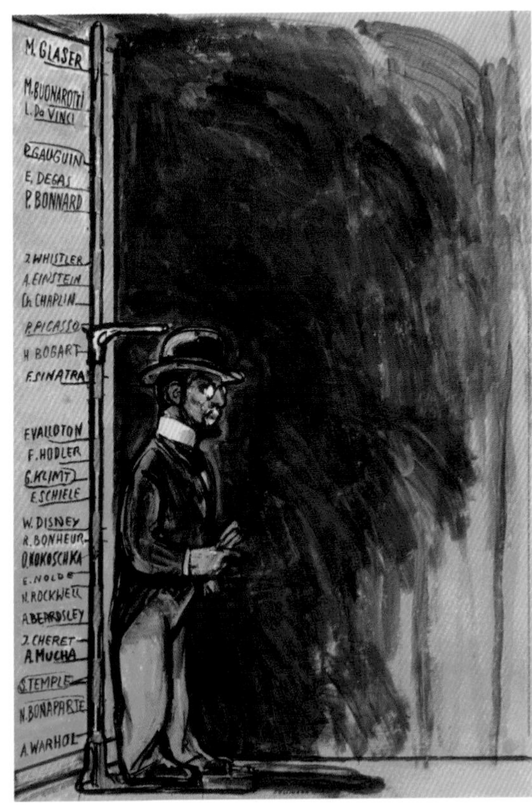
M. GLASER
M. BUONAROTTI
L. Da VINCI
P. GAUGUIN
E. DEGAS
P. BONNARD
J. WHISTLER
A. EINSTEIN
Ch. CHAPLIN
P. PICASSO
H. BOGART
F. SINATRA
F. VALLOTON
F. HODLER
G. KLIMT
E. SCHIELE
W. DISNEY
R. BONHEUR
O. KOKOSCHKA
E. NOLDE
N. ROCKWELL
A. BEARDSLEY
J. CHERET
A. MUCHA
S. TEMPLE
N. BONAPARTE
A. WARHOL

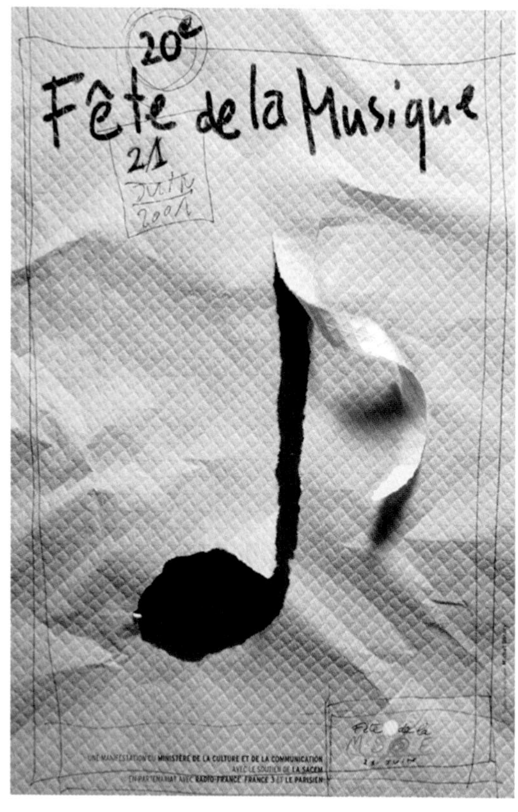

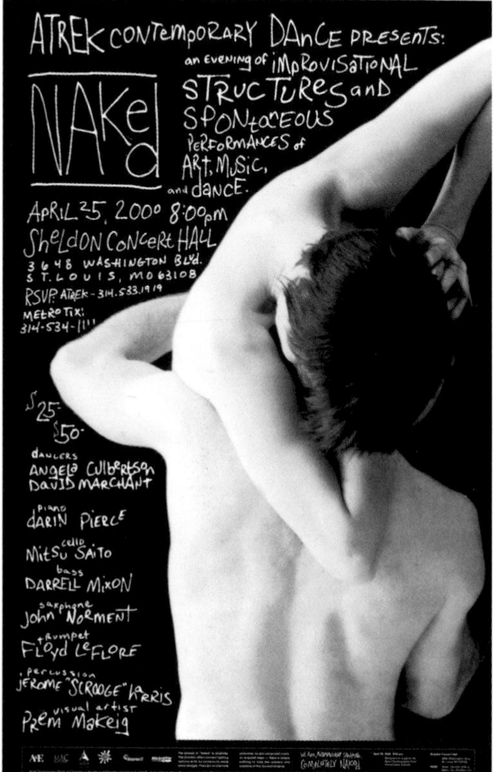

ABOVE **The primary graphic showing an angel** is rendered in a quick linear scrawl and the lettering, though far from heavenly, still perfectly complements the drawing style on this theatre poster.
Designer, letterer, illustrator: Thomas Matthaeus Müller Client: Büro für Off-Theater

TOP LEFT **The scrawl on this poster has great appeal** to the masses because it is an unpretentious, quotidian handwriting that anyone would be able to accomplish.
Designer, letterer, illustrator, photographer: Michal Batory Client: Ministère de la Culture, France

LEFT **The starkest use of scrawl** is white on black, especially when placed next to a dramatic photo like on this poster for the dance performance *Naked.*
Designer, letterer: Steve Hartman Photographer: Gregg Goldman Client: Atrek Dance Company

ABOVE **The surreal image** is the most important graphic element here. However, the lettering not only informs but also provides a contemporary atmosphere for the classic drama being advertised on the theatre poster.
Designer, letterer, illustrator: Feliks Büttner Client: Volks Theater Rostook

TOP RIGHT **An absurd concept** certainly deserves an equally absurd handlettered accompaniment; this lettering for the poster 'June Crawfish' looks like it was done by intelligent lobsters.
Designer, letterer, illustrator: Scott Ray Photographer: Doug Davis Client: Dallas Society of Visual Communications

RIGHT **Due to type shortages** in Poland in the period during and after World War II, Polish artists mastered the art of handlettering better than any designers in the world, transforming it into a wildly expressive style, as is evident on this poster for an exhibition on Wojciech Korkuc.
Designer, letterer, illustrator: Wojciech Korkuc Photographer: Wlodek Krzeminski
Client: Municipality of Minsk Mazowiecki

Scrawls can be powerfully demonstrative graphic elements. On this poster for the play *Kot Martin*, the scrawl is in fact both the word and the picture, at once representational and abstract – a real *tour de force*.
Designer, letterer, illustrator: Martin Klaus, personal work

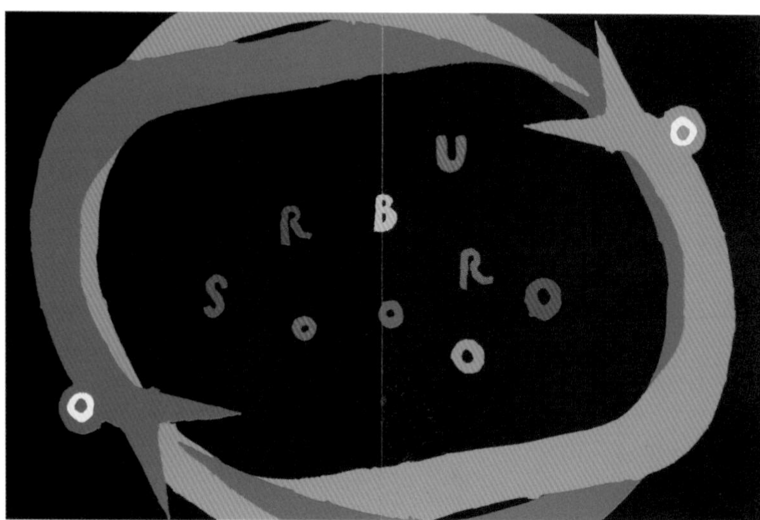

Scrawls like these are seamlessly integrated into the illustration. This is a subtle yet eye-grabbing use of simple letterforms that is consistent with the dominant drawing style on this poster, 'April Wind Works No. 80'.
Designer, letterer, illustrator: Shin Matsunaga Client: Cross Brand

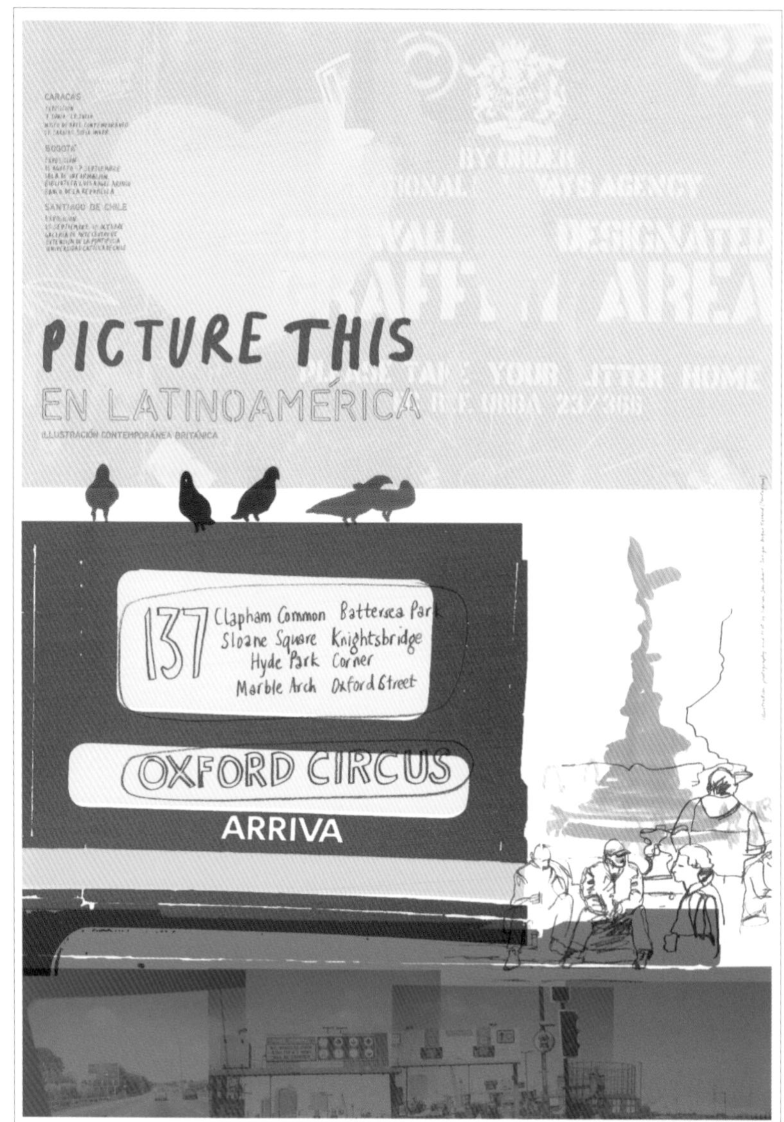

Composition is everything in this design because the lettering acts as pattern, texture and information. The layered text and image on this poster for the exhibition 'Picture This En Latino América' presents the reader with a lot to take in.
Designer: Angus Hyland Design assistant: Charlie Smith Illustrator: Marion Deuchars Client: The British Council

Due to its improvisational nature, scrawled lettering is virtually a requisite to any graphic design related to jazz, as shown on this poster for the photography exhibition 'Wojciech Kusy – Foto Jazz'.
Designer, letterer, illustrator: Marian Oslislo Client: Municipal Museum, Zabrze

This image of a male figure is akin to the German expressionist characters made popular by Saul Bass in his 1950s film adverts. The lettering, on a poster advertising the Greenwood Art Walk 2000, is similarly expressive and perfectly appropriate.
Designer, letterer, illustrator: Robynne Raye Client: Greenwood Arts Council

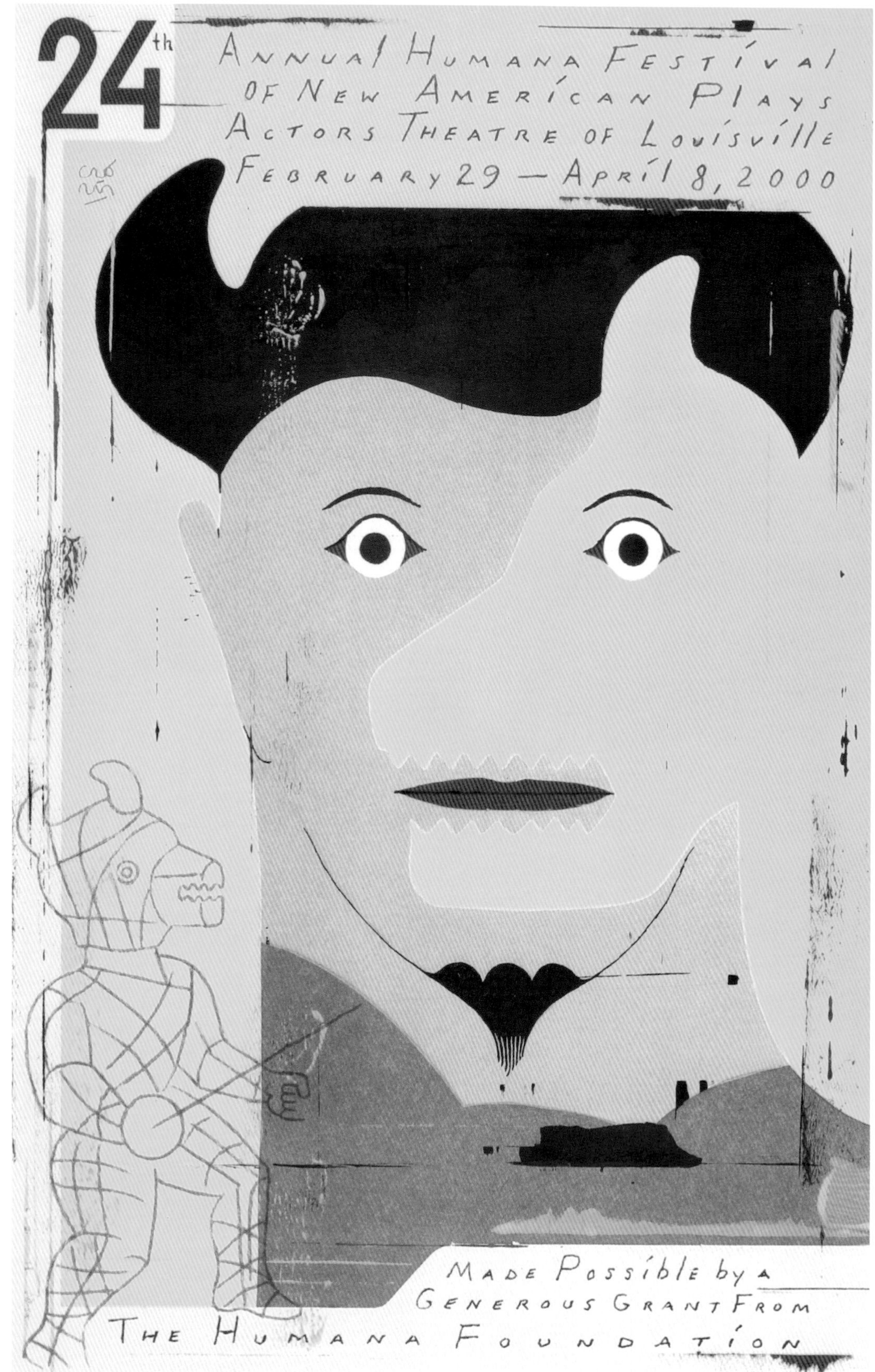
24th
Annual Humana Festival
of New American Plays
Actors Theatre of Louisville
February 29 — April 8, 2000
Made Possible by a
Generous Grant From
The Humana Foundation

LEFT **Very carefully letter spaced**, this simple print does not appear too crass and nor does it detract from the image on this poster for the 24th Annual Humana Festival of New American Plays.
Designer, letterer, illustrator: Brian Cronin
Client: The Actors Theatre of Louisville

OPPOSITE, TOP **These extremely rough** but decidedly comical drawings on two advertisements, 'Flexibility' and 'Balance', are courageously fettered except for the minuscule scrawled word and handmade logo.
Art director: Sandra Scher Creative director: Carol Holsinger
Illustrator: Sara Schwartz Client: Crunch

OPPOSITE, BOTTOM LEFT **Informal Japanese scrawls** are well suited to the sketchy drawing that exudes a light-hearted good nature in this brochure, 'How To Make the Chair'.
Art director: Nob Narumi Designers: Riwa Fujiwara, Nob Narumi
Letterer, illustrator: Dr. Nova Client: Comfortable Chair Company

OPPOSITE, BOTTOM RIGHT **Consistently inconsistent**, Absolut Vodka is known for its adverts that use the Absolut bottle as an icon for many different visual approaches, including the handlettered variety.
Designer: Estudio Mariscal Illustrator: Javier Mariscal Client: bddp@tbwa

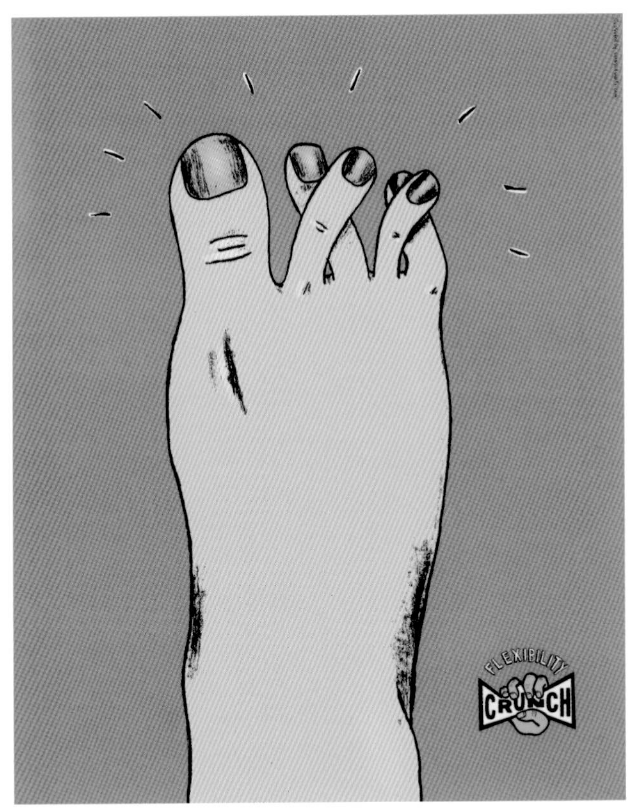
FLEXIBILITY
CRUNCH

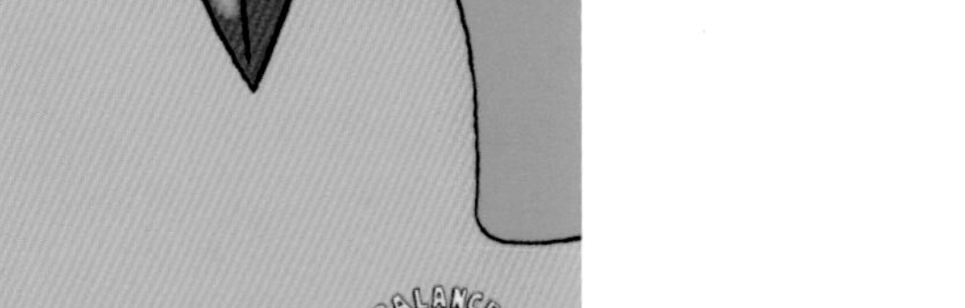
BALANCE
CRUNCH

いすのタマゴ

ABSOLUT
VODKA

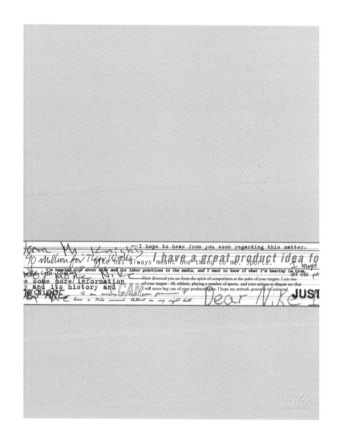

ABOVE **Genuine scrawled comments** on the Rolodex cards showing Sillicon Valley Bank's business associates have been used in the design of the cover and interior of the company's annual report (2000).
Designer: Michael Braley Photographers: Jock McDonald, Graham MacIndoe Client: Sillicon Valley Bank

LEFT **Excerpts from handwritten letters** to Nike coalesce into a unique design concept for the cover of Nike's 1998 annual report.
Designer, illustrator: Valerie T. Smith Client: Nike

OPPOSITE, TOP LEFT **It seems paradoxical to find scrawls** on a website, but, owing to the inconsistent type display, handlettering works best with the pictures on this page from 'tidycats.com'.
Creative director: Joe Duffy Art director: Kobe Suvongse Design director: Dan Olson
Letterer, illustrator: Lourdes Banez Client: Purina

OPPOSITE, BOTTOM LEFT **The options for handlettering on the web** are infinite because, as long as the creators know how animation programs work, the text can be made to jump, jiggle and shake, as shown on this website for 'campheartland.org'.
Creative director: Alan Colvin Design director: Dan Olson Designer, letterer, illustrator: Sida Phungjiam
Client: Camp Heartland

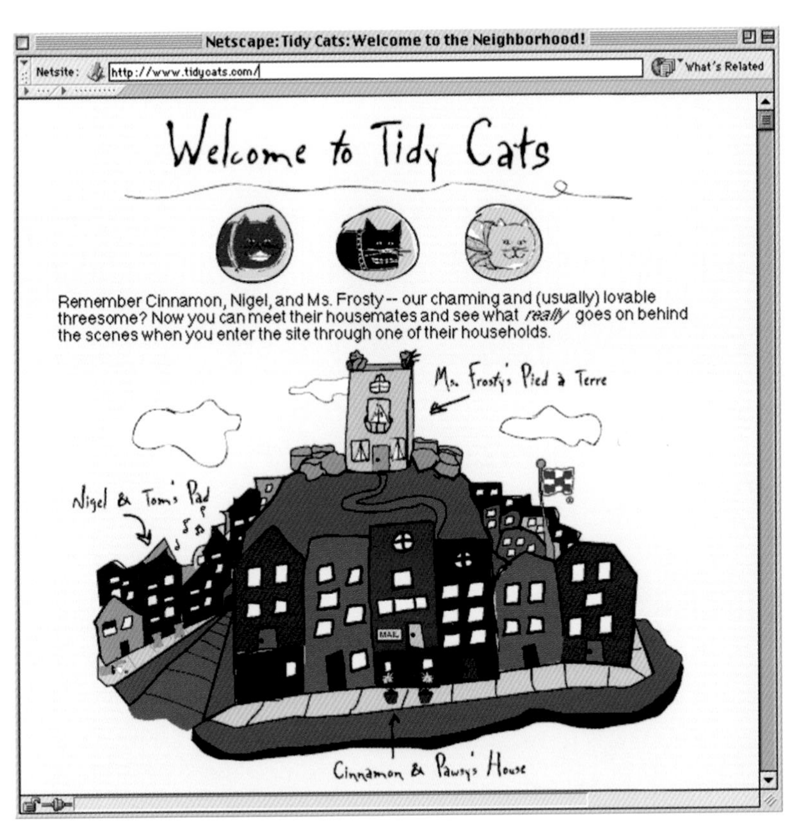

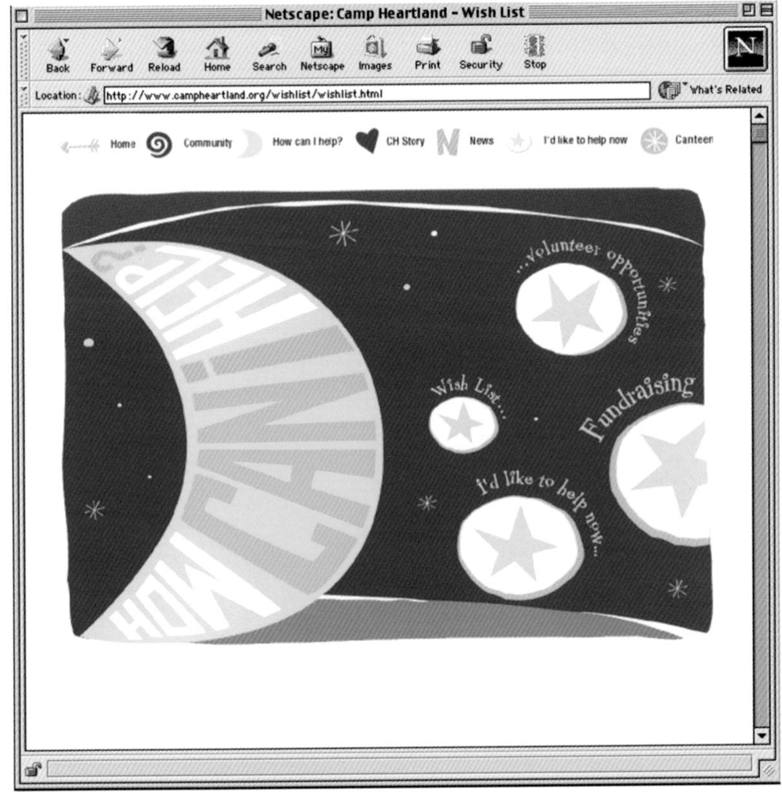

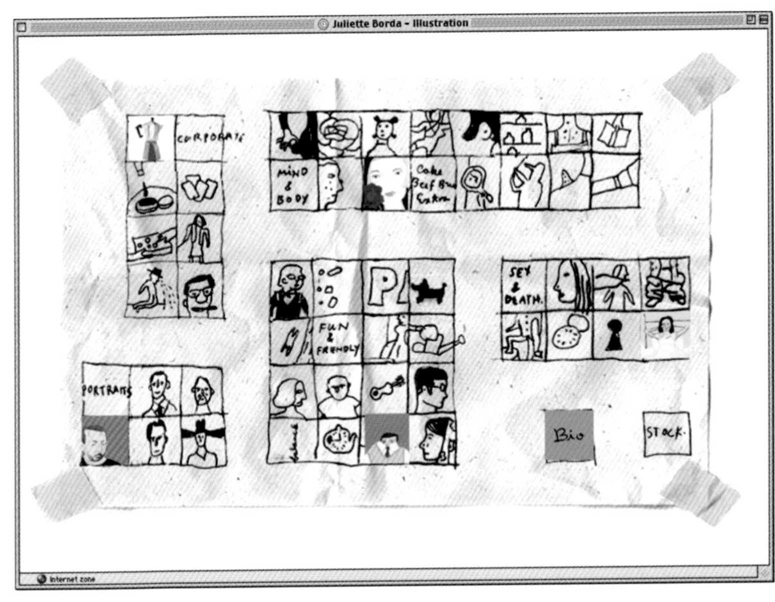

ABOVE **There is no doubt that the web** is a major example of high technology. Many illustrators, therefore, use handlettering to set a more informal tone that gives their work human sensitivity, as indicated here on the website 'www.julietteborda.com'.
Designer: Bernard Uy Letterer, illustrator: Juliette Borda

RIGHT AND BELOW RIGHT **Rough and untutored handlettering on billboard advertisements** as a complement to illustrations has increased in recent years.
'A Quick Bite' Designer: Norm Shearer Letterer, illustrator: Mike Sukle Photographer: Mark Laita
'A Saucy Little Number' Designer, letterer, illustrator: Mike Sukle Photographer: Joe Hancock
Client: Noodles & Company

BOTTOM RIGHT **Against an awesome backdrop** of mountain slopes, an extreme skier receives a scrawled command that cannot be ignored; all in all, a very effective advertisement aptly named 'Skip Lunch'.
Art director: Allison Burton Copywriter: Jon Dietrich Photographer: Hank de Vre Client: K2 Skis

BELOW **The idea that two cows** are writing headlines for advertisements is a stitch; it does not matter that this scrawl is too neat for cows.
Creative director: Doug Rucker Art director: Kyle Friedel Copywriter: Cynthia Duxbury
Designer, letterer: David Ring Client: Chick-fil-A

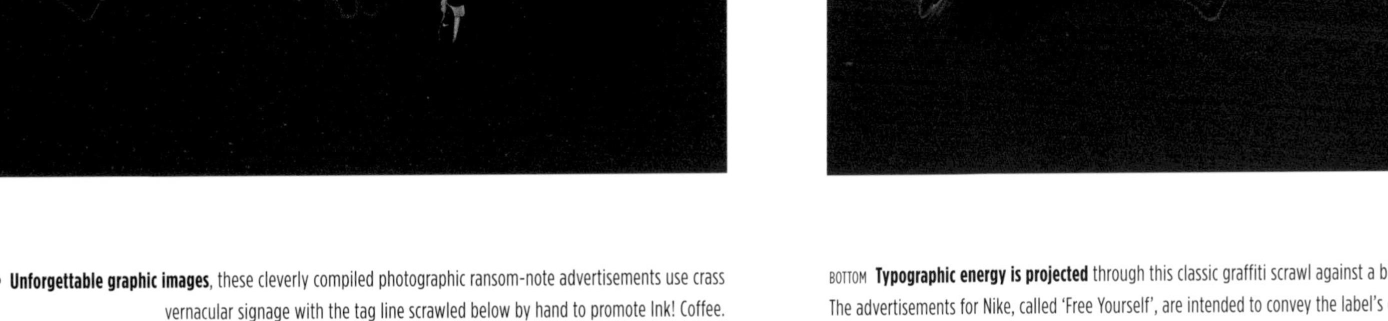

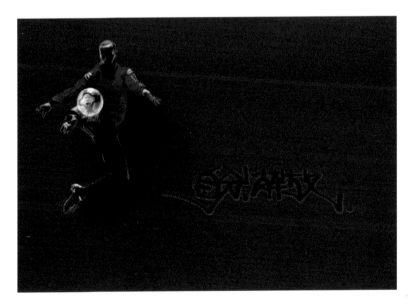

TOP **Unforgettable graphic images**, these cleverly compiled photographic ransom-note advertisements use crass vernacular signage with the tag line scrawled below by hand to promote Ink! Coffee.
Creative directors: Tim Abare, Chris Beatty Art director: Marco Pipere Writer: Tim Abare
Photographers: Scott Coe, Marco Pipere, Matt Neren Client: Ink! Coffee

BOTTOM **Typographic energy is projected** through this classic graffiti scrawl against a blood-red background. The advertisements for Nike, called 'Free Yourself', are intended to convey the label's coolness.
Creative director: John Jay Art director, designer: Joshua Berger Writer: Barton Corley
Letterer: Shotaro Photographer: John Huet Client: Nike

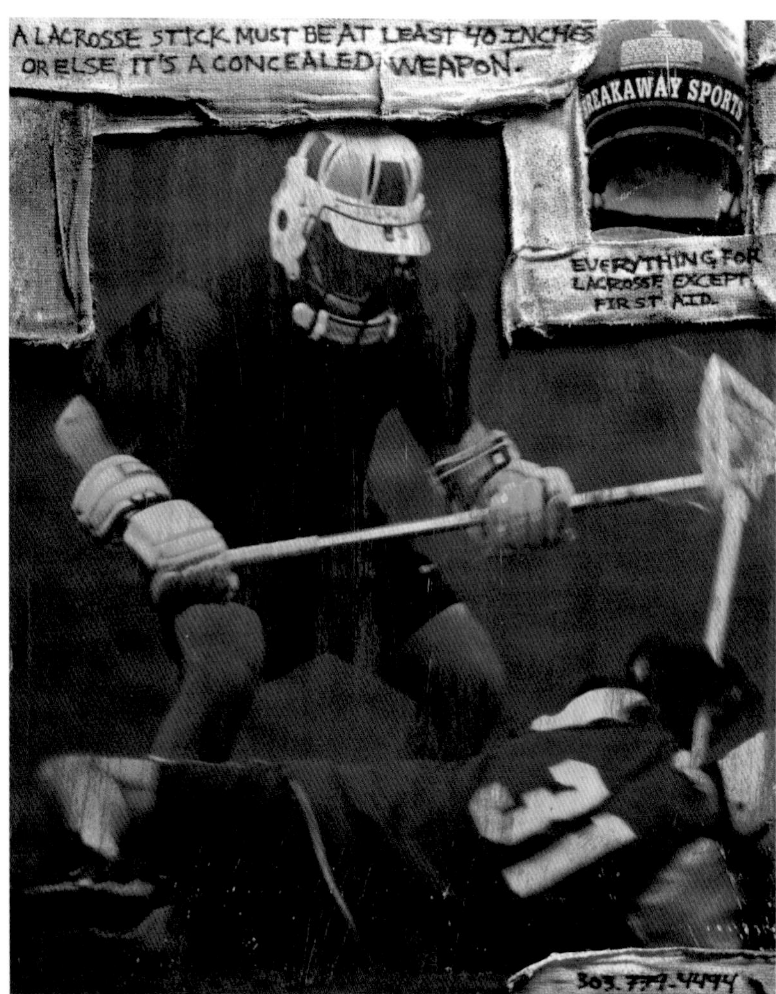

Athletes often write phrases on their equipment; thus, using this kind of lettering motif to convey the lacrosse message, as on these advertisements for Breakaway Sports, appeals to anyone who has ever played the sport.
Art director: Dan Richardson Copywriter, letterer: Jonathan Schoenberg Photographer: Brooks Freehill
Client: Breakaway Sports

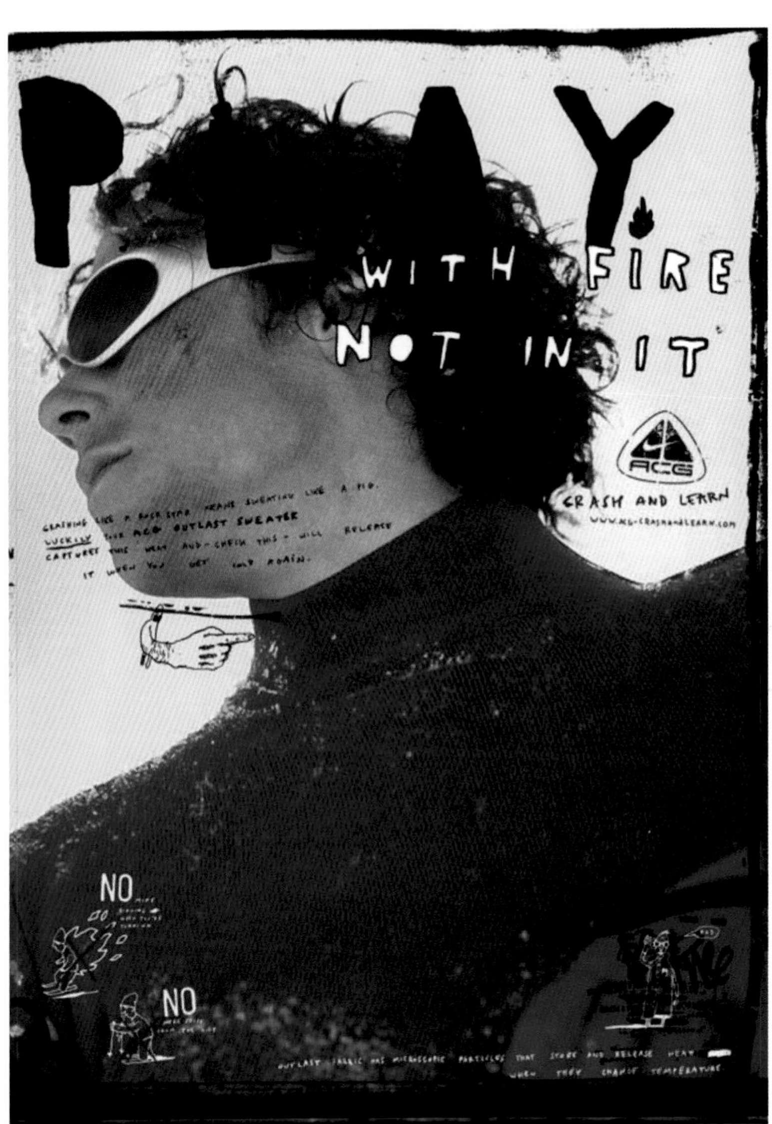

Amusing photographs with scribbled narratives and scrawled headlines give this Nike campaign for ACG its comically shrill and fashionably snotty voice.

Art director: Frank Hahn Copywriter: Tim Wolfe Illustrator: David Foldvari Photographer: Trevor Graves

Client: Nike

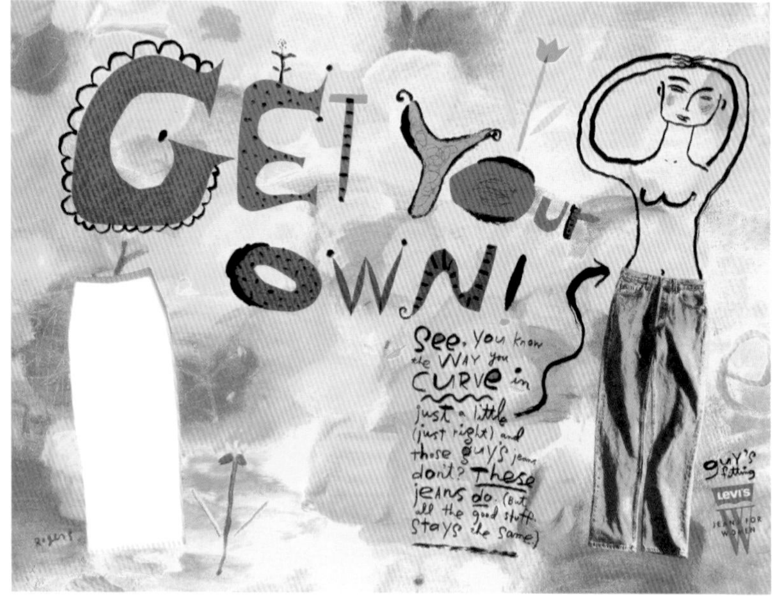

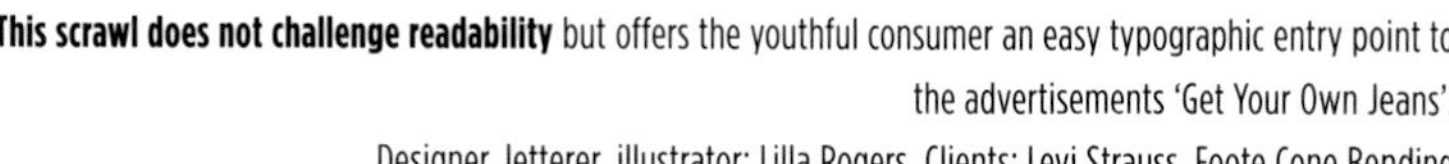
This scrawl does not challenge readability but offers the youthful consumer an easy typographic entry point to the advertisements 'Get Your Own Jeans'.
Designer, letterer, illustrator: Lilla Rogers Clients: Levi Strauss, Foote Cone Bending

The carefully scrawled trademark on this stylistically crude illustration advertising the Calvin Klein spring/summer 2002 collection is a code for youth culture.
Designer, letterer: M/M (Paris) Photographers: Inez van Lamsweerde, Vinoodh Matadin
Clients: Calvin Klein Inc., CRK Advertising 2002

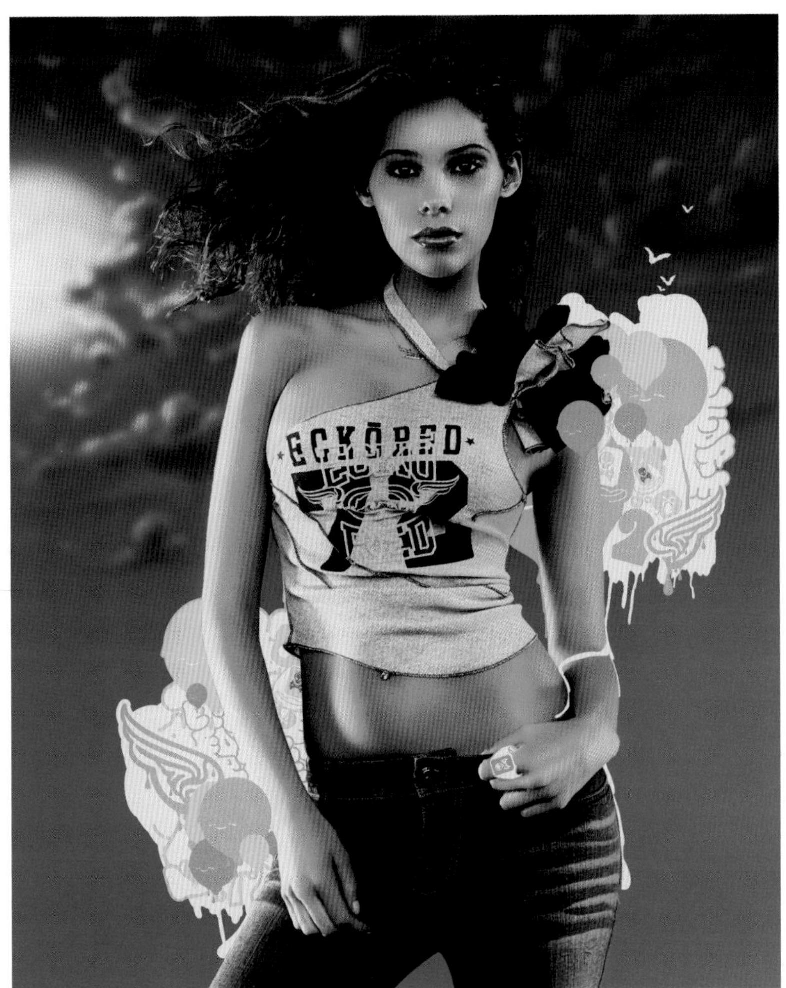

Incorporating scrawls on high-fashion photographs, as in this magazine advertisement for Ecko, is gaining popularity and quirky handlettering is being tamed as a result.
Designer, letterer, illustrator: Justin Fines Client: Ecko

To convey a sense of immediacy and to set off the surreal imagery, an ad-hoc scrawl is needed for this advertisement for the 2003 Video Music Awards.
Creative director: Jeffrey Keyton Design director: Jim deBarros Art director: Thomas Berger
Letterer: Lance Rusoff 3-D portraits: Kevin O'Callaghan Photographer: Dewey Nicks Client: MTV

OPPOSITE, TOP **Buyers are encouraged to think** that this CD for System of a Down, called *Steal This Album!*, is an amateur mix. In fact, it is a clever put-down of the pretence of most mainstream CD design.
Art director: Brandy Flowers Letterer: Shavo Odadjian Client: Sony Music

OPPOSITE, BOTTOM **The brushed letter used as a frame** for the photographic illustration is a smart way of tying these CDs together as a unique series.
Designer, illustrator: Michal Batory Photographer: DR Client: Radio France

BELOW RIGHT **The children's lettering** on this album jacket and record for Danger Gens seems authentic, but increasingly children's letterforms are exploited for adult graphics.
Designer: Art Chantry Letterers: Morgan Day (age 5), Brian Edwards (age 7) Illustrator: Brian Edwards (age 7)
Clients: Danger Gens, Church Melody Records

BELOW **Scrawled letters on this record sleeve** for Lord High Fixers are but one component of a multi-layered visual mystery. It evokes the look of defacement and, by extension, triumph over conventional typographies.
Designer, letterer: Art Chantry Photographer: The Federal Bureau of Investigation (FBI) Client: Estrus Records

SYSTEM OF A DOWN
SYSTEM OF A DOWN
CD-36
STEAL THIS ALBUM!

1. CHIC 'N' STU
2. INNERVISION
3. BUBBLES
4. BOOM!
5. NÜGUNS
6. A.D.D.
7. MR. JACK
8. I-E-A-I-A-I-O
9. 36
10. PICTURES
11. HIGHWAY SONG
12. F**K THE SYSTEM
13. EGO BRAIN
14. THETAWAVES
15. ROULETTE
16. STREAMLINE
6 9699-87062-2 4
PRODUCED BY RICK RUBIN AND DARON MALAKIAN
MIXED BY ANDY WALLACE*
WWW.SYSTEMOFADOWN.COM

France musiques
SIGNATURE
OLIVIER MANOURY
Solo

LE MOUV'
SIGNATURE
BOOTY TIME
BUMCELLO

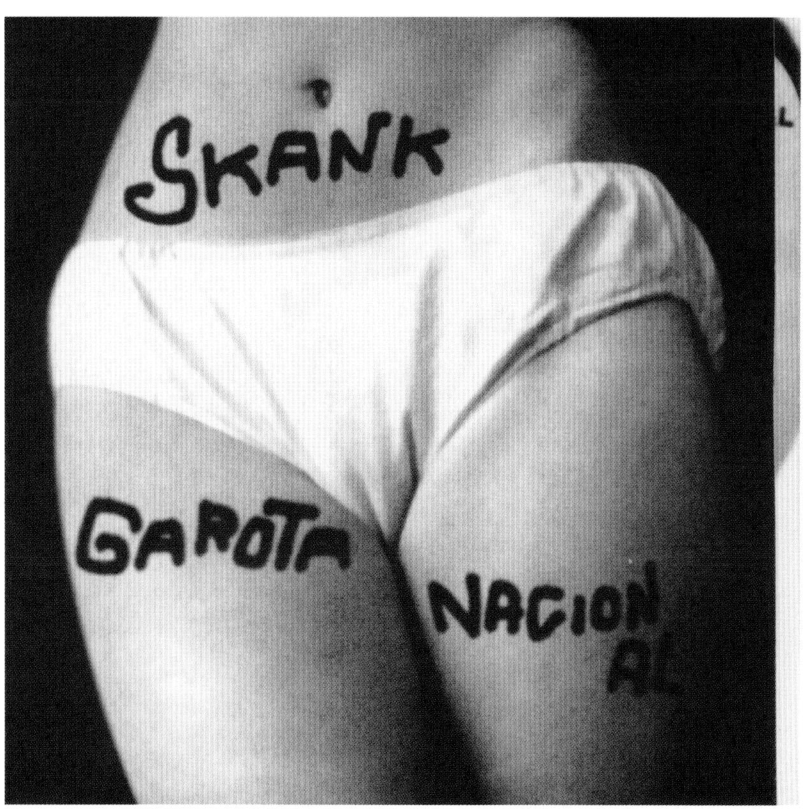

THIS PAGE **It was common to see colourful body** painting on record albums in the 1960s. The practice continues to a degree on this CD for Skank, called *Garota Nacional*, but a simple marker pen takes the place of more elaborate methods.
Designer, letterer, photographer: Gringo Cardia Client: Sony Music Brasil

OPPOSITE **This parody of soft-core porn** exudes the spirit of an old pornographic Tijuana bible and the verisimilitude of an erotic *fumetti* or comic book. The lettering on this CD for Marisa Monte is almost professional in the same way that the artwork is almost 'good'.
Designer, letterer: Gringo Cardia Illustrator: Carlos Zefiro Client: EMI Brasil

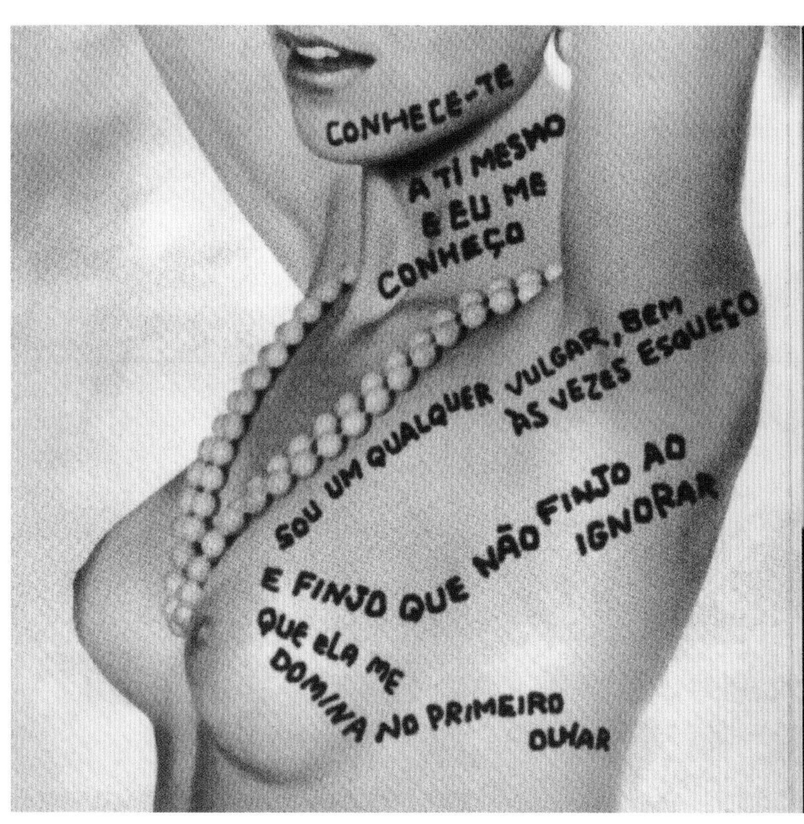

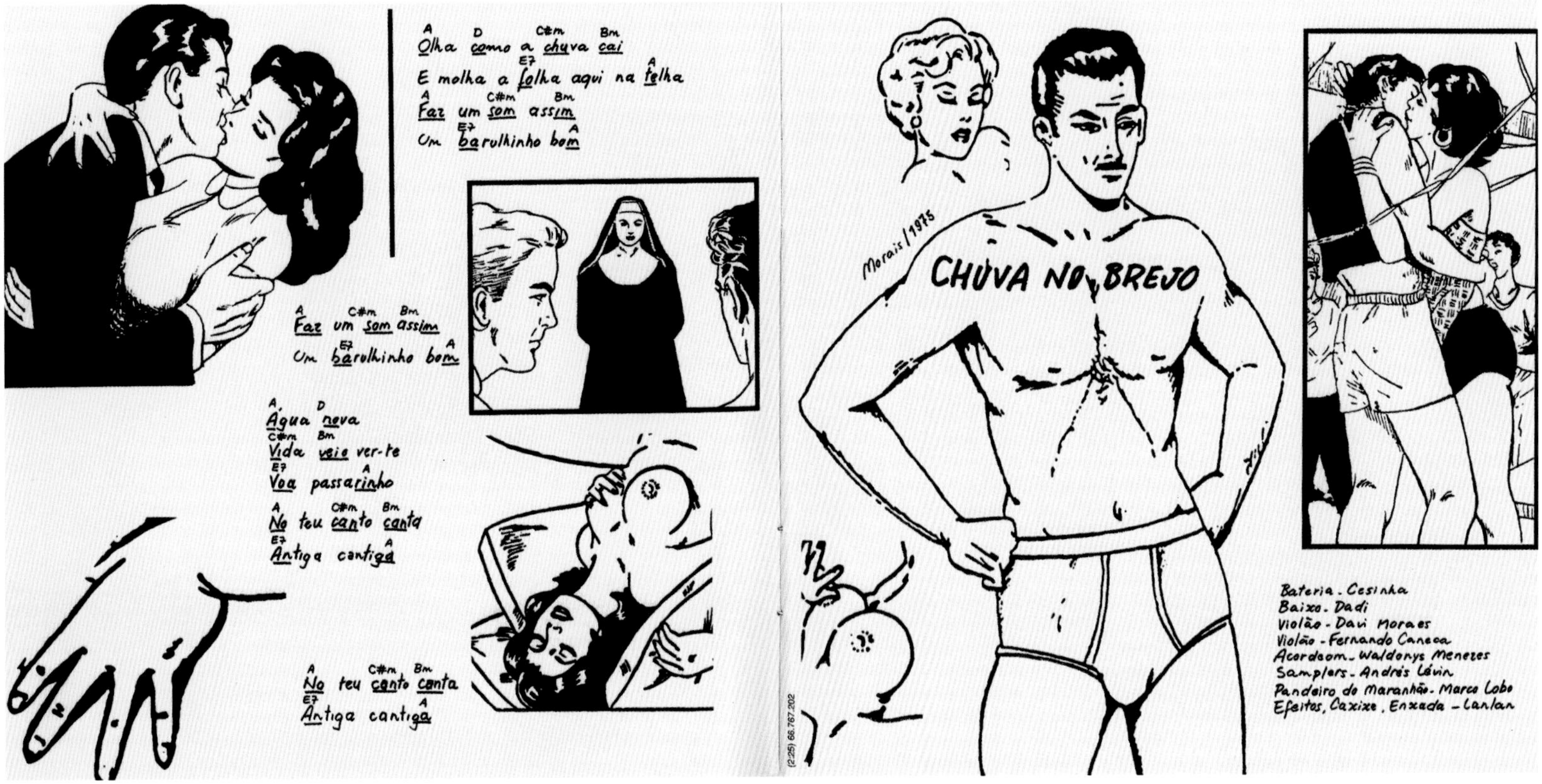

Olha como a chuva cai
E molha a folha aqui na telha
Faz um som assim
Um barulhinho bom

Faz um som assim
Um barulhinho bom

Água neva
Vida veio ver-te
Voa passarinho
No teu canto canta
Antiga cantiga

No teu canto canta
Antiga cantiga

Morais / 1975

CHUVA NO BREJO

Bateria - Cesinha
Baixo - Dadi
Violão - Davi Moraes
Violão - Fernando Caneca
Acordeom - Waldonys Menezes
Samplers - Andrés Lévin
Pandeiro do Maranhão - Marco Lobo
Efeitos, Caxixe, Enxada - Lanlan

(1996) and Filosofia (1996). Designed by Zuzana Licko, the former with elegant ligatures and the latter inspired by Bodoni (c. 1785), both fonts replaced quirkier novelties and provided designers with the impetus to return to the typographic sophistication they had eschewed in favour of fashionable disharmony. Type as visual art was settling down, but disquiet for something different remained. Scratch away the top layer of much design born at the tail end of digital typography's exuberant epoch in the late 1990s and hints of personal expression were still apparent. Orthodox modernists aside, designers cannot live on Bodoni, Univers or even Template Gothic alone, and not all messages profit from elegance, balance or harmony. In the aftermath of fervent experimentation spawned by *Emigre*, put forward by *Fuse* (the digital type 'journal' edited by Neville Brody and Jon Wozencroft), popularized by *RayGun* (the alternative music magazine designed by David Carson) and adopted by MTV, music channel VH1 and the rest of youth culture, eclecticism was unstoppable. But, rather than find an outlet in digital clichés, eclecticism became manifest in the most fundamental hand work.

At this point in the history of graphic art, the scratch was not a completely novel mark. Etchers regularly scratched words and phrases into their metal plates as captions or slogans for engraved pictures. Scratching on paint-sopped canvas or ink-laden paper has long been a means of making verbal compliments to narrative and abstract images. Some scratches are incredibly artful, others are coarse and still others are artfully coarse; but all are distinctly individual signatures. Most handlettering is a signature, but the scratch is more powerful because it is achieved by applying pressure. Generally, writing or scrawling is done with an easy hand motion, whereas scratching requires the determined and continuous stress of the hand on the surface.

Could this be too much hoopla for an otherwise simple mark that is possibly no more consequential than a fallen eyelash? Not at all: the scratch has become a significant contemporary lettering element (and style), which demands at least semi-serious consideration. What distinguishes a successful scratch from a common scrape is the designer's ability to transform the pedestrian into the extraordinary.

The scratch may currently be the most radical alternative to conventional type (as well as formal calligraphy) because it has considerable power to be interpretative yet curiously universal, expressive yet legible. Unlike the distressed type experiments of yore in which readability was challenged, the scratch is now almost always readable. Naturally, scratched letters are not the most appropriate for continuous text settings, but as headlines or pull quotes they have much the same function as a typeface, plus, they are more eye-catching. Whereas pure type requires the right words to telegraph meaning, a scratch (large or small) invariably draws the reader to it to decipher the meaning. Typeset words are easy to overlook even as they are being read because the average typefaces are so familiar that one perceives them in a reflexive way. Conversely, the scratch signals warning: even if the message is benign, the cut of the scratch is inherently violent.

The film title sequence for *Seven* (1995), designed by Kyle Cooper, was the precursor of current scratchy lettering. The theme of decapitation that pervades director David Fincher's thriller served to stereotype the scratchy style as a mnemonic for grotesquery, and a subsequent increase in the use of scratches for the titles of horror and mystery films and books was evident. Yet the style was also applied to other real-life themes endemic to struggles of any kind. A powerful example is David Croy's poster, 'Talk Therapy' (see p. 70), which boldly faces the horror of rape and expresses a narrative of pain born of intimate violence. Printed in black and white, the scratchy lettering carved into rectilinear speech boxes (which at once resemble quotation marks and pointing fingers) represents the voice of the victim or survivor. Overall, the exclusive use of handlettering gives the piece an immediacy and emotional quality that type could not. The word 'rape' is achieved by cut or torn lettering, suggesting the enormity of the criminal act; the scratched personal testimony though angry is more vulnerable. Such is the power of the scratch to be more than a design conceit.

In a similar vein, Jeff Hopfer art-directed and lettered the advertisements for the Episcopal New Church Center in Texas (see p. 73). He scratched, graffiti-style, the short statement, 'Of Course People with Pierced Body Parts are Welcome in Our Church' over a Renaissance painting of the crucifixion in a manner that is at once

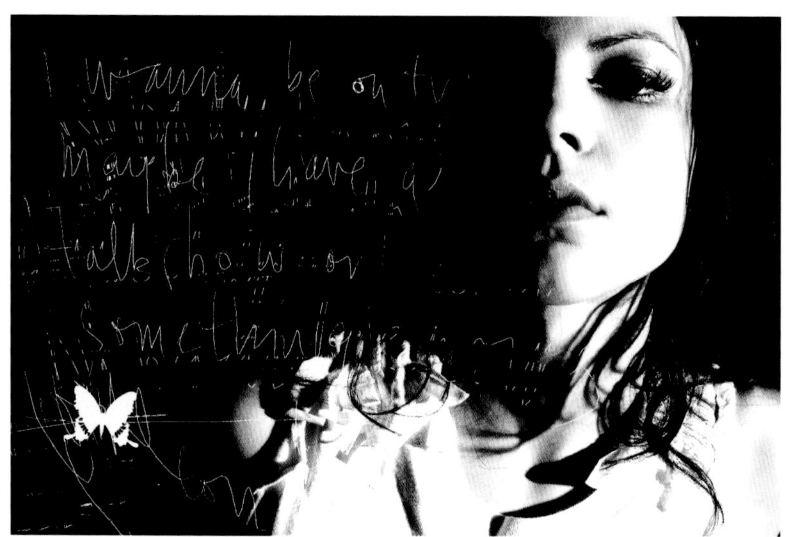

ironic and poignant. Furthermore, in a complementary advert with the headline 'Get In Here for Christ's Sake', the scratchy scrawl seems like a personal plea from the Saviour himself. Rather than plaintive cries, these scratches are a demonstrative counterpoint to more official church graphics. In the first advert, the contrast between classical image and ad-hoc lettering suggests rebellion against the uptight strictures expected from organized religion. The lettering in the second image, showing a grainy photograph of a simple handmade wooden cross (the kind that might have been employed as a symbol after the crucifixion), is in sync with the tenor of the message: christianity was always and should continue to be a grass-roots movement. Note that even the 'logo' is the handscratched words 'Episcopal New Church Center' in the form of a cross.

Not all scratchy work is as weighty as this, but, as the Episcopal Church posters reveal, the scratch is routinely used to contradict formal and official modes of lettering. Joshua Berger's application of the scratch on the cover of *Plazm* magazine and on an interior spread (see p. 61) runs counter to every tenet of traditional magazine design. Although the title is fairly conventional on the cover, the dropped-out scratched writing indiscriminately scrawled over a layout of butted photographs fails to inform the reader as to the contents of this particular issue. As if written by a person in a dark cell, the text is void of logical line breaks or word spacing and is filled with false starts and crossings out; readability is, therefore, extremely challenged. The interior spread, though a tad more legible because the lettering is printed in black, is as insanely anarchic as the cover. All the same, something about these compositions draws readers' attention and compels them to decipher the narrative. Given that the scratches appear in the same space as the barcode, there is certainly an element of artifice but the marks also project a kind of intimacy that standard type alone could never hope to achieve.

Art Chantry has been a long-time recidivist in the anti-type movement. One of many examples, his CD packaging for Phone Dummy, a neo-punk rock group (see pp 80–81), includes a booklet covered in scratchy, scrawled and simulated handlettering reversing out of colour photographs. Given the punk penchant for DIY (do-it-yourself) graphics, this ad-hoc technique is not as surprisingly employed here as on the Episcopal New Church advertisements but it is no less engaging. Chantry has built a personal vocabulary on found and handmade graphics that assaults prevailing rules of balance and harmony. In his booklet, excerpts from the band's songs are scratched to approximate the lyricist's own scribblings. Each lyric is punctuated by a song title that is hand drawn in a parodic simulation of actual type. Despite the informality, the compositions have a distinct logic that enhances the allure.

Brad Holland's scratches for the poster 'How to Create A Newspaper Ad' (see p. 66) appear wild at first glance but are also built on an armature of logic that allows the reader to follow the narrative without distraction. Holland, whose surrealist paintings and drawings have been mainstays of editorial and advertising media, has discovered a way to surrealistically integrate his scratchy letters as both texture and information. In this advertisement, the hand-wrought marks tell the first-person story of Lee Clow, an advertising executive famous for his commercial to launch the Apple Macintosh, and his quest to create the most eye-popping and memorable advertisement possible for a newspaper. Holland's visual exposition is the model of Clow's thesis because it not only surprises the reader but it also transforms the page into an urgent message demanding attention.

The purpose of the scratch is to dislodge pretensions and to alter the perceptions of what the printed page has been or should be. In a period when perfection is a keystroke away, imperfection is bound to have appeal. Of course, if the scratch appeared everywhere, designers would be itching to return to good old formality.

Scratchy lettering is more than a messy façade; at best it is spontaneity without conceit as illustrated here in these posters with black-and-white photographs and scratched expressionist markings.
[pp 56, 57] 'Pretty Baby 1' and 'Pretty Baby 2' [opposite] 'I Wanna Be on TV' [above] 'I Love Gossip'
Letterer, illustrator: Andy Simionato Photographer: Karen Ann Donnachie Client: *This is a Magazine*

LEFT **Physical scratches on plaster** produce the most tactile surface on this magazine cover for *Print*, which uses a variety of scratches and scrawls as headlines.
Creative director: Steven Brower Art director: Stephanie Skirvin
Designer, letterer, photographer: Frédéric Rey Client: *Print*

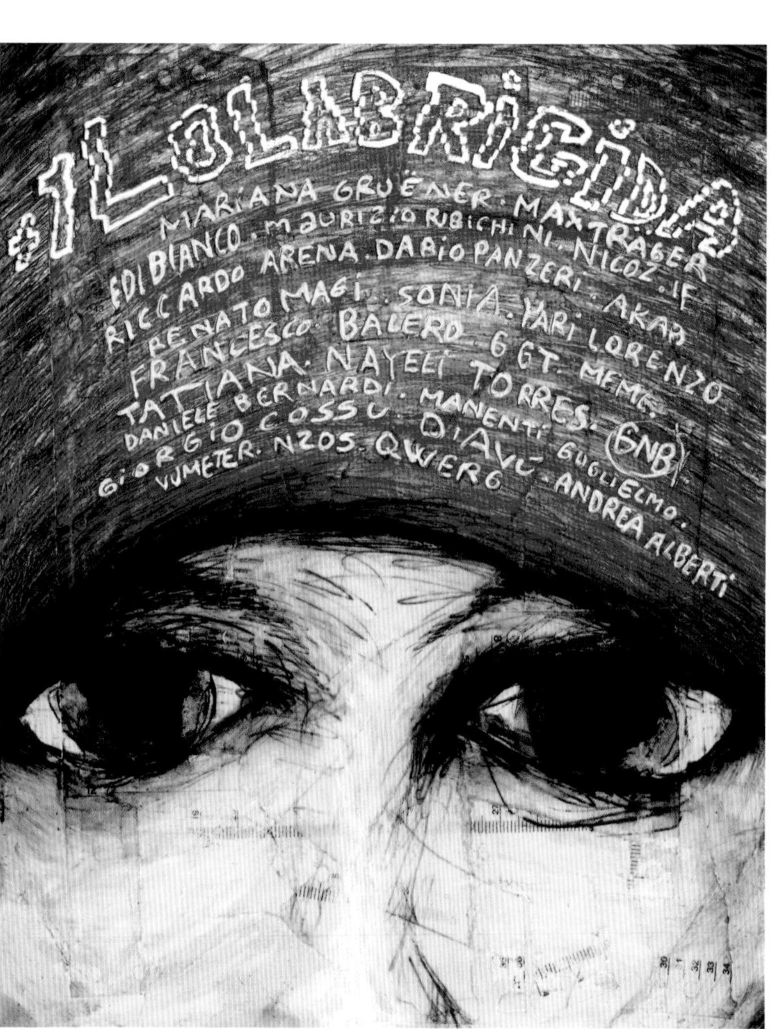

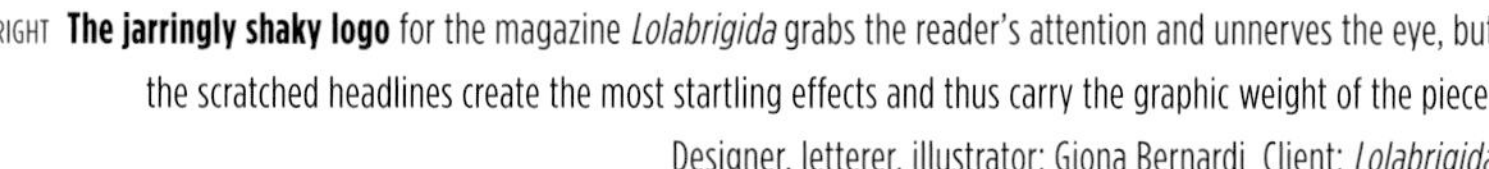
RIGHT **The jarringly shaky logo** for the magazine *Lolabrigida* grabs the reader's attention and unnerves the eye, but the scratched headlines create the most startling effects and thus carry the graphic weight of the piece.
Designer, letterer, illustrator: Giona Bernardi Client: *Lolabrigida*

LEFT AND BELOW **Oozing a devil-may-care sensibility**, the design of issue 27 of *Plazm* is barely readable yet beckons the reader to follow the meandering path of the words.
Creative directors: Joshua Berger, Niko Courtelis, Pete McCracken, Enrique Mosqueda
Art director, designer: Enrique Mosqueda Letterer, photographer: Mark Borthwick Client: *Plazm*

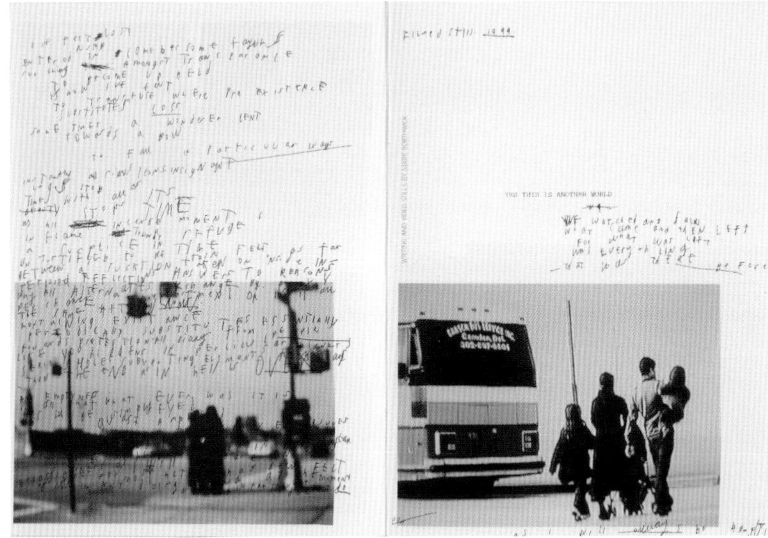

ABOVE AND LEFT **Filling a magazine with scratches** and other handlettered forms, as shown on this cover and spread from *Big Magazine*, turns what is standard journalism into a personal diary.
Designer: David Carson Letterer, illustrator: George Bates Client: *Big Magazine*

BELOW LEFT AND RIGHT **The contrast of beautiful colour reproductions** and scratched words on 'Things Worth Looking Into', a promotion for a paper company, begs the question as to whether this is a design conceit because the lettering is elegantly crafted to accentuate the virtues of the paper.
Art director, designer, letterer: Rob DeLuke Photographer: Mark McCarty Client: Finch Paper

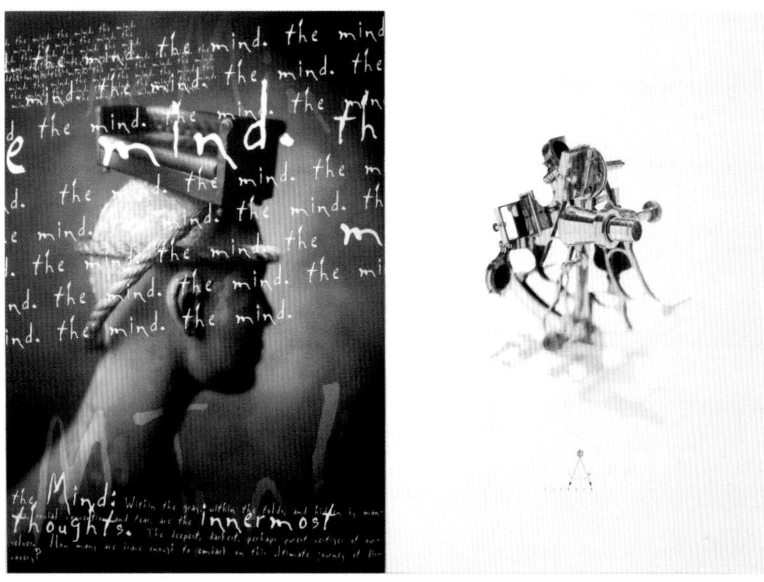

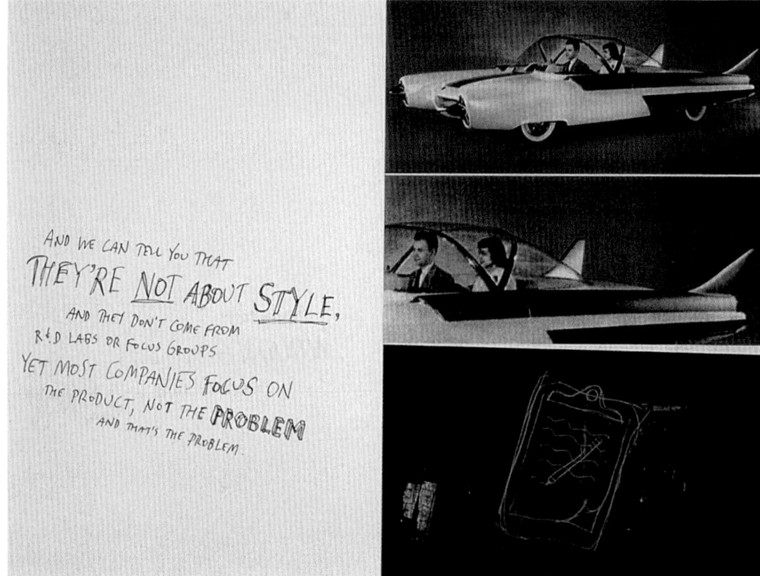

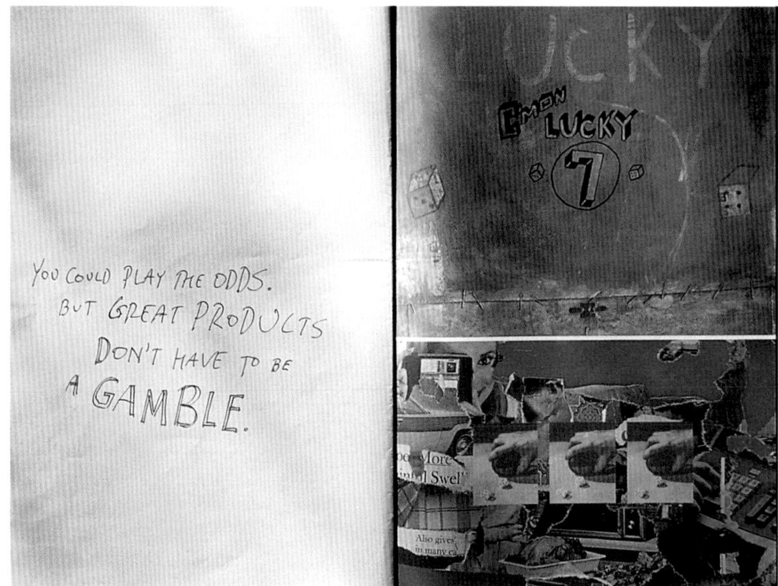

ABOVE LEFT AND RIGHT **The juxtaposition of slick and raw** makes this scratched design for the GVO brochure at once fetching and ironic.
Creative director: Bill Cahan Art directors: Bill Cahan, Bob Dinetz Designer: Bob Dinetz
Illustrators: Bob Dinetz, Gary Baseman Client: GVO Inc.

Lettering for the headline announcing a story about David Koresh, the leader of the Branch Davidian cult who was killed by the FBI, befits the eerie treatment on the magazine spread 'David Koresh and the Myth of the Alamo'.
Designer: DJ Stout Letterer, illustrator: Henrik Drescher Client: *Texas Monthly*

Conveying the insanity of violent acts, scratchy letters seem well suited to the depiction of violence on this magazine spread entitled 'The Horse Killers'.
Designer, letterer: DJ Stout Illustrator: Matt Mahurin Client: *Texas Monthly*

The desperation of the lost outsider and the untutored marks of someone who has not learned how to write in the schooled manner are suggested by these scratched words for 'The Outsiders', a magazine spread.
Designer, letterer: DJ Stout Photographer: Judy Walgren Client: *Texas Monthly*

Put together, the primitive sensibility of the photo illustration and the scratched headline, on the magazine spread 'The Evolution of Daniel Lee', evoke a sense of mystery and perhaps evil.
Designer: Scott Farestad Letterer: David Butler Photographer: Daniel Lee Client: *Photo Insider*

LEFT **Stream-of-consciousness writing** offers both information and texture in this decidedly ad-hoc composition.
Creative director: Alon Shoval Designer, letterer, illustrator: Brad Holland
Art directors: Michael Wright, Mark Braddock Client: The Newspaper Association of America

BELOW **A contradictory combination of formality and expression**, the painted textures are at once violent and serene on this poster called 'Acupuncture'.
Designers: Brad Holland, Jim McCune Letterer, illustrator: Brad Holland Client: Art Directors' Association of Iowa

LEFT **The tip of this kitchen knife** appears to have scratched the lettering on this theatre poster, which has the distinct look of a confessional note that might have been written by Medea herself.
Creative director: Drew Hodges Art director: Gail Anderson Designer, letterer: James Victore Client: SpotCo

LEFT **The violently scratched lettering complements** the cluttered and emotionally complex layered imagery. Steadman is well known for carving texts into his illustrations and this approach works well on the poster for the lecture series 'Inside the Heads of Film Directors'.

Art director, designer: Warren Johnson Letterer, illustrator: Ralph Steadman Client: Intelefilm

RIGHT **Running counter to the spontaneous nature of the style**, this scratchy lettering contained in orderly boxes gives the quirky poster for the tenth Annual Potato Festival its charm and offers the eye a structure for reading the text.

Designer, letterer, illustrator: Woody Pirtle Client: Hampton Day School

RIGHT **The most commonly used tool** in the scratch genre is the simple scratch board. Letters are scratched out of the black-over-white material to give a rough and ready look to this theatre poster for *We Are Them. They are Us.*
Designer, illustrator: Eric Belooussov Letterer, client: Ima-press

BOTTOM RIGHT **This map has three typographic layers**: strict formal typography, sketchy street and park names and an overall scratchiness that draws the eye to a single spot on the map. The theatre poster is advertising a production called *Dom-map*.
Designer, illustrator: Eric Belooussov Client: Cultural Centre Dom

BELOW **A bite from this fly** would definitely cause its human victim to scratch, which may or may not have anything to do with why the lettering on the poster, promoting a theatre production called *Noise & Fury*, is scratched on the fly's wing.
Designer, illustrator: Eric Belooussov Letterer: Dmitriev Nick Client: Cultural Centre Dom

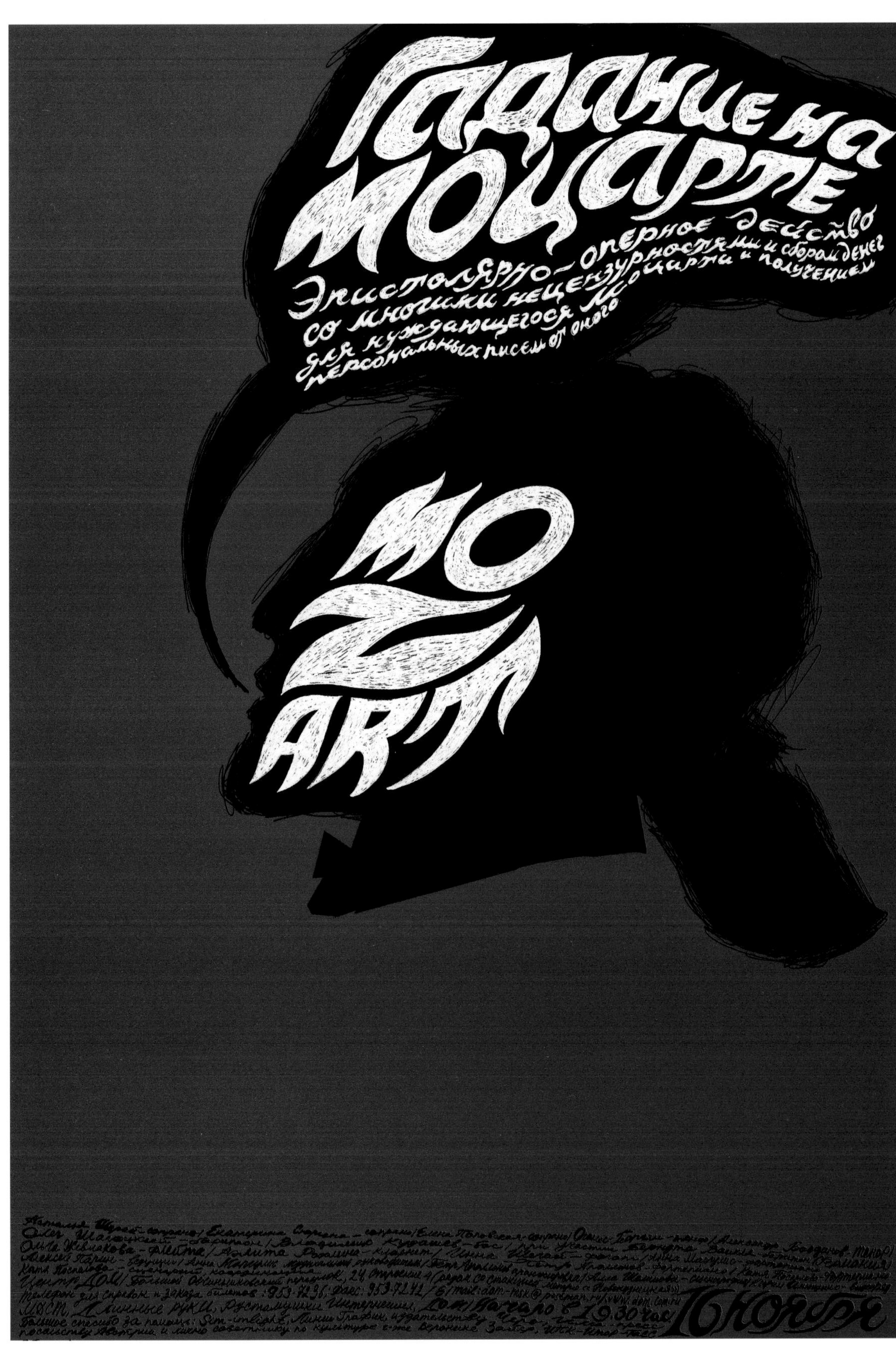

Mozart is not a figure in history about whom the word 'scratch' immediately comes to mind. But, Eric Beloussov uses scratched lettering to add mystery to this curious poster for an event about the composer.
Designer, illustrator: Eric Belooussov
Letterer: Dmitriev Nick Client: Cultural Centre Dom

ABOVE **With its incomprehensible, violently scratched words**, this expressive poster for an exhibition called 'The City Museum of Vukovar in Exile' suggests the handwriting of an artist facing the onset of madness.
Designer, letterer, illustrator: Boris Ljubicic Client: Council of the City of Vukovar in Exile, Zagreb

ABOVE RIGHT **Stark lettering and bold quotation marks** simulate the rape victim's inner voice on this poster, which is aptly named 'Talk Therapy'.
Designer, letterer: David Croy Client: Rape and Sexual Abuse Center, Minneapolis

RIGHT **Picasso, probably one of the first painters** to introduce the scratched letterform to modern art, could not have written this quotation better in his own hand; it appears on a poster called 'Project Guernica'.
Designer: Dpild af Tid Aps Letterer: Jenz Koudahl Clients: Tim Feldmann, Wilda Dance

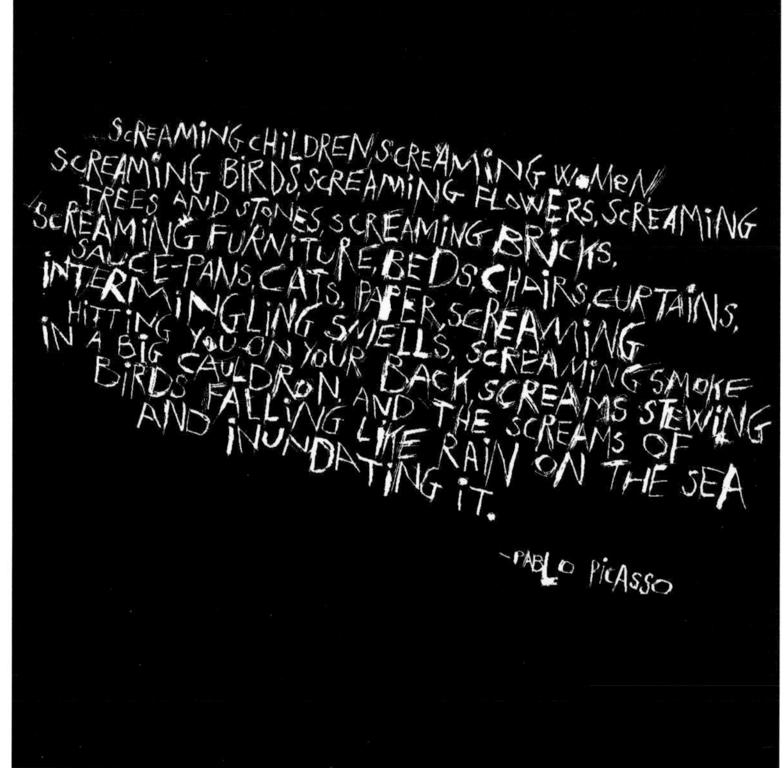

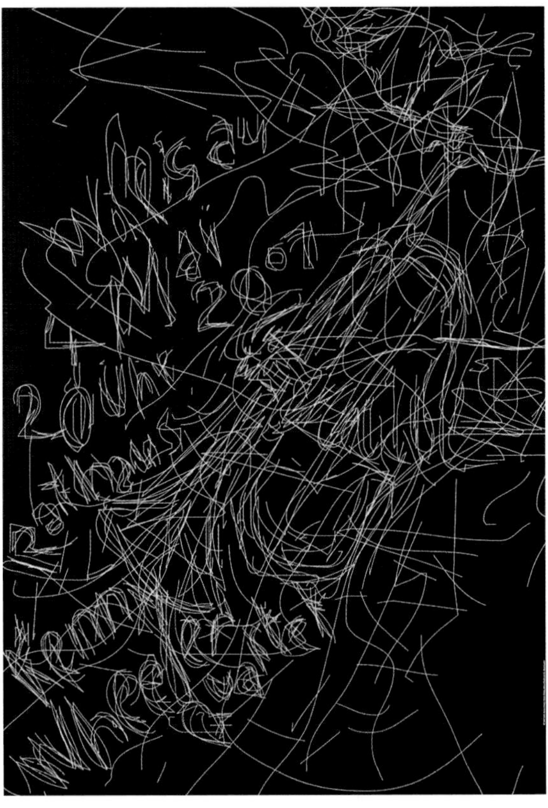

LEFT **If the viewer looks hard enough** at this poster for the jazz festival in Willisau, the image of a trumpet player appears through the frenetic scratches.
Designer, letterer: Niklaus Troxler Client: Jazz in Willisau

BOTTOM LEFT **There is perhaps no better way** to announce a play with a virtually unprintable title than to make the reader search out the words amidst a mass of furious scratches, as proved on this poster for *Fucking A*.
Designer, letterer: Paula Scher Client: The Public Theater

BELOW **After decades of manipulating real type**, Paula Scher does not always feel the need to make everything aesthetically pure. The scratched letter is a respite from the rigours of convention on this poster, 'So Far'.
Designer, letterer: Paula Scher Clients: Art Institute of Boston, AIGA Boston

A. STRINDBERG

HRVATSKO NARODNO KAZALISTE SPLIT

OTAC

RIGHT **As a face emerges from a marsh of dense scratches** it becomes clear that formal lettering would reduce the overall shock value of the theatre poster for *Otac* (*Father*); scratches give it a dynamic dimension.
Designer, letterer, illustrator: Boris Bucan Clients: Hrvatsko Narodno Kazaliste, Split (Croatian National Theatre)

BOTTOM RIGHT **One of the most common forms of pictorial vandalism** is to scratch on a photo portrait. It works well here, adding an aura of mystery to Björk's CD, *Hidden Place*.
Designer, letterer, illustrator: M/M (Paris) Photographers: Inez van Lamsweerde & Vinoodh Matadin
Client: One Little Indian Records Ltd.

BELOW **Scratches do not have to be ferocious or violent.** The dreamy lettering – seen as a transparent mask over this tranquil face – heightens a curious sense of calm on this poster, 'Butterflies & Zebras'.
Letterer, illustrator: Andy Simionato Photographer: Karen Ann Donnachie Client: *Qvest Magazine*

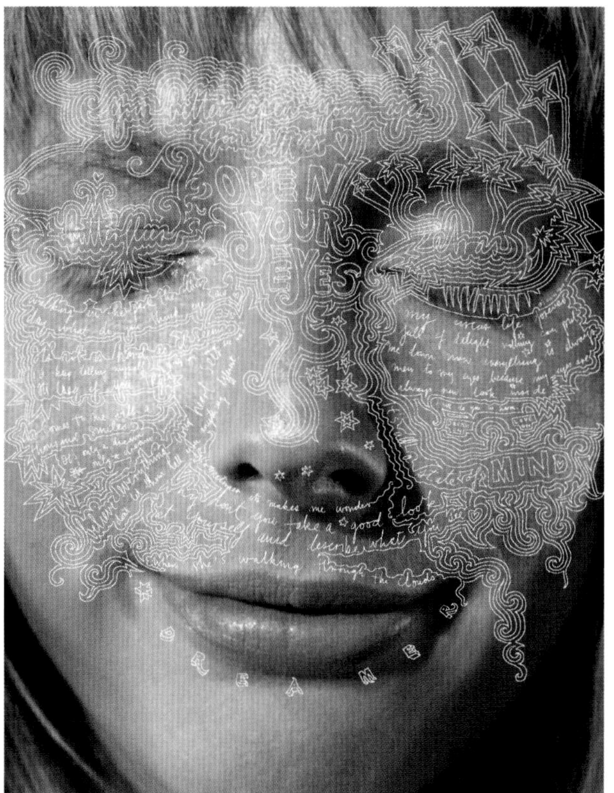

LEFT **More than a superficial scratch and certainly more painful than a tattoo**, carving on the skin with a razor blade (presumably sterilized) is the ultimate example of sacrificing one's body for typography: Stefan Sagmeister advertises one of his lectures.
Designers, letterers: Stefan Sagmeister, Martin Woodtli Photographer: Tom Schierlitz Client: AIGA Detroit

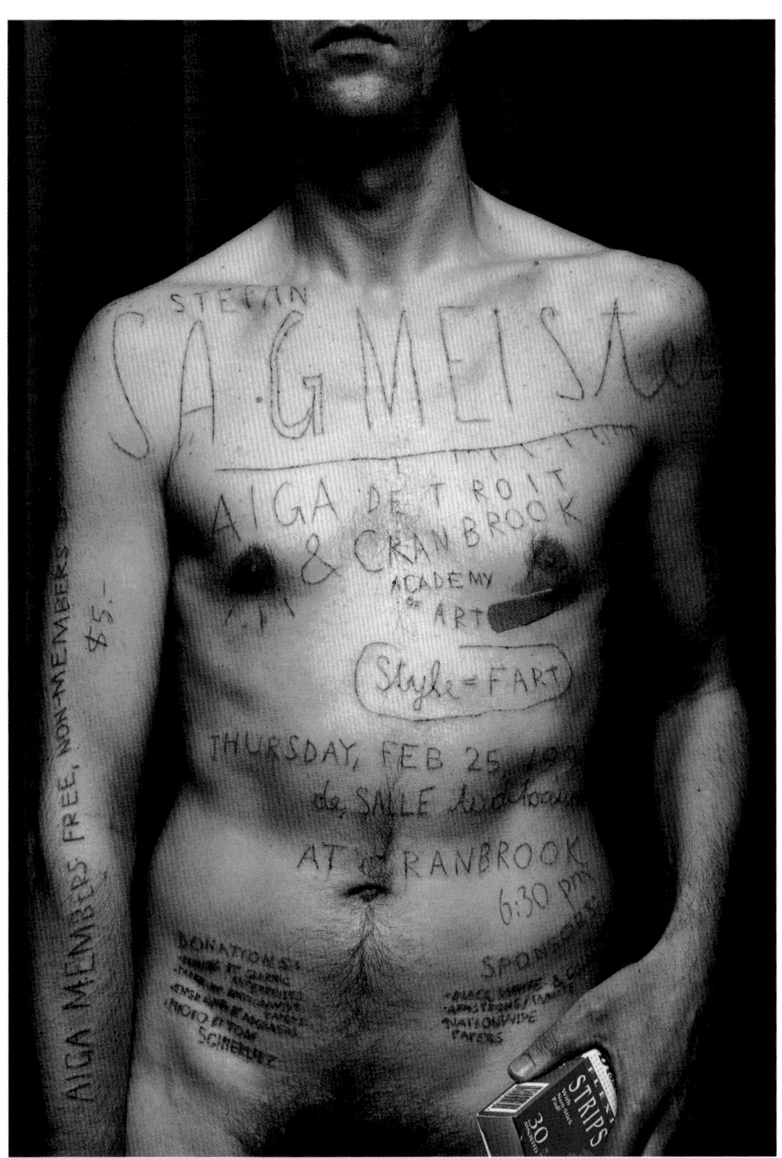

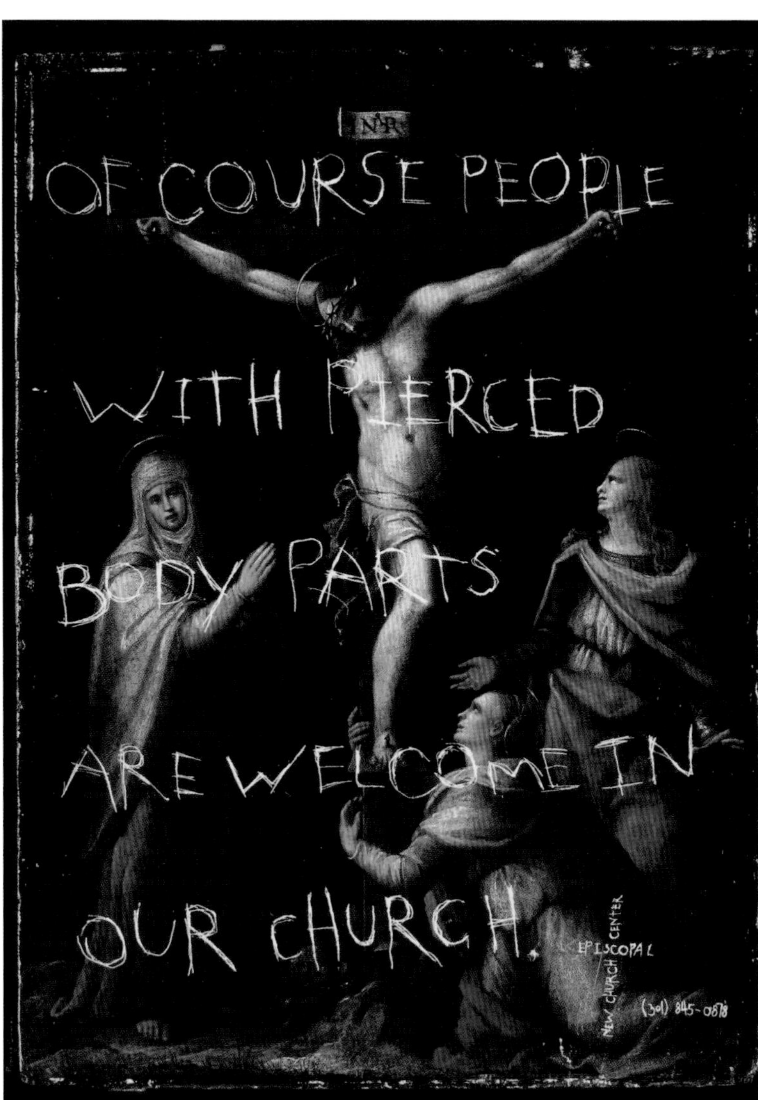

RIGHT **Designs for religious themes often rely on rather stereotypically** sacred iconography, but this poster, 'Of Course People with Pierced Body Parts Are Welcome in Our Church', introduces an alternative approach through the application of coarsely carved, scratchy words.
Art director, letterer: Jeff Hopfer Copywriters: Jeff Hopfer, Ron Henderson Photographers: Stock, Christie's Client: Episcopal New Church Center

It may not be the easiest text to read, but this lettering for two theatre posters exudes a feeling of insanity that fits the theatrical and graphic theme of the play. The viewer is forced to take an active role in deciphering the posters; likewise the audience has to work at understanding the performance of *Cardinal Virtues*.
Designer: Studio Dumbar Letterer: Bob van Dijk Illustrator: Monica Peón Client: Zeebelt Theatre

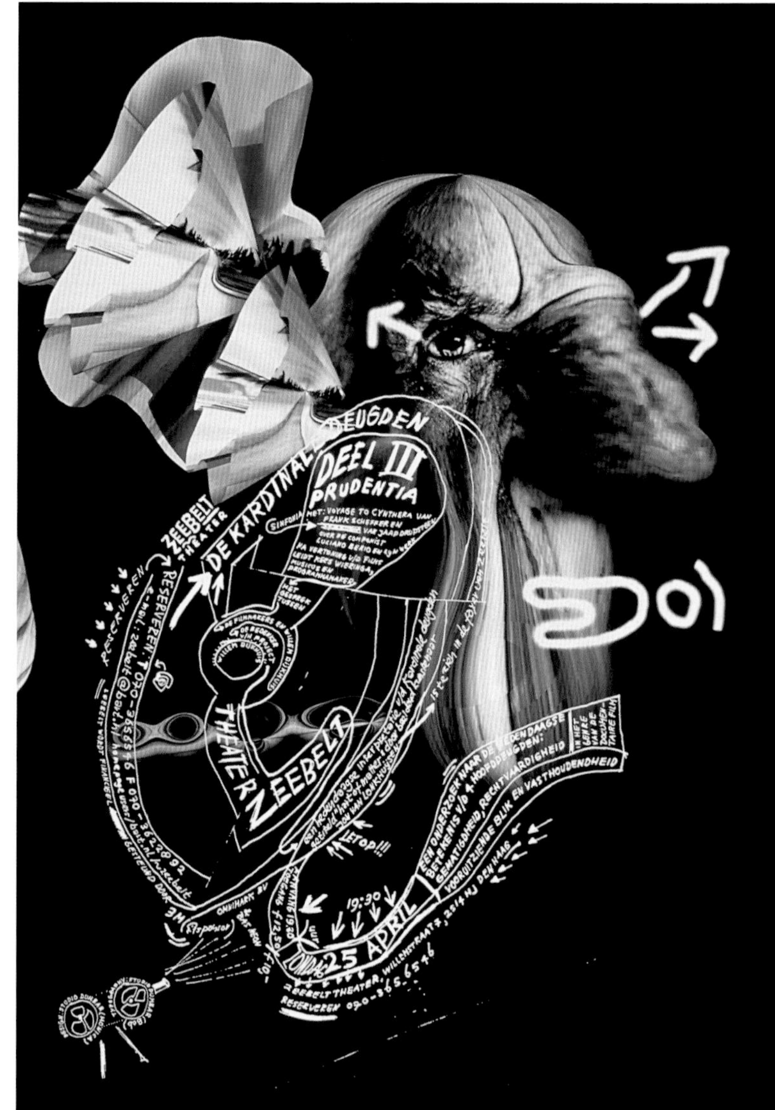

LEFT **The chicken-like scratches found on this poster**, advertising the lecture 'Variations on a Rectangle' by magazine art director DJ Stout, are consistent with the thumbnail-sized pages used to map out the pace and flow of magazine layouts.
Designer, letterer: DJ Stout Photographer: Michael O'Brian Client: Art Directors Club of Tulsa

BELOW **Scratchy script complements the hirsute fellow voraciously sucking** on the frothing toes. Since the entire image is raw, this type of lettering, including the scratched out portion, is the only typographic option for the billboard art project.
Designer, photographer: Jelena Kovacevic Letterer: Goran Juresa Client: Eye Gallery, Novi Sad

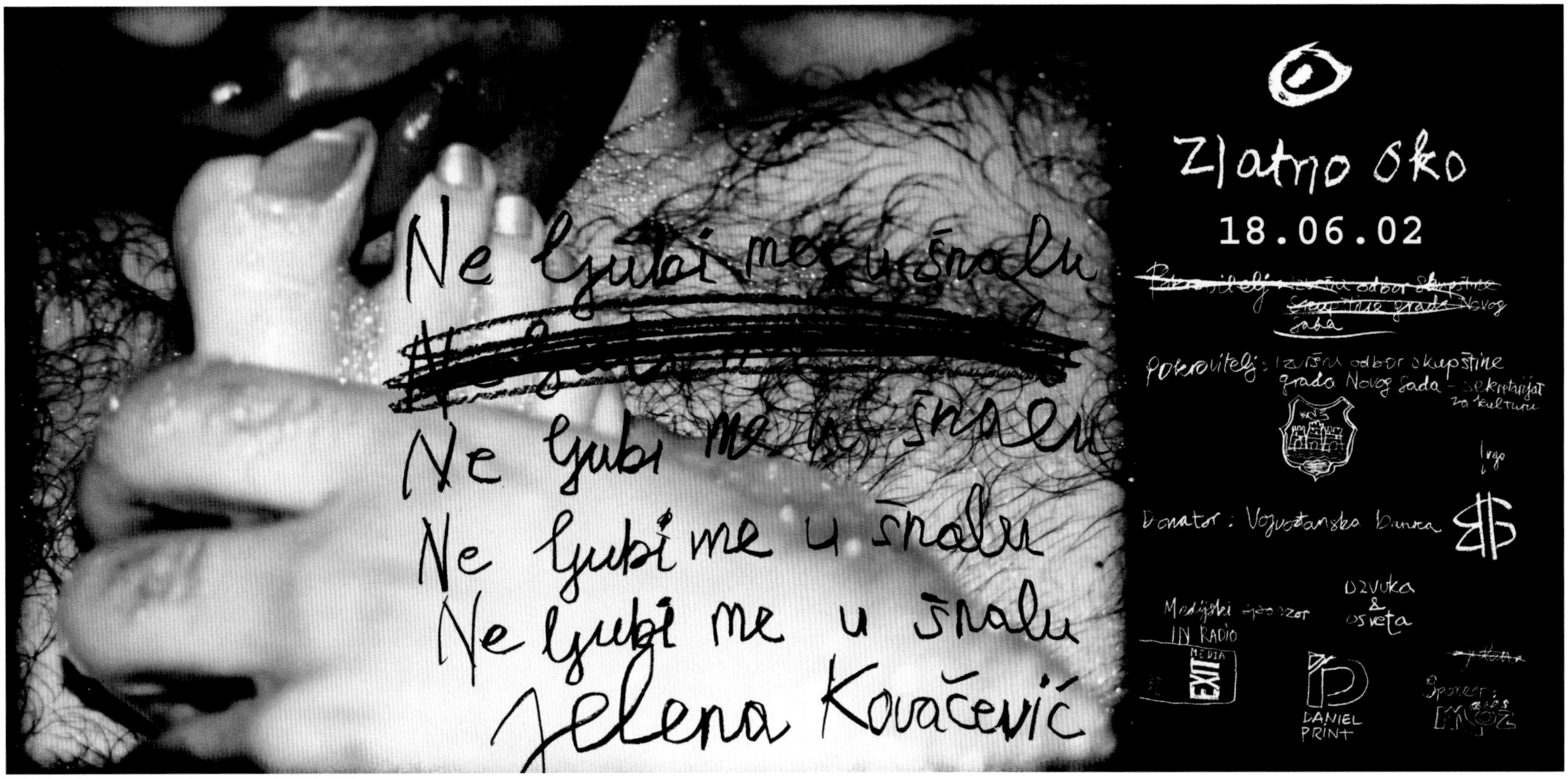

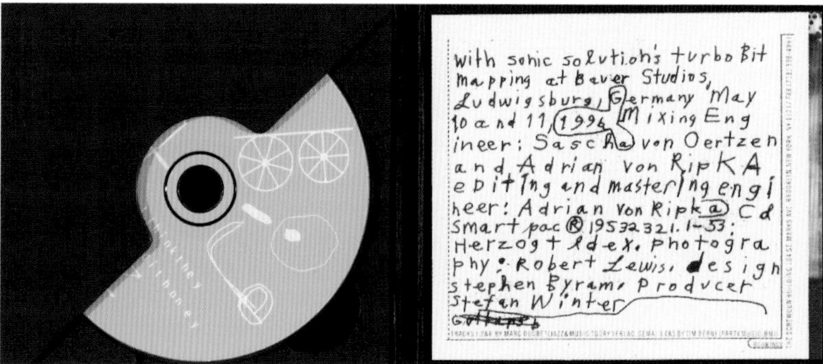

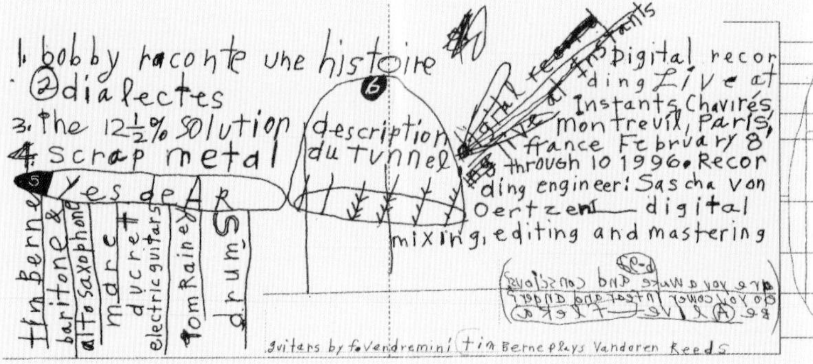

The name Big Satan is both ominous and hilarious. Surely a modern-day Satan would use this kind of untutored lettering, which features throughout this otherwise elegantly produced CD package for the album *I Think They Liked It Honey.*

Designer, letterer, illustrator: Steve Byram Photographer: Robert Lewis Client: Winter & Winter

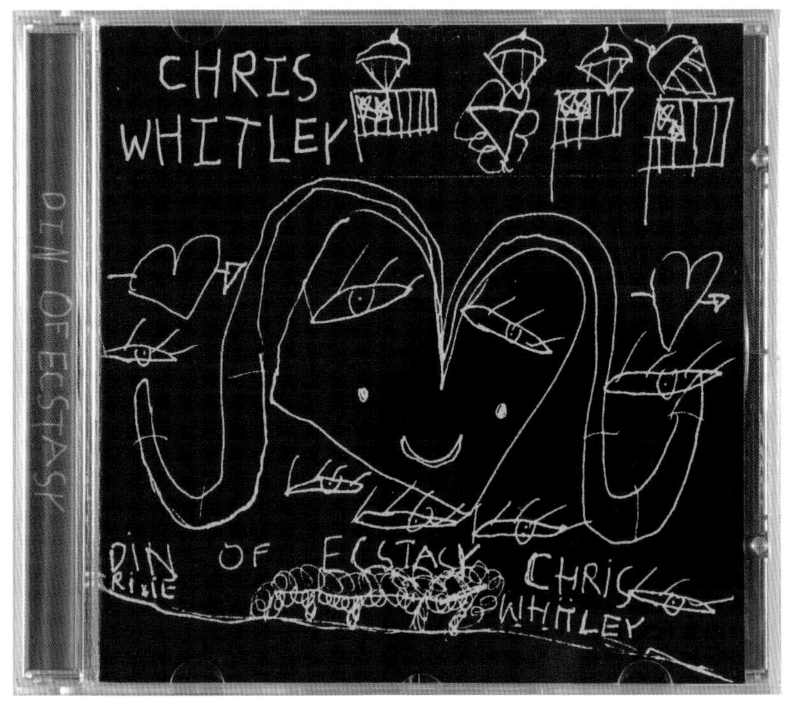

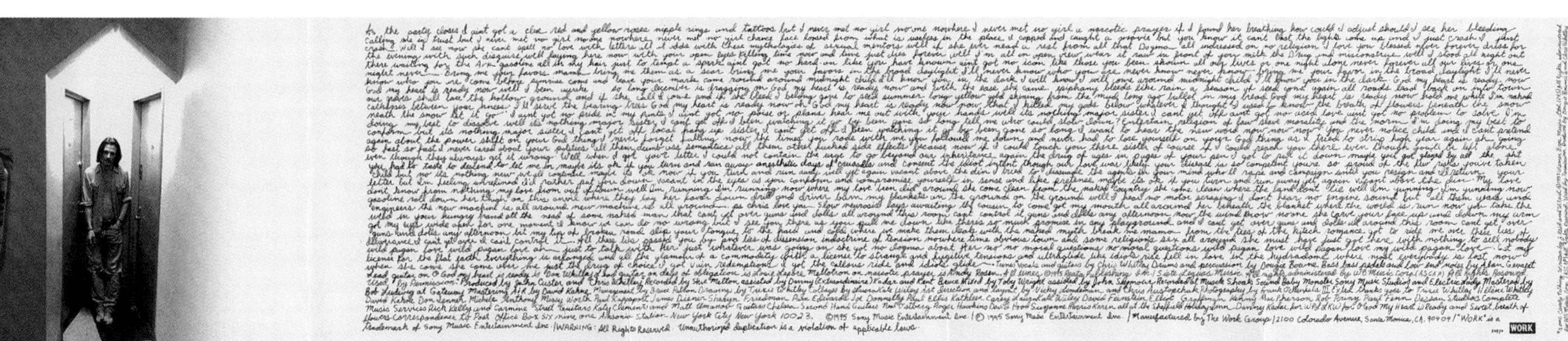

Scratching sentences, phrases and paragraphs in long, unrelieved lines is often considered the work of a madman, but on this CD for Chris Whitley's album *Din of Ecstacy* it adds an aesthetic quality.
Art directors, designers: Nicky Lindeman, Chris Austopchuk Illustrator: Trixie Whitley
Client: Sony Music Entertainment Inc.

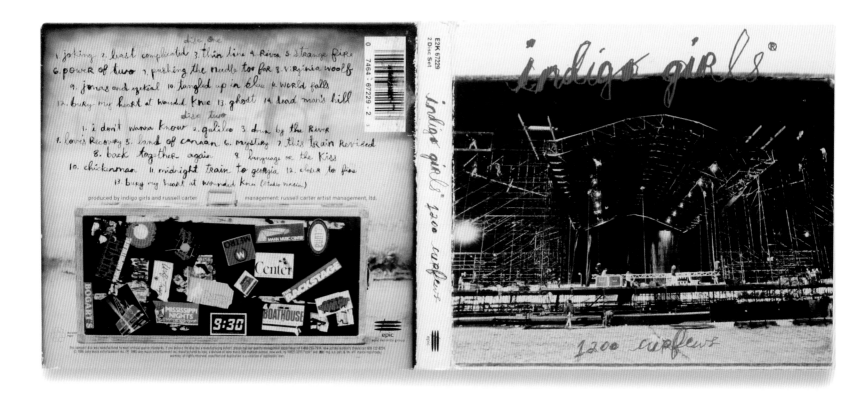

Scratchy lettering is but one component of this hand-wrought album package for Indigo Girls' *1200 Curfews.* Everything is designed to feel ad hoc and spontaneous but it is only an illusion.
Art director, designer, letterer: Risa Zaitschek Photographers: Jason Stang, Susan Alzner, Lance Mercer
Client: Sony Music Entertainment Inc.

LEFT **Often, it is as painful to read scratched letters** as it is to listen to someone stutter. The lettering has such a strained look on Tim Berne's CD *Nice View* that it seems as if the writer has had a difficult time expressing himself.
Designer, letterer, illustrator: Steve Byram Photographer: Robert Lewis Client: JMT Records

BELOW **This design underscores the fashion in art brut illustration**; the scratching acts as a counterpoint to the artwork, which was produced for Train's CD *Train.*
Designer: Richard Stutting Letterer, illustrator: Tommy Dougherty III Art concept: Charles Colin
Client: Sony Music Entertainment Inc.

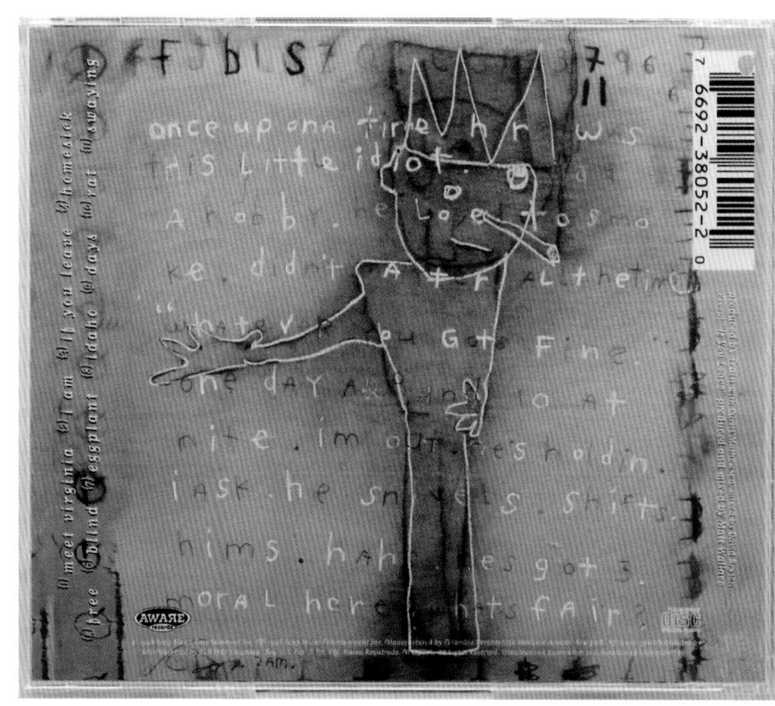

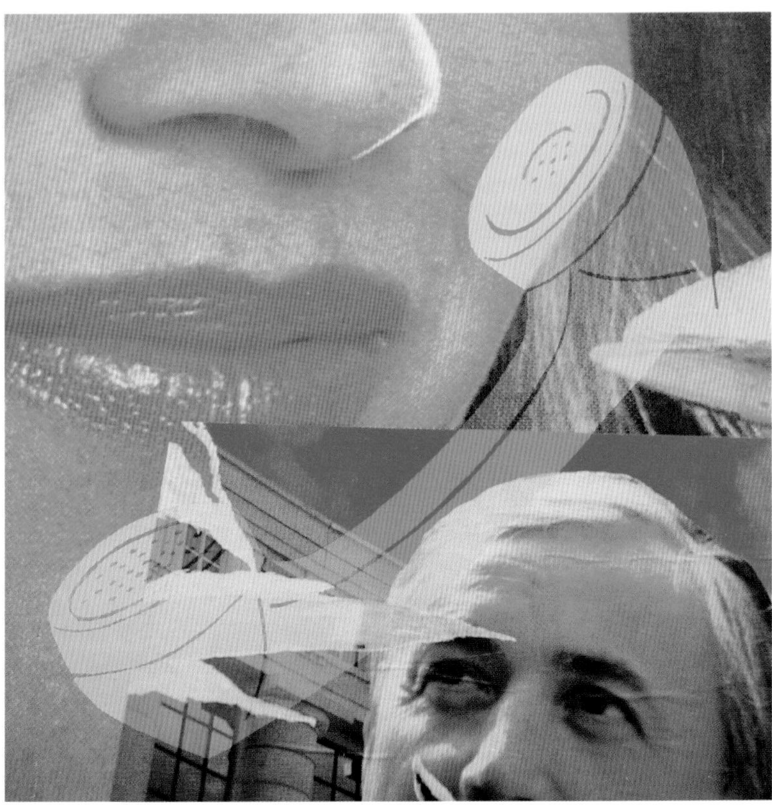

ABOVE **The CD is a sly commentary on religious fervour in rural areas.** The words are scratched in the same style as the lettering on makeshift signs on makeshift chapels in remote areas. The group Reverend Horton Heat are making an important statement with this CD design for their album *The Full-Custom Gospel Sounds of the Reverend Horton Heat.*

Designer, letterer, illustrator: Art Chantry Photographer: James Bland Client: Sub Pop Records

RIGHT AND OPPOSITE **Punk has a strong do-it-yourself sensibility** and these pages from the CD booklet for Phone Dummy's album *Answer the Phone Dummy* combine a feeling of alternative professionalism with mannered ad hocism.

Designer: Art Chantry Letterer: Kurt Bloch Photographer: David Wilds Client: Sub Pop Records

KIM - vocals and BASS
LULU - vocals and GUITAR
KURT - guitar and ETC.

Written and produced by KURT BLOCH for the "I would like to do that" Brothers. Recorded at HANZSEK audio, Seattle by Kurt and PETE GERRALD. Additional recording at PRIVATE RADIO by PAT GRAY. Songs published by Energy House Music (BMI), administered by BUG music.

JOHN MOEN played drums on "brd "COATED""
MIKE MUSBURGER helped get the ball rolling and played tambourine and ETC. thanks again, MIKE!

Cover by KURT and ART CHANTRY

photography by DAVID WILD except ⑤⑧⑬⑭ by CHARLES PETERSON and ②⑪ by AYNE ST. MARTIN

RUSTY WILLOUGHBY and NATE JOHNSON courtesy FLOP and FRONTIER/EPIC rec'ds
MIKE POSY and KEN POSY courtesy POSIES and DGC rec'ds
JASON FINN courtesy LOVE BATTERY and ATLAS rec'ds
DAN PETERS courtesy MUDHONEY and REPRISE rec'ds
JOHN MOEN courtesy the MAROONS
KIM SHATTUCK courtesy the MUFFS and WARNER BROS. rec'ds

SUB POP

BACK TO NOWHERE

AS THEY SAY I'M BACK TO NOWHERE AS OF YESTERDAY AT LEAST THEY'RE TELLING ME THAT AGAIN AND I'M FINE KNOWING IT NOW
DAYS THEY SAY ARE LONG BUT THERE'S NO OTHER WAY TO GET THROUGH ONE HAVE A HAPPY DAY OR SOMETHING LIKE THAT
BACK TO NOWHERE I AM GOING BACK TO NOWHERE I'LL BE THERE NOWHERE IS WHERE YOU'LL FIND ME BECAUSE I'M THERE ALL THE TIME.
TIMES DON'T CHANGE ENOUGH FOR ANYONE TO SAY "EVERYTHING WILL TURN OUT OKAY IT ALL WILL BE FINE"
DAN PETERS ON THE DRUMS

5

6 "COATED" instrumental

i've not done anything at all since i last saw you
and i haven't had a thing to eat for a day or two
I found the star that led me to the planet where you are
drums - mike musburger

I Found the Star

7

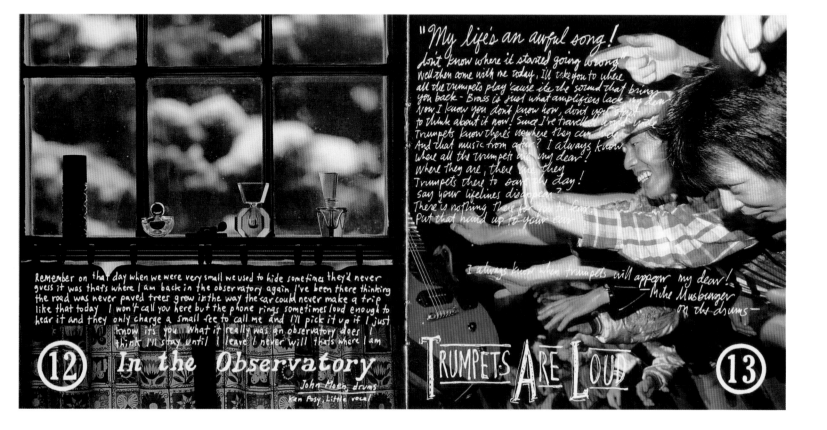

Remember on that day when we were very small we used to hide sometimes they'd never guess it was that's where I am back in the observatory again I've been there thinking the road was never paved trees grew in the way the car could never make a trip like that today I won't call you here but the phone rings sometimes loud enough to hear it and they only charge a small fee to call me and I'll pick it up if I just know it's you what it really was an observatory does I think I'll stay until I leave I never will that's where I am

12 In the Observatory

John Moen, drums
Ken Posy, Little vocal

"My life's an awful song!
don't know where it started going wrong"
Well then come with me today, I'll take you to where
all the trumpets play 'cause it's the sound that brings
you back - Brass is just what amplifiers lack my dear
now I know you don't know how, don't you start
to think about it now! Since I've travelled
Trumpets know there's nowhere they can
And that music from afar? I always know
where all the trumpets are my dear!
Where they are, there they
Trumpets there to save the day!
say your lifelines disappear?
There is nothing there for you to fear
Put that hand up to your ear

I always know when trumpets will appear my dear!
—Mike Musburger on the drums—

TRUMPETS ARE LOUD

13

ornate, curlicue, sinuous

In some quarters, calligraphy is one of those handy crafts, like crocheting or basket-weaving, the tools for which come in a kit often purchased at craft fairs or flea markets. People create calligraphy for fun in their spare time or as part of cottage businesses addressing wedding and Bar Mitzvah invitations. In other quarters, it is seen as the highest level of cursive handlettering, an art of expression and precision intensely studied and practised following age-old traditions. Both are reasonable assessments. The Sunday calligrapher dabbles in craft, while the professional engages in art, or vice versa. Anyway, whatever the operative designation, calligraphy is the art and craft of drawing ornate, curlicue and sinuous scripts by hand, and it takes talent and dedication to flawlessly master it. This section, however, is not strictly about calligraphy, but it does draw upon and often rejects some of the medium's heritage.

Modern calligraphers honour Chinese, Japanese, Arabic and Medieval European scribes as wellsprings of the craft. A passion for the written word and its spiritual connotations drive the most serious practitioners, while rote methods of penmanship appeal to the less devoted. In addition to these ancient origins, the calligraphic sensibility underwent a surge of utilitarian popularity during the first half of the twentieth century when commercial artists relied almost entirely on their hands, as a substitute for expensive photostats and other convenient reproduction tools, to create all the design components that are taken for granted in the computer age (such as borders, hairlines, dingbats). In the 1920s and 1930s, custom-made cursive alphabets were frequently employed for book covers, jackets and title pages, as well as for logos, brochures and advertisements. William Addison Dwiggins (1880–1956), the master typographer and letterer of this era, created unique curlicue and swash scripts that defied the laws of typographic gravity and projected the calligraphic art light years ahead. He further spawned a legion of followers who copied or adapted his calligraphic methods. Yet, calligraphy was still an anathema to orthodox modernists (Dwiggins once called them 'those Bauhaus Boys'), who held that even the most artistic manifestations were based on archaic or ornate sensibilities that ran counter to contemporary machine aesthetics. Modern typography was a rejection of formal handwork as a remnant of bourgeois privilege. Therefore, the new sans-serif faces abandoned any hint of calligraphic fussiness (and handwork entirely). Nonetheless, orthodoxy did fill every corner of the commercial art field and various approaches to flexible steel nib or broad-edged pen and brush calligraphy were commonplace, especially on book jackets, until the early 1950s after which advancements in cold type technology (and shifts in general style) made them passé.

However, script lettering has long retained a certain currency because not every script is purely calligraphic. During the nineteenth century, for example, so-called banknote scripts were in fashion for a variety of commercial printing needs, including banknotes, diplomas, stock certificates and other official documents. They were also used on unofficial materials, such as calling cards, invitations and personal notices. Derived from formal (probably regal) penmanship, scripts were made into typefaces that became the common stock at printing shops for all kinds of quotidian use.

Scripts are routinely represented in various styles in most type catalogues even today. Around the turn of the twentieth century, script-inspired letters were imbued with the sinuosity typical of the Art Nouveau style. A vogue emerged during the early-twentieth century for perfume script, the generic style of a number of typefaces used for, as the name underscores, perfume, lingerie and other fashion advertisements – in short, anything with a feminine audience. Do not be misled that scripts are exclusively ascribed to one gender; strangely, the codifier of the New Typography, Jan Tschichold (1902–74), often combined light-line (or monoline) banknote scripts with bold modernist Gothic type on his book jackets and title pages to intensify the contrasts between headlines and subheadings. The marriage of machine-age type and pre-industrial lettering was a curious, if critical, commentary on old and new typesetting mannerisms. It was doubtless influenced by avant-garde Futurist and Dada typography, which involved a hotchpotch of standard commercial typefaces, including scripts, composed in atypical combinations.

Scripts also have a long history as product trademarks for such companies as Coca Cola and General Electric. The word 'champagne' on Moët & Chandon labels dating back to the nineteenth century has nearly always been set in a script face. By the 1950s, scripts were being used for many commercial logos on high-ticket products from Cadillac to Frigidaire (and they looked impressive when made into illuminated three-dimensional objects engraved or carved out of metal or wood).

Script faces can be formal or informal, mannered or free-hand and, for that matter, light or dark. Whatever the typographical intention, however, historically they have been sidelined in the same way, and perhaps for the same reason, that italics are relegated to secondary status in type hierarchies: because they are not as demonstrative as other faces. This has not entirely marginalized scripts, but readers are prone to take the messages they convey less seriously as though the content is subordinate to that of Roman faces. Scripts imply a lack of substance (or a parenthetical idea). Certain lettering and typography should connote or underscore meaning, but this should not demean those typefaces that were designed as integral scripts without links to larger type families. Hermann Zapf's Zapf Chancery (1979) and Medici Script (1974) and Robert Slimbach's Poetica (1992), which have a strength and beauty of their own, are very good examples. It does mean, however, that scripts have a certain amount of symbolic baggage that designers should understand when working with them. This said, the lettering surveyed in this section ignores for the most part the problems in favour of focusing on the positive graphic effects derived from scripts and, especially, on what simulated handwriting brings to the page.

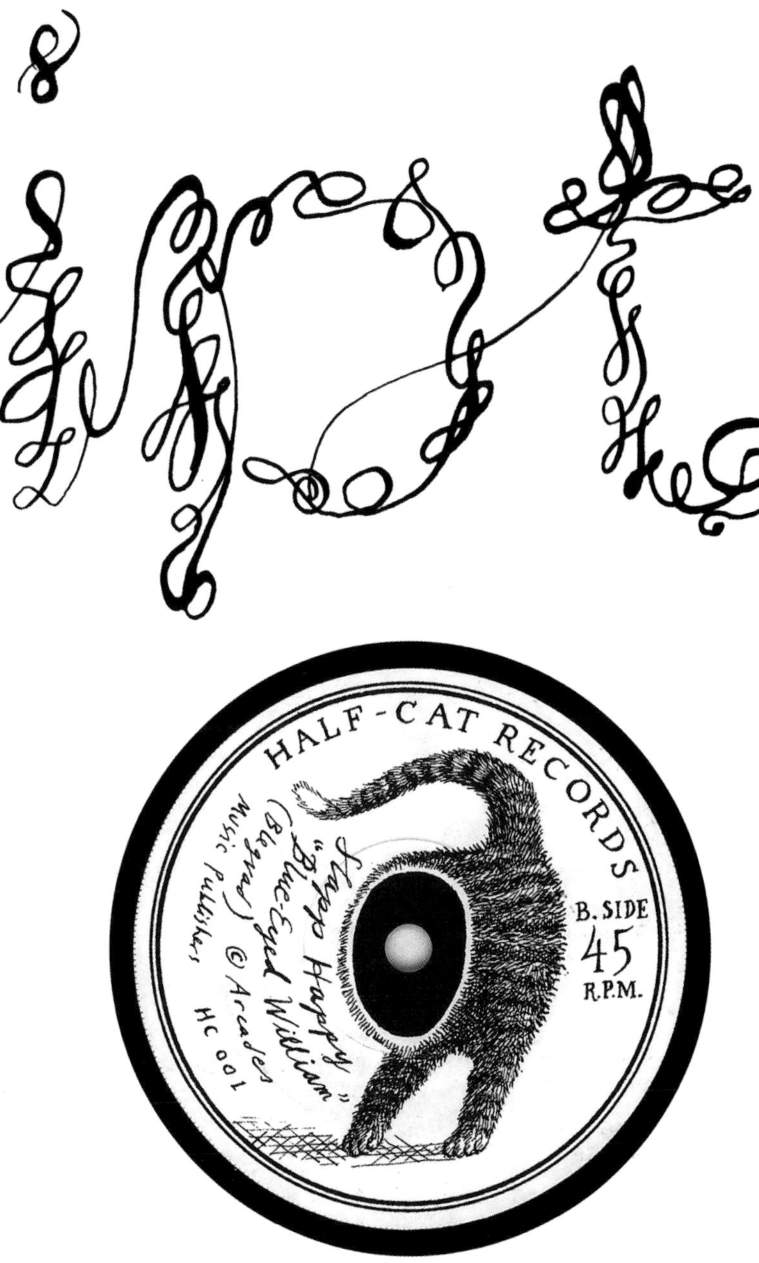

The pseudo-elegant handlettered formal script on Half-Cat Records' logo serves as a striking aesthetic contrast to the other handmade Roman letters.
Designer, letterer, illustrator: Peter Blegvad Client: Slapp Happy

Although scripts are not best suited to being read in large text blocks (remember how difficult it is to read Babar the Elephant books in which all the text is in cursive), they can, as I have said, be efficiently used as large headlines in newspapers and magazines or on posters, book jackets and CD covers. Furthermore, the current variety of hand-drawn, eccentric scripts adds quirkiness to layouts. Whereas script may lack authority, it contributes a distinct graphic personality and introduces an individual artistic character onto a page. Designer and inveterate hand-scrawler Art Chantry notes that, since script evolved from handwriting (as opposed to the chiselled-on-stone origins of Roman typefaces), 'I've always felt a closer, more "human" connection to script forms. The primary strength of script is in its emotional closeness to the human hand (and mind).' By virtue of script's fluidity it might also be described as lettering with sex appeal; few other type styles are more fundamentally alluring than the flowing cursive line that forms a smooth and supple string of words.

Some of the scripts surveyed in this section are erotically motivated. Others are rough and untutored, while still others are more refined in a calligraphic sense. Most adhere to existing models, a few are invented and occasionally there are swashes, ligatures and curlicues thrown in to add personality to the form. Perhaps the most common script today, like those of yesteryear, are born of pure handwriting: good and bad penmanship.

Designers often draw upon the artless vernacular for sophisticated design. This is apparent in Michael Bierut's poster for the seventh

A strand of wool is transformed into the name and registered trademark of this sock company.
[top] Smartwool Corporate Logo [bottom] Socks Identity Creative director: Joe Duffy Senior designer: Neil Powell
Designer, letterer, illustrator: Missy Wilson Client: Smartwool

BELOW LEFT **Here is a mark that blends the audacity of graffiti** with the sinuous nature of calligraphy. It works well as both a trademark and a startling monogram for Bad Cat.
Designer, letterer, illustrator: Kostja Gatnik Client: Emzin

BELOW RIGHT **This Japanese character is not a script in the Western sense**, but it is a curvy pictographic drawing of the kind that formed the basis of the Western calligraphic tradition. Here, it is used as Ko's logo.
Designer, letterer: Touru Shigenari Client: Okunoseimeido

annual book fair to help the homeless (see p. 87), which injects an artless childlike script into an otherwise conventional layout. The script is not as free flowing as informal handwriting, but Bierut conveys the idea that he probably failed his school penmanship class. Regardless, the result is as natural as any personal signature.

Speaking of natural, Lynn Buckley's cover for *The Natural* (see p. 90) interprets the title of this great novel about a mysterious baseball slugger both literally and figuratively. Her unpretentious handwriting underscores the word 'natural', but it is composed of string unravelling from the baseball that the protagonist hits out of the ballpark. Conversely, but no less impressively, each of the CPB Group's advertisements for the bike-helmet manufacturer Giro (see p. 103) contains one simple, unadorned and undramatic handwritten word – 'passion', 'breathe', 'beauty' – by a striking conceptual image. Standard type alone could not convey the same intimacy, something that is true about most of the penmanship conceits found in this section.

The next most common neo-script is of the brush or thick-nibbed-pen variety, charged with kinetic power and impromptu energy. Milton Glaser's poster for 'Camus: Rebellion, Resistance and Death' (see p. 91) is an example of this more refined method. Rick Meyers's poster, 'Fluidity Diagram' (see p. 90), and Turkish-born Bülent Erkmen's surrealist poster, 'Fake Identities 5' (see p. 99), use the same technique but lack the aforementioned refinement if not the intensity. Eric Belooussov's poster for the exhibition 'Busidoremi' conveys a seeming total abandon, yet while this method suggests the hand of a renegade

BELOW LEFT **Script in the purely aesthetic meaning** of the style is not exclusive to Roman alphabets. This rounded linear composition, used for Kamaburo's logo, is an exotic example of a non-Western application.
Designer, letterer: Touru Shigenari Client: Oharameya

BELOW RIGHT **This Cyrillic logo is derived from the ornately official** penmanship of the seventeenth and eighteenth centuries. Although it is clearly mannered, the swashes give the logo a certain charm.
Designer, letterer: Rastko Ciric Client: Bosko Buha Theatre, Belgrade

graffiti artist, it also projects more sophistication. As spontaneous as all these approaches seem, it is only an illusion.

On the subject of sophistication, not all scripts even give the illusion of improvisation. Some are unmistakably studied to achieve a result that seems either cooked or overcooked. Such is the case in Louise Fili's logo for The Mermaid Inn [right], a New York restaurant, which relies on deftness of hand to produce an accurate result that in its formal informality is both readable and identifiable. Likewise, Laetitia Wolff and Nick Dewar's poster 'Objets Inanimés' (see p. 96) is scripted in the literal sense of the word: while it retains a casual appearance it demands calligraphic precision to achieve balance and harmony.

In addition to the raw and harmonious, there are two kinds of, let's call them, ostentatious scripts: those that evoke egotistical confidence and those that suggest flamboyance. The former is represented by Tom Hautekiet's poster for the book *De Geverfde Vogel* (*The Painted Bird*, see p. 90), in which his casual script is given monumental proportions by the vivaciousness of the 'g', 'f' and 'l'. In fact, anything with a circular or oval swirl is imbued with a confidence matching that of John Hancock's signature on the American Declaration of Independence (1776). Similarly, Polish-born Roman Kalarus's poster 'Image of Jazz in Polish Poster' (see p. 92) reveals premeditated brazenness in the way the word 'jazz' is stretched out. Kalarus's kind of ostentation is characterized by swash letters, once the province of ornate illumination and inscription but now commonly used for noble and common functions alike. Pepe Gimeno's scripts (see p. 97) are a veritable orgy of delightful excess; Kostja Gatnik's Bad Cat logo (see p. 84) is the swash as graphic icon; and UK-based Teamwork Design's 'Merry Christmas' (see p. 95), with the festive words transformed into Santa's white beard on Mao Tse-tung, turns the swash into the perfect visual pun.

It is fascinating to contrast traditional Western typography (chiselled) with Japanese typographic traditions (brush). Since so much of Western script borrows from Chinese, Japanese and Arabic calligraphic techniques, it is very interesting to compare the Western examples in this section to Ghobad Shiva's poster for an art lecture in Tehran (see p. 89). While the letterforms are different, the ebb and flow of the letters clearly influences the most sophisticated specimens in this book.

Overall, the hand script expresses the full gamut of typographic emotion and is never neutral. Unlike formal calligraphers, new script letterers care more about aesthetic expedience than formal perfection. The results are a perfect antidote to gloss and purity.

Curlicue lettering reflects the curvaceous contours of the mermaid used as the logo for The Mermaid Inn.
Art director: Louise Fili Designers: Louise Fili, Chad Roberts
Letterer: Chad Roberts Illustrator: Anthony Russo
Client: The Mermaid Inn Inc.

To the Western eye, Cyrillic lettering evokes a feeling of mystery particularly when drawn with a brush. On this exhibition poster, it also creates a curious pattern that frames a bizarre image.
Designer, illustrator: Eric Belooussov Letterer: Dmitriev Nick Client: Cultural Centre Dom

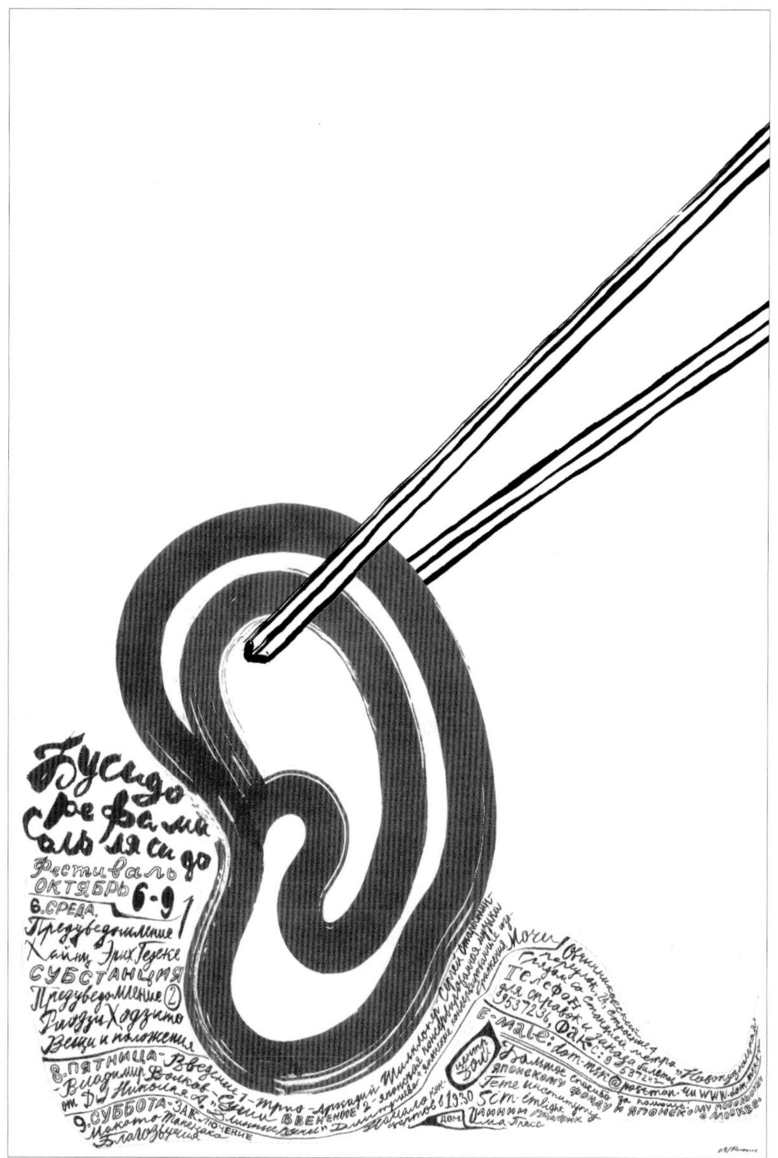

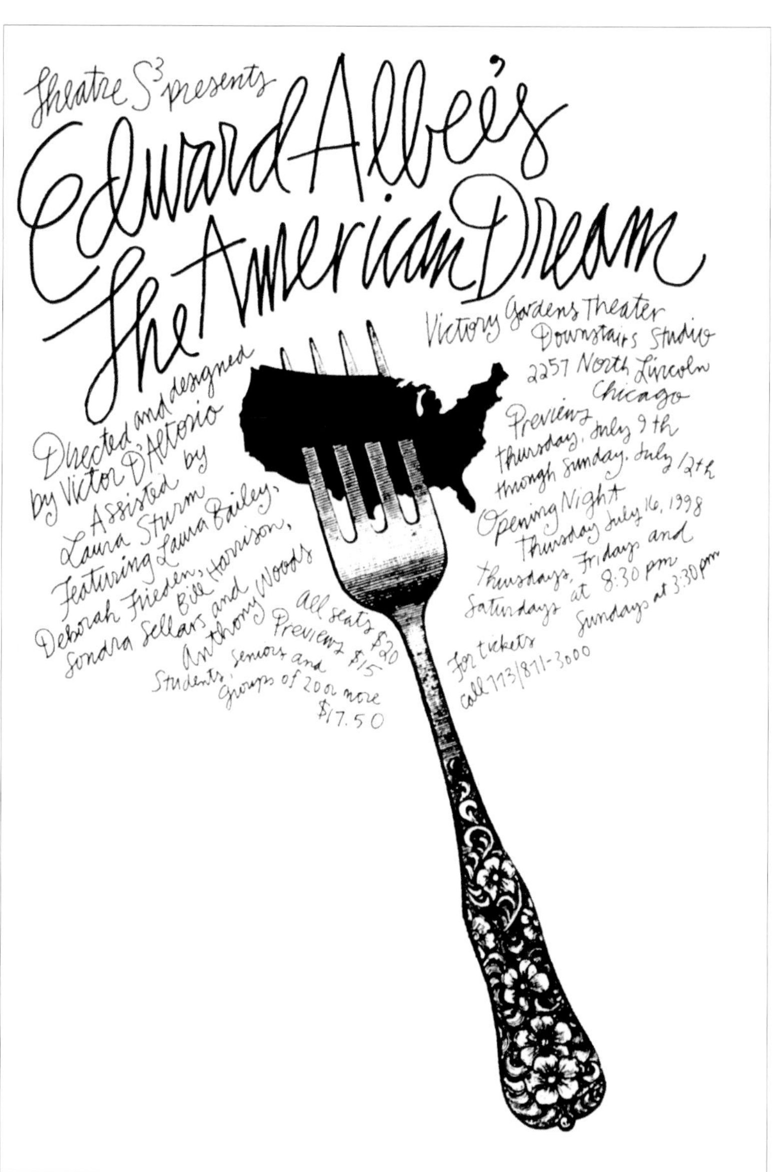

Stylized penmanship is used to emphasize the impropriety of this poster promoting veteran playwright Edward Albee's dark and satiric play on American morals and mores.
Designer, letterer: Michael Bierut Client: Theatre S³

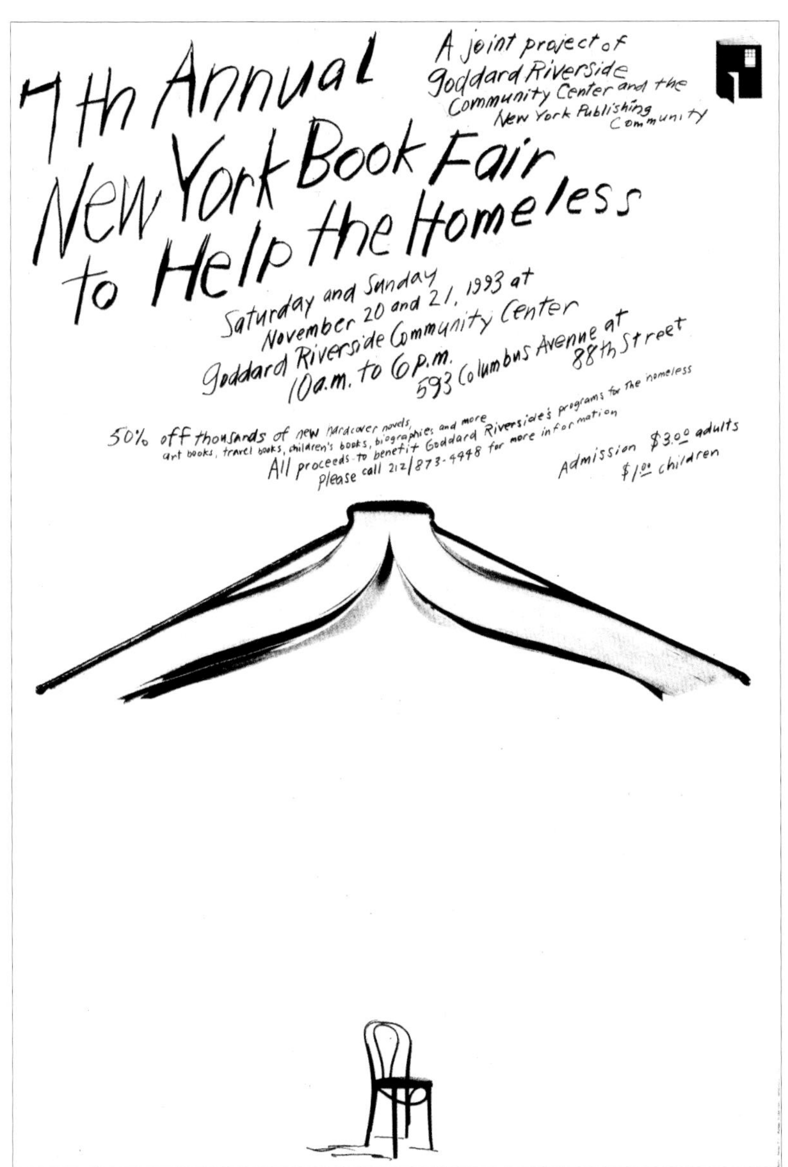

The handwriting on this poster is not script per se, rather it is italic, a cousin of script. It is used to give the impression of immediacy, which is in keeping with the book fair's theme of homelessness.
Designer, letterer: Michael Bierut Photographer: Reven T. C. Wurman Client: Goddard Riverside Community Center

Adhering to the principles of early-nineteenth-century poster design, James McMullen's swirling calligraphic script frames his decidedly fluid watercolour drawing on this theatre poster for *Grande Ecole*.
Designer, letterer, illustrator: James McMullen Client: Theatre 14, Paris

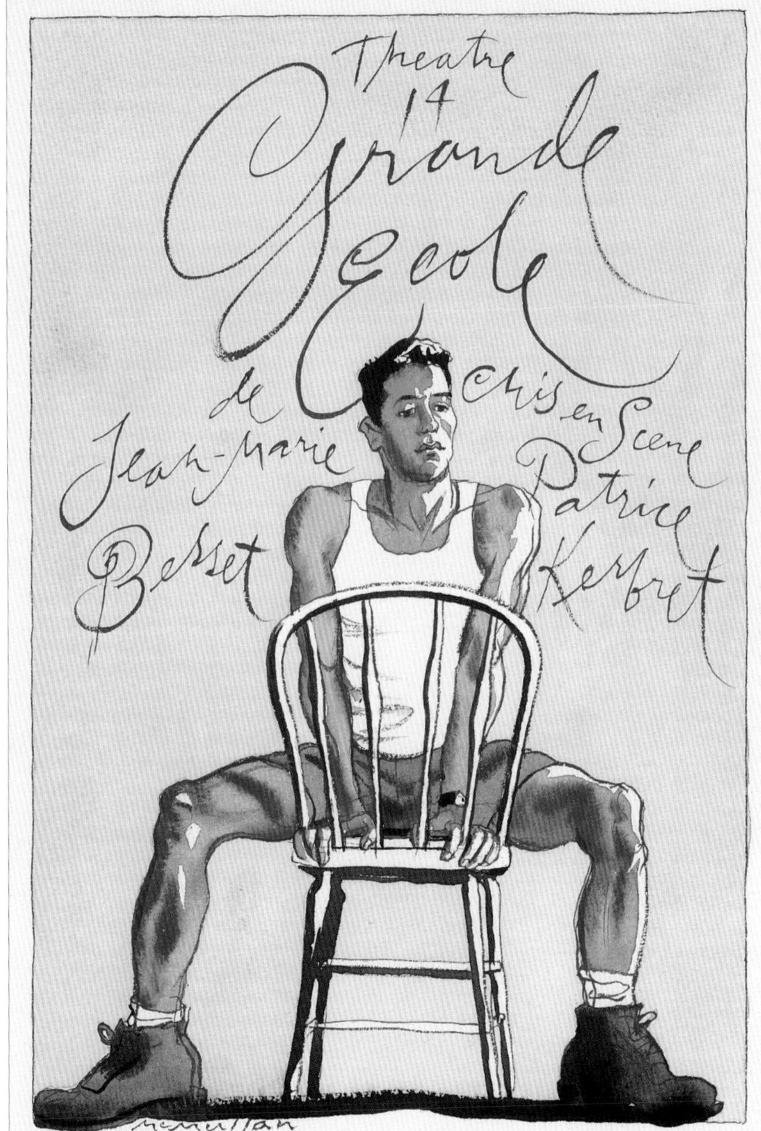

LEFT **Full of ironic contrasts**, especially the relationship between the innocent script and the bright-red blood, this poster, entitled 'Stop Torture in Peru!', deals with a very serious issue effectively.
Designer, letterer, illustrator: Woody Pirtle Client: Amnesty International

RIGHT **By adopting the look of Arabic calligraphy**, the script combines many traditions in one poster for the theatre production *On the Carpet*.
Designer, illustrator: Eric Belooussov Letterer: Dimitriev Nick Client: Cultural Centre Dom

LEFT **Western letters sit comfortably alongside Iranian calligraphy** to form an impressively contemporary composition on this poster advertising an art lecture.
Designer, letterer, illustrator: Ghobad Shiva Client: Tehran Museum of Contemporary Art

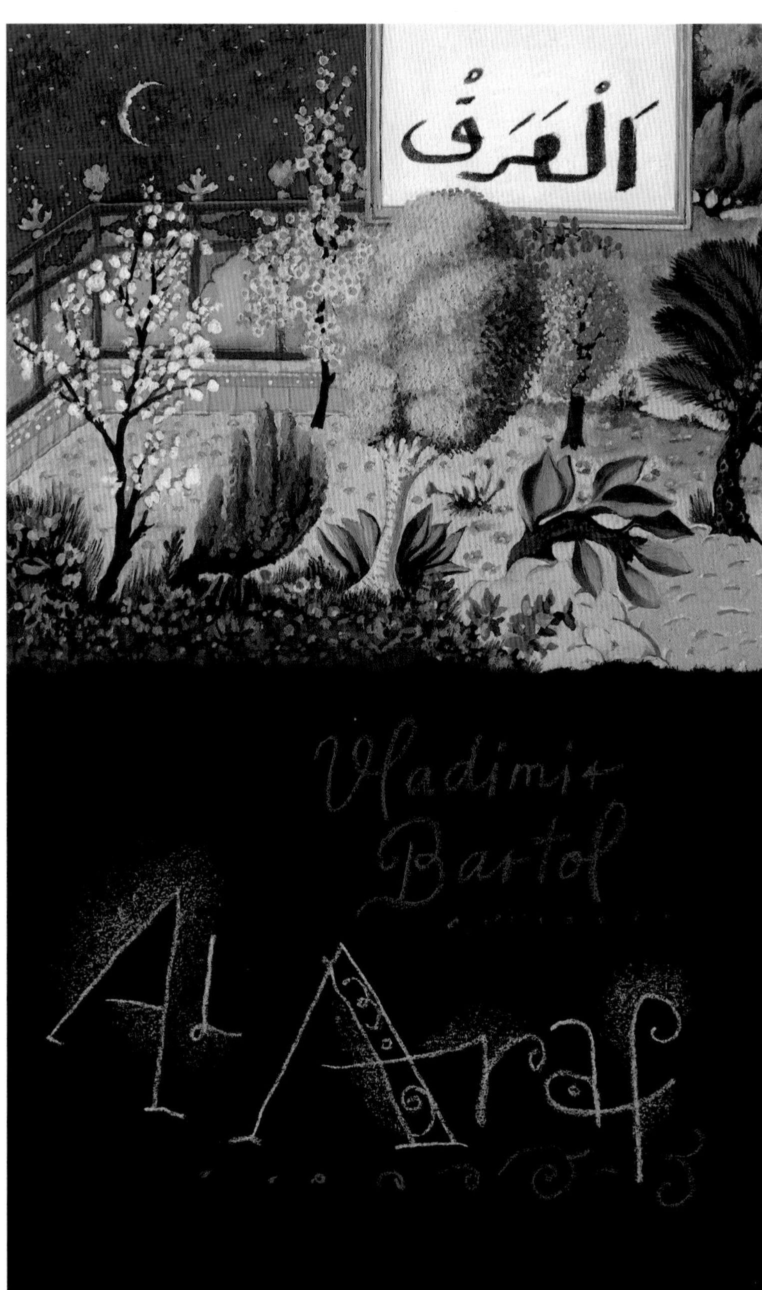

RIGHT **The exotic blend of old and new script lettering** makes this ancient Persian miniature more contemporary. The poster is promoting a theatrical piece called *Al Araf*.
Designer, letterer, illustrator: Radovan Jenko Client: Sanje, Ljubljana

RIGHT **Handwriting analysts judge the writer's character** by the curvature of the script – it would be interesting to know what they would deduce from this clearly pronounced example on the poster 'Fluidity Diagram'.
Designer, letterer, client: Rick Meyers

BOTTOM RIGHT **Deliberately scribbled**, this brush script is difficult to make out but is nonetheless striking on the book cover for *De Geverfde Vogel* (*The Painted Bird*).
Designer, letterer: Tom Hautekiet Client: Theater Company De Onderneming

BELOW **This script is cleverly spun** around the unravelling of the stitching on a baseball; it was used on the book cover of *The Natural*.
Designer, letterer, illustrator: Lynn Buckley Client: Farrar, Straus and Giroux

OPPOSITE **Colour adds dimension to all script**, and here it also echoes the multi-coloured portrait of Albert Camus on the poster, 'Camus: Rebellion, Resistance and Death'.
Designer, illustrator: Milton Glaser Client: School of Visual Arts, New York

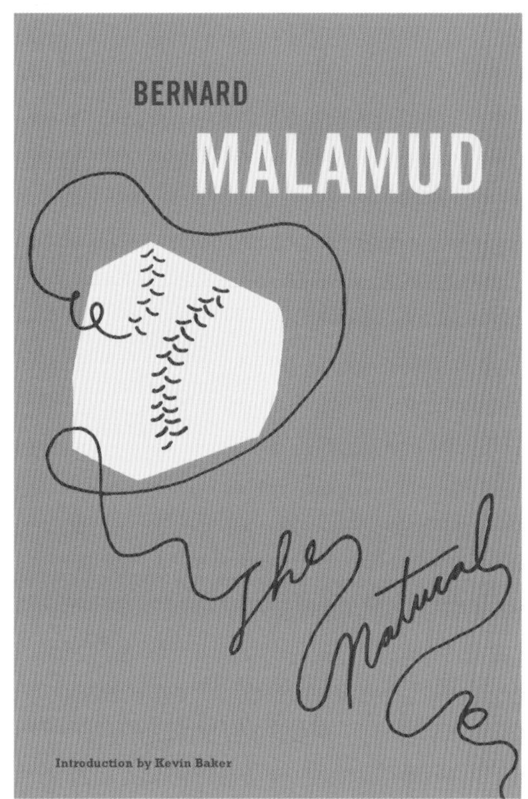

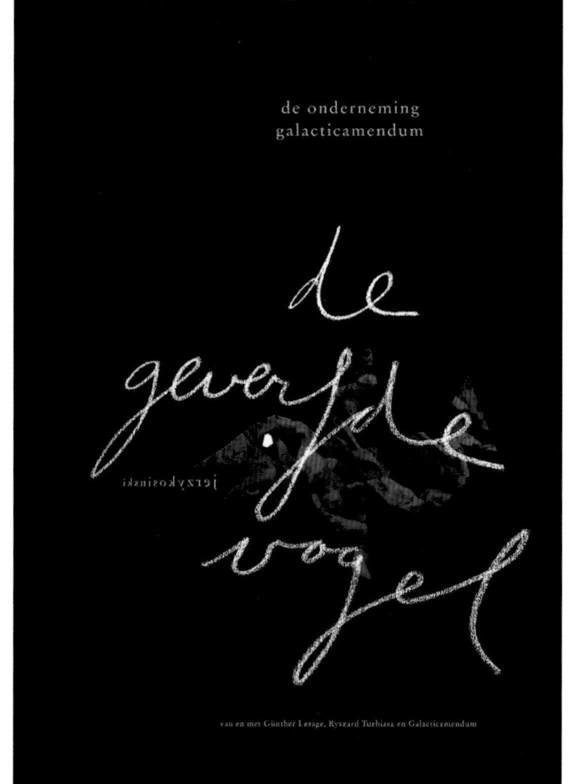

IN HONOR OF DAVID RHODES 25TH YEAR AS PRESIDENT OF SVA
THURSDAY DECEMBER 11, 2003 SVA AMPHITHEATER
A DISCUSSION OF ALBERT CAMUS, HIS LIFE, HIS WORK, AND HIS INFLUENCES
Camus: Rebellion, Resistance and Death
Milton Glaser

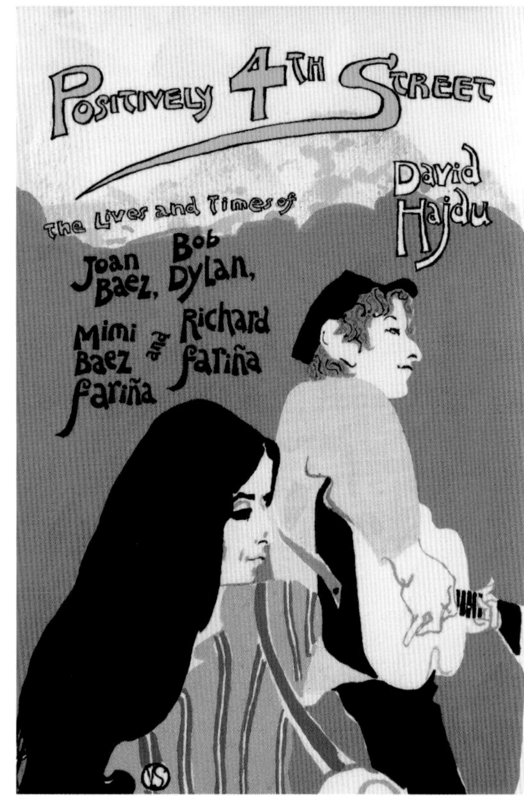

ABOVE **Late-nineteenth-century Art Nouveau style** was adopted by the psychedelic designers of the 1960s for rock concert posters and has been reprised here on the book cover for *Positively 4th Street*, which focuses on the era's musical icons.
Designer, letterer illustrator: Eric Von Schmidt Client: Farrar, Straus and Giroux

TOP LEFT **This hard-edged handwriting is void of artifice** and is totally consistent with the tone, texture and character of Lightnin' Hopkins's portrait on his CD *In the Key of Lightnin'*.
Designer, illustrator: Milton Glaser Client: Tomato Records

LEFT **The script is much too deliberate to be improvised**, but the word 'jazz' does spring like music from the jazzman's trumpet on this poster advertising the exhibition 'Image of Jazz in Polish Poster'.
Designer, letterer, illustrator: Roman Kalarus Client: *Emzin Magazine*

What more appropriate way is there to package the words of the peripatetic Beat writer Jack Kerouac on a CD of his readings than to simulate his own cursive handwriting on these ersatz postcards?

Designer, letterer: Chika Azuma Photographers: John Cohen, Allen Ginsberg, Burt Goldblatt Client: Verve

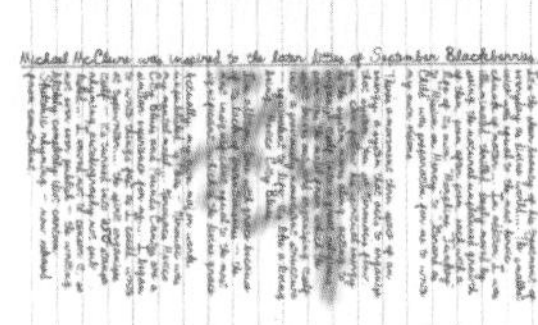

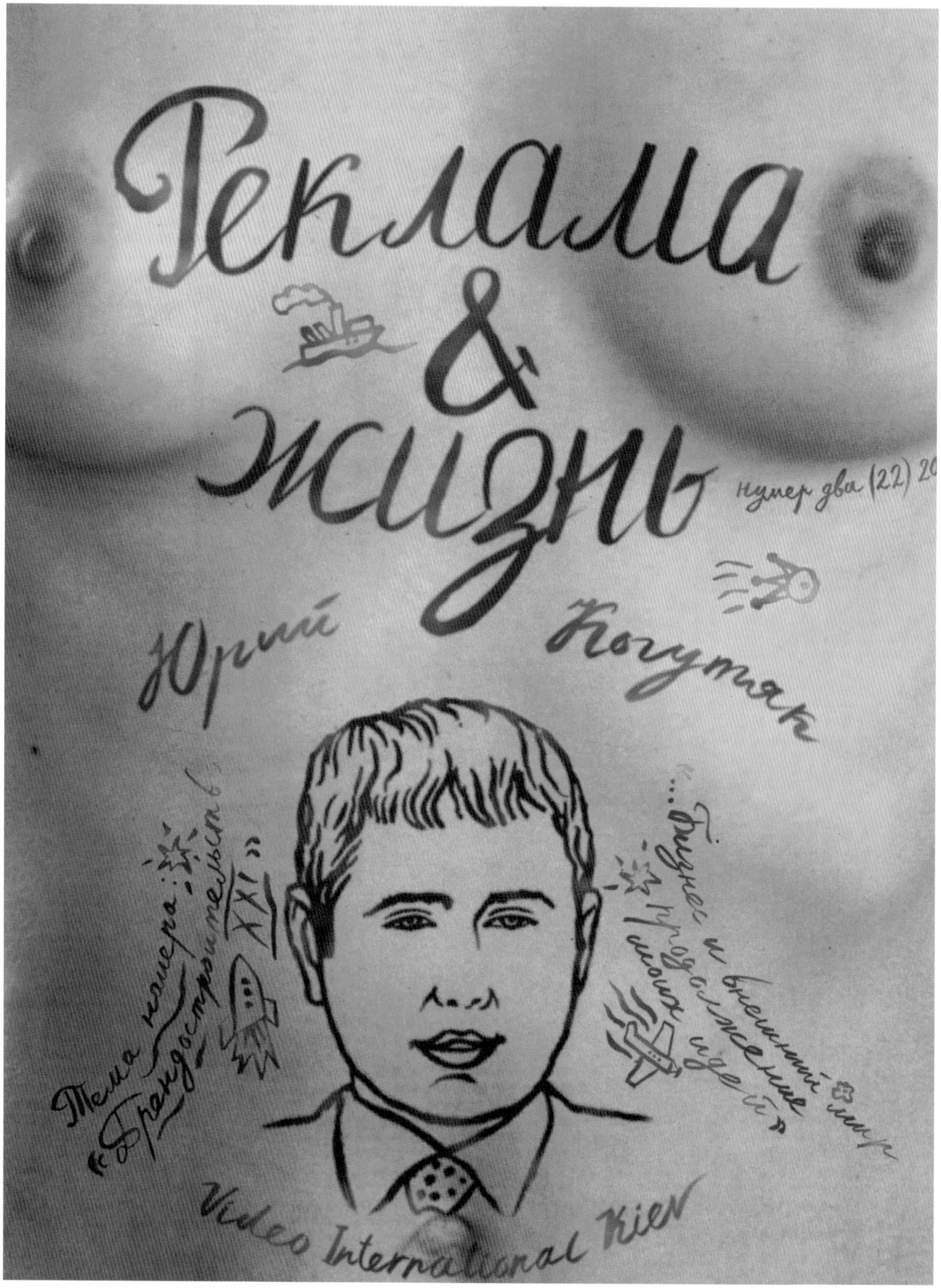

Tattooed writing most commonly takes the form of script lettering. On this magazine cover for *Advertising & Life*, the body art is a beautifully casual Cyrillic script.
Designer: Petr Bankov
Letterer, illustrator: Vlad Vasilyev
Photographer: Andrey Gutnik
Client: *Advertising & Life*

RIGHT **The brush script used here as a pun is a little bit too hairy**, but the combination of unmistakable icons – Father Christmas and Mao Tse-tung – on this Christmas card hits the conceptual mark.
Art director: Gary Tam Designers, illustrators: Gary Tam, Joey Ong Client: Teamwork Design Ltd.

ABOVE **A clumsily rendered brush script** surprisingly complements the grotesquely hairy and mysterious image that dominates this eye-catching Russian poster advertising International Woman's Day.
Designer, photographer: Petr Bankov Letterer: Vlad Vasilyev Client: Design Depo

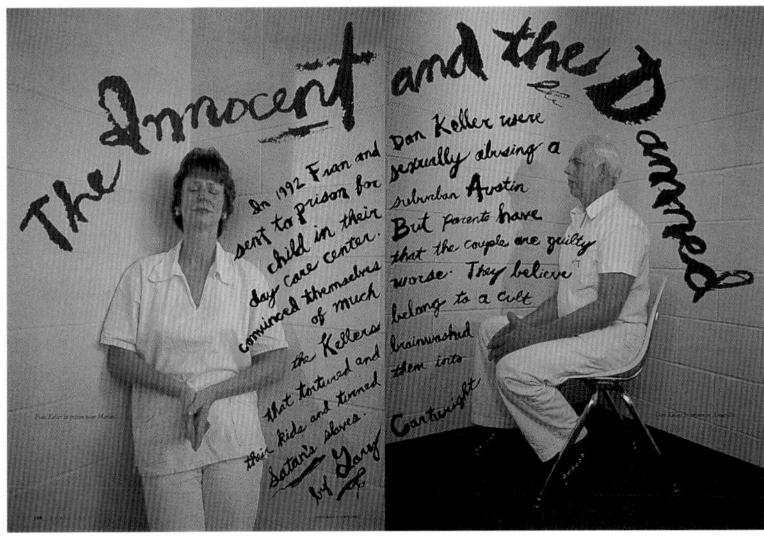

ABOVE **Editorial design often incorporates script** to signify and reveal personal testimony; in this magazine layout, the script conveys both desperation and innocence and is in keeping with the title of the piece.
Designer, letterer: DJ Stout Photographer: Joseph Vento Client: *Texas Monthly*

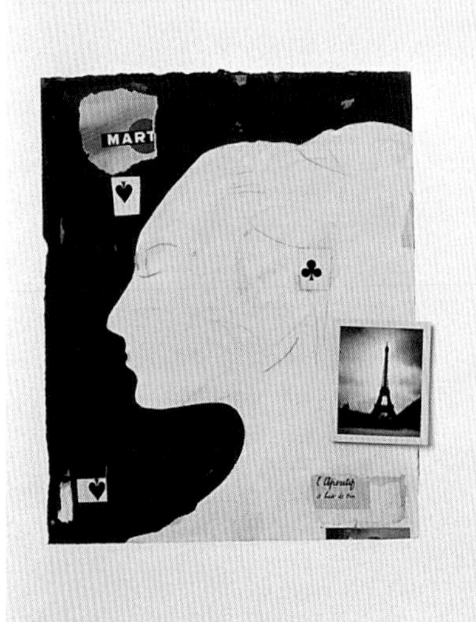

TOP **Script lettering was often embroidered onto fabric** in the form of curious (and homy) amateur designs during the nineteenth century. This poster, entitled 'Objets Inanimés', pays homage to that traditional form of folk-art lettering.
Art director: Laetitia Wolff Illustrator: Nick Dewar Client: Olafur Thordarson

BOTTOM **Sometimes script is a conceit used to give the appearance of casualness**; in this case of purposeful informality for an annual report called 'What's Love Got to do With it?', the result, while pleasing to the eye, is also somehow mannered.
Art directors: Bill Cahan, Kevin Roberson Designer: Kevin Roberson Illustrator: Nick Dewar Client: GVO Inc.

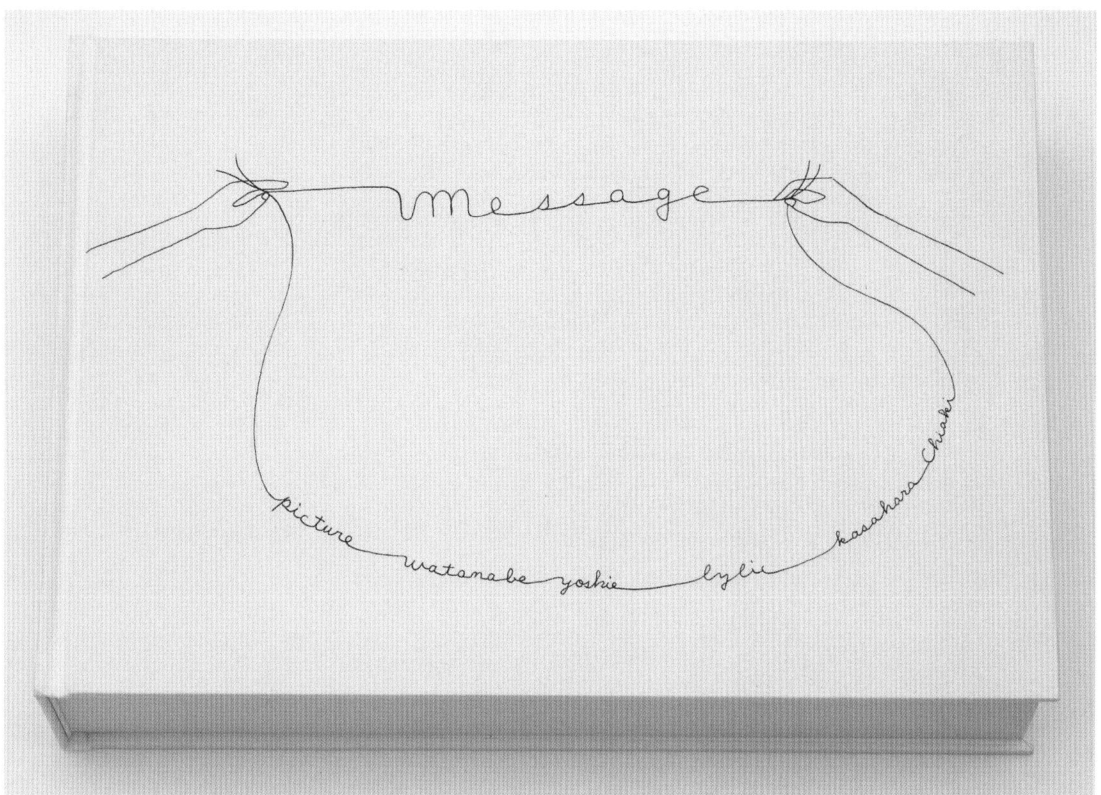

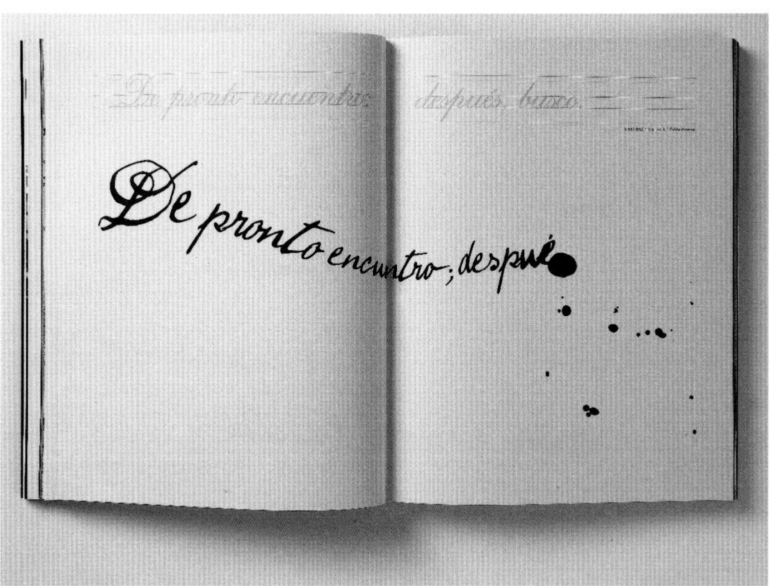

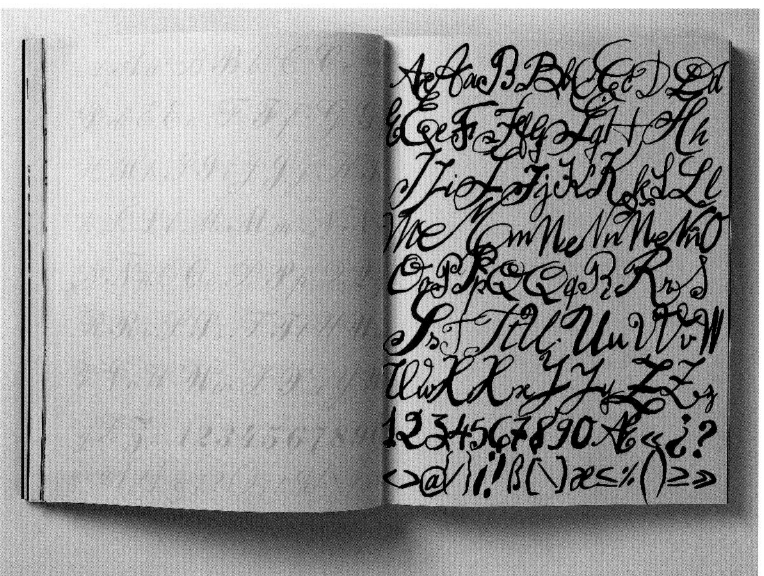

TOP **Thread is supple and perfectly suited to making sinuous script letters**. This understated book cover for *Message* shows that even the thinnest weight of thread is imbued with typographic impact.
Art director, designer, illustrator: Yoshie Watanabe Copywriter: Chiaki Kasahara Client: D-BROS

BOTTOM **This script lettering has all the calligraphic flourish** that characterizes an eighteenth-century diary entry; here, it is featured in the book *Cali-Tipografía*.
Designers, letterers: Pepe Gimeno, José Gil, Didac Ballester, Suso Pérez
Clients: Pepe Gimeno, La Imprenta Comunicación Gráfica

LEFT **Swirly and swashy scripts go well** with these light-hearted, fashion-oriented images that have the look of paper-doll cut-outs; the piece is called 'Glam It Up Vogue Girl!'.
Creative director: Gene Krell Editor: Hye Ju Lee Letterer, illustrator: Sara Schwartz Client: Korea *Vogue Girl Magazine*

BOTTOM LEFT **Everything is just one big happy doodle.** Simplicity gives this catalogue cover for the Chelsea Day School auction its graphic allure and the informal script provides an air of familiarity.
Designer, letterer, illustrator: Christina Sun Client: Chelsea Day School

BELOW **Stark handlettering like this suggests informality**, but it is actually standardized and manoeuvred on these stickers, which are collectively called 'Typolover'.
Designer, letterer, illustrator: Mina Zabnikar, self promotion

RIGHT **Dirty Girl's identity is entirely based on** the curlicue hairstyle of the cosmetic company's mascot, which is reflected in the flowing script lettering on the packaging.
Designer, letterer, illustrator: Haley Johnson Client: Dirty Girl

BELOW **Scripted handwriting provides more than information**, it is also a visual texture. Here, on a poster entitled 'Fake Identities 5', it helps to heighten the surrealist sensibility.
Designer, illustrator: Bülent Erkmen Letterer: Bilge Barhana Photographer: Fethi Izan
Client: Kum, Pan, Ya Theatre Group

Handwritten words are sometimes better at expressing ideas than any other typographic style. The bottle's outline, in this illustration called 'Rose', is only suited to a handwritten accompaniment.
Designer: Christy Salinas Letterer, illustrator: Juliette Borda Client: Hay House Books

Real type would only serve to depersonalize the idea presented in the illustration; this watercolour and gouache painting, 'Ms Average Canadian', demands script for the lettering.
Designer: Dave Donald Letterer, illustrator: Juliette Borda Client: *Chatelaine Magazine*

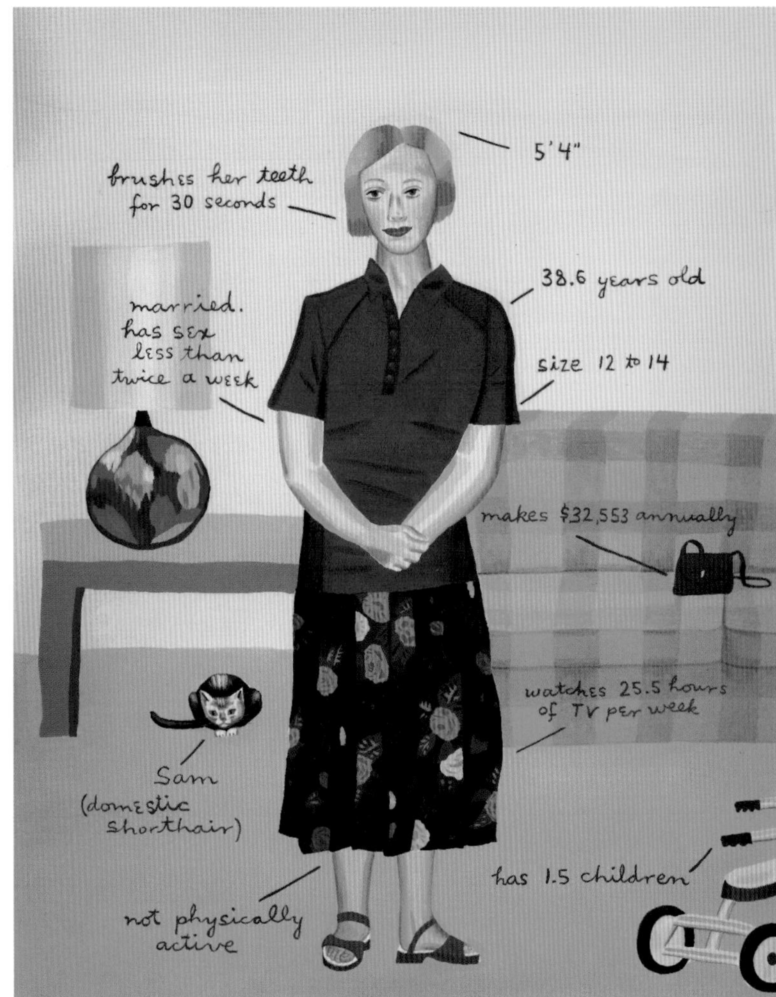

TOP **Like the cursive lettering in Babar the Elephant books**, the writing in this children's series adds texture and increases the visual experience. The characters convey their own unique personality in these flyers for [left] 'Pirate juillet 2001' and [right] 'Pirate septembre 2000'.
Letterer, illustrator: Marc Boutavant Client: Le Pirate Guingette

BOTTOM **It is not easy for a very young child to follow script writing**, so this book, *Les Fantômes de la Maison*, which is entirely written in this lettering style, is intended to be deciphered and read out loud by an adult.
Letterer, illustrator: Marc Boutavant Client: Mila Editions

Simulating the objects the words are describing, calligraphic script is used in a sophisticated way. The adverts for the Bernhardt Furniture Company are beautifully lettered and portray a sense of class and lavishness.
Art director: Jeff Hopfer Letterer: John Stevens Copywriter: Mike Renfro Photographer: Alderman
Client: Bernhardt Furniture Company

If these single words were set in a formal typeface (or even a grittier form of handlettering), the elegantly simple concept – headline as caption – would not succeed as wittily as it does in these adverts for Giro helmets.
Art director, letterer: Tony Calcao Copywriter: Rob Strasberg Photographer: Mark Laita Client: Giro

Samplers remain a popular, timeless craft (like knitting, weaving and crocheting) but they are not considered as highbrow (or even middlebrow) art. Samplers are discussed (indeed embraced) in the histories of early folk art but they are not seriously explored by the rarefied flame-keepers of modern typography. Samplers cannot be ignored, however, either as a possible inspiration for bitmapped type forms or as an aspect of symbolic letterforms. They are celebrated not for their quaintness but for their parody of that characteristic.

Throughout this book are myriad examples of customized letterforms used as metaphors, puns and illusions. The stitched letter can be all of these, and it is also dimensional. This kind of lettering increases the visceral sensation of a design and enables sentences, words and ideas to leap off the page in surprising ways. Arguably, the stitched letter is the most artistic of all the handlettering genres exhibited here. The size of this section should not adversely reflect on the significance of the work. Fewer designers are applying themselves to stitching because it is so, well, funky. While pen and brush scrawls more easily fit into contemporary designs, this arduous handwork is more of an anomaly. Moreover, it takes time, effort and skill to achieve the best results. It demands intelligence to smartly integrate a sewn composition into an otherwise contemporary piece of design. It is amusing to note that the early-twentieth-century modernists rejected hand-drawn letters as being too fussy, but they were not against making unprecedented letters from materials like yarn if the effect indicated a break from bourgeois tradition.

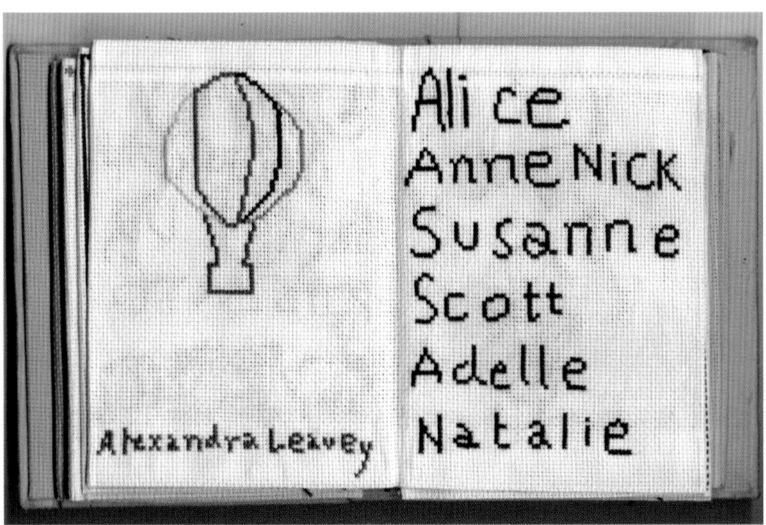

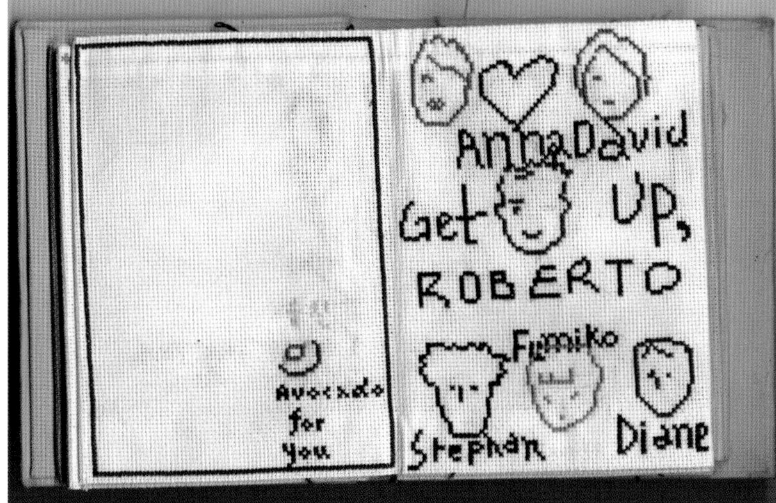

Stitched lettering is primarily crude, although this is not always the case. Compared to scrawled lettering, stitched forms often have a more amateurish aura. Nevertheless, there is something aesthetically compelling about pieces like Sarah Doyle's unselfconscious and curiously witty letter and image combination for the group Lyrical Cru (see p. 113), which looks as though it was done by a kid in a nursery-school crafts period. As there is no pretence about creating accurate type simulations, the resulting letters are refreshingly absurd and serendipitous. Similarly, Chosil Kil's *I Made This For You*, a book of lettering entirely made from coarsely stitched embroidery (see pp 104–07), seems to send up both the antique sampler and modern pixelated lettering. What makes this piece even more fascinating is that the designer has tried so hard to get the letters as perfect as possible, but owing to the unforgiving nature of the medium she did not stand a chance. Angus Hyland's poster 'Fabric of Fashion' (see p. 108) is about as crude as the pieces by Doyle and Kil but not nearly as absurd because his sewn lettering has a clear logic in its representation of a fashion theme.

Remember the old saying 'a stitch in time saves nine'? Well, the stitching here saves little time but demands that the viewer spend a little more of their precious moments admiring the results. It is hard to peel one's eyes away from this work because it is, frankly, ridiculous in many ways and truly exquisite in others.

Thread and yarn produce a very fluid line that makes for a uniquely expressive lettering medium. A good example of thread type is Maja Bagic's poster 'Wake Up!' (see p. 109), which required letters to be painstakingly sewn to form a simple script. The design succeeds because of its artless innocence and its funny commentary on the superfluities of a high-end design competition. Conversely, some designers use thread in less carefree and more ominous ways. The sutured lettering in Tomato Kosir's 'Helvetica' poster (see p. 112) is a wry and ironic commentary that makes the word Helvetica out of the stitches of a wound, stitches that are not even in Helvetica itself.

Parodies of conventional needlepoint are common but no less potent when made with dry wit. This is brilliantly evidenced in Min Uong's art direction of Margaret Cusack's colourful cover illustration for *The Village Voice* (see p. 115), which flawlessly and comically imitates a real sampler and stitches everything on the cover from logo to headlines. The sampler language is also an acerbic counterpoint to the sadomasochist theme it illustrates. Also masterfully produced with a more literal take on needlepoint are Lizzie Fin's CD covers for the Moloko albums (see p. 110). The band's logo is designed from real buttons (i.e. metaphoric lettering), while the title of the CDs – *Indigo* and *Pure Pleasure Seeker* – are spot-on copies of quintessential needlepoint stitching. The most bizarre of these parodies is, however, Croatian-born Melina Mikulic's needlepoint kit (complete with yarns) to promote the novel *Ear, Throat, Knife* (see p. 114). It takes Mirko Ilic's image of an eerily erotic tongue and transforms it into real embroidery, type and all; even the artist's signature has to be embroidered.

Due to its arcane nature, stitched lettering is inherently imbued with comic attributes. Some of the work described here has

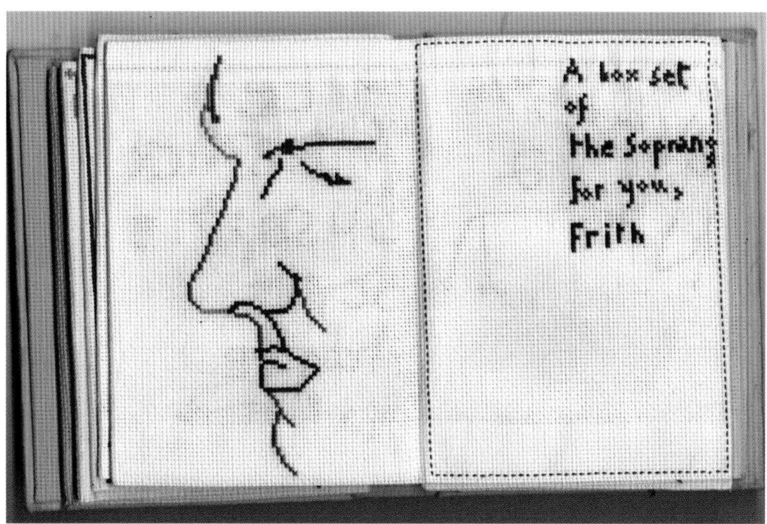

been approached in a very serious way by the designers, yet the results invariably evoke a smirk, a smile and, at times, a full-throated laugh. There is something sincerely (and perhaps deliberately) ridiculous about making letters the way our grandmothers made quilts or patterns on holiday sweaters. Contemporary graphic design demands this kind of self-conscious rule-busting activity, and because most rules have been broken, one of the few remaining ways to induce shock and awe is to revert back to this venerable method.

Although design history books have blatantly ignored it, embroidered, sewn and sutured lettering has a small but significant place in typographic and lettering legacies. Stitching certainly does not enjoy the same ubiquity as today's scrawls, scratches, scripts and simulations, but it does provide the opportunity designers have always needed to bring quantitatively and qualitatively more weirdness, absurdity and wit to the current panoply of hand-produced graphic design.

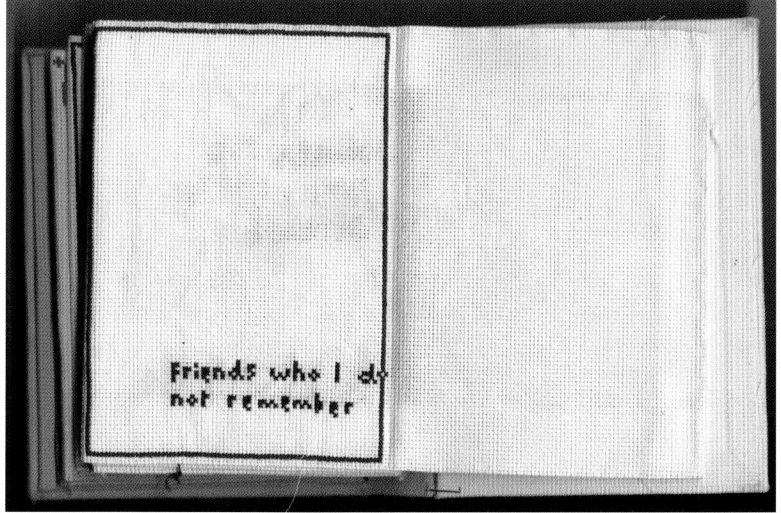

pp 104–07 **Needlepoint samplers are always precise** but not always innovative; however, this book, *I Made This For You*, has an imaginative narrative that uses the language of the sampler in a raw and expressive way. Designer, letterer: Chosil Kil, personal work

Crafts Council Gallery
44a Pentonville Road
Islington, London N1 9BY
Tel 020 7278 7700
5 minutes from Angel tube
Free entry
Tues to Sat 11-6
Sunday 2-6
Closed Monday
Disabled Access
Closed from 6.00
Saturday 23 December
Re-opens Tuesday
2 January 2001
FABRIC OF FASHION
CRAFTS COUNCIL GALLERY
9 NOVEMBER 2000 - 14 JANUARY 2001
A BRITISH COUNCIL EXHIBITION INCLUDING HUSSEIN CHALAYAN, CAROL FRASER,
ELEY KISHIMOTO, JESSICA OGDEN, UNIFORM, VEXED GENERATION
The British Council

Visceral spontaneity was achieved by stitching the main text for a poster promoting an exhibition about the relationship between mass-printing and hands-on textile design.
Designer, letterer: Angus Hyland
Design assistants: Charlie Smith, Emily Wood
Photographer: Michael Danner Client: The Crafts Council

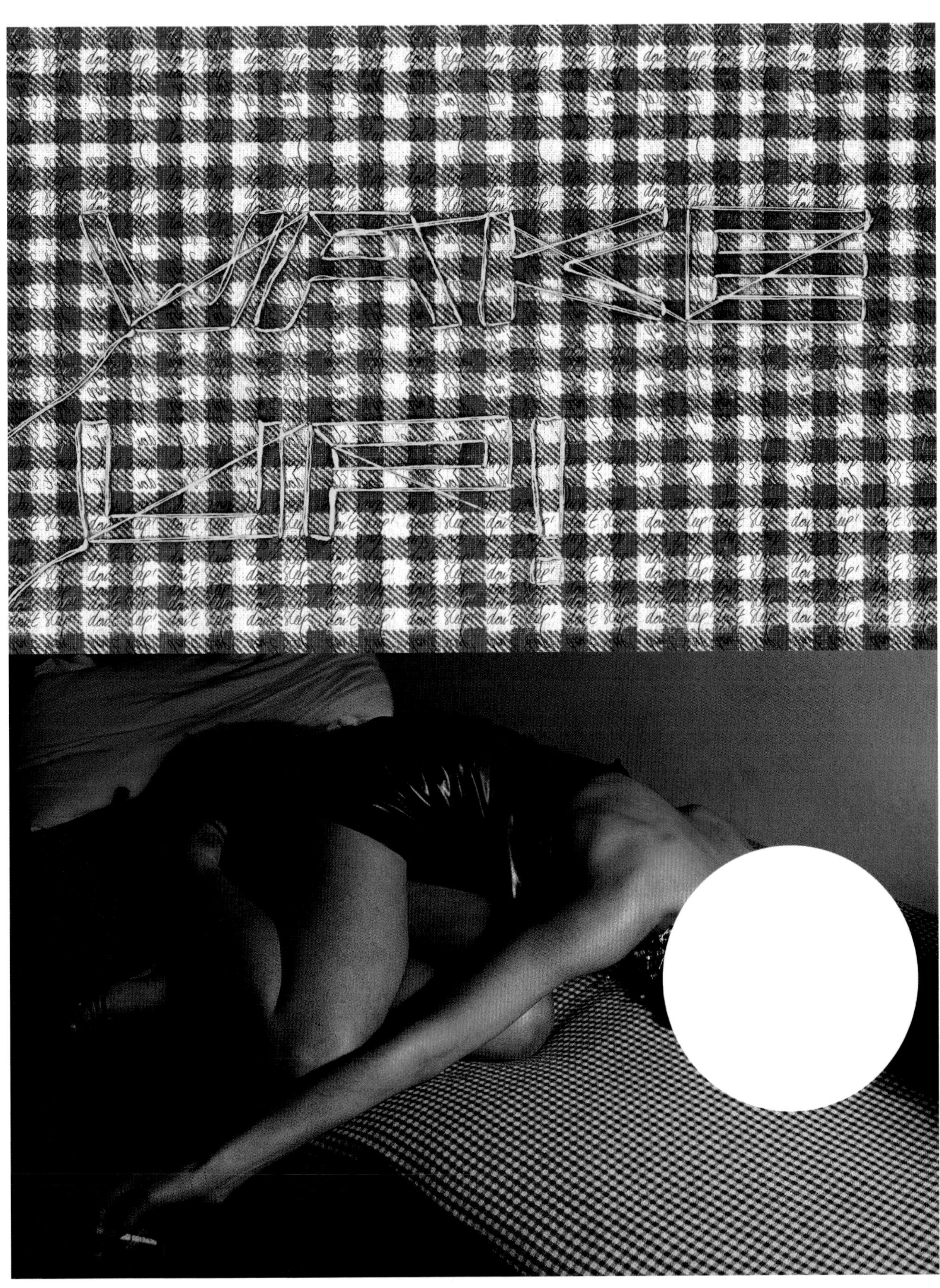

This image is notable for its curious dimensionality. The woven checkerboard pattern dominates and reflects the cushion in the photograph, while the stitched headline adds to the overall allure of the poster 'Wake Up!'.
Designer, letterer, photographer:
Maja Bagic, self promotion

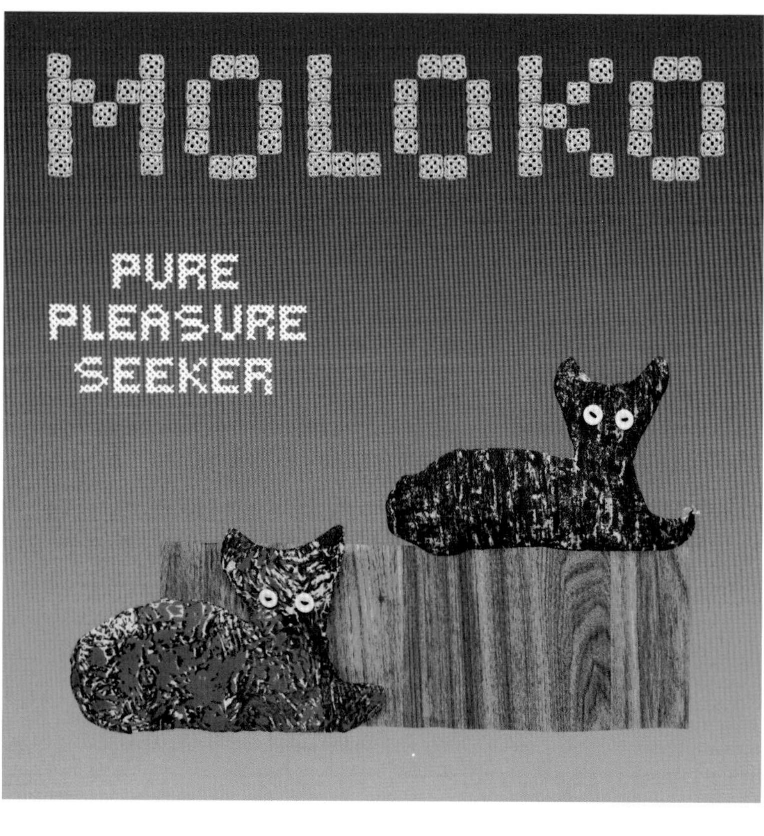

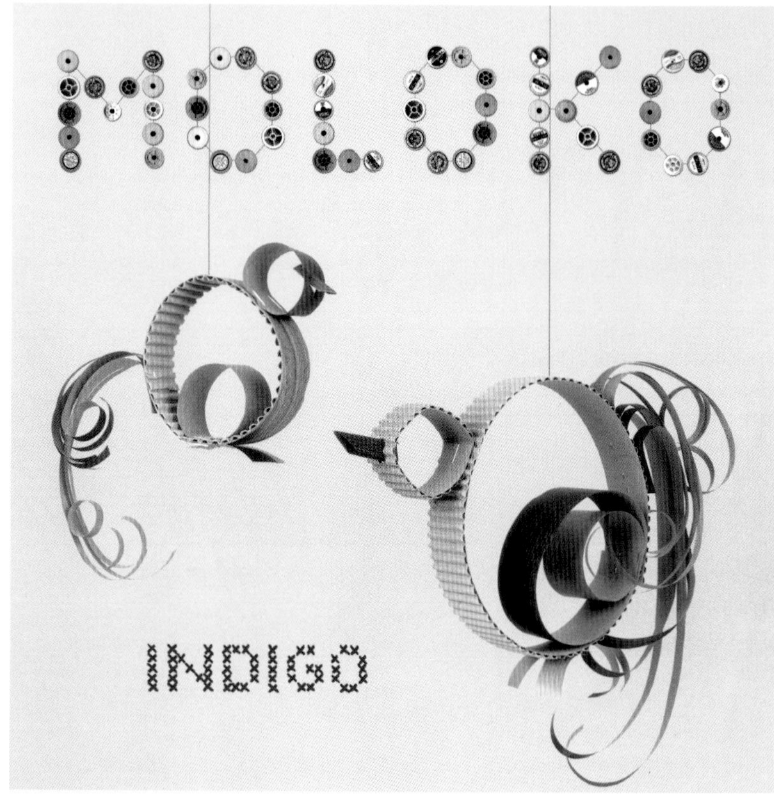

ABOVE **Heightening the craft sensibility of the illustrations** is the simulation of embroidered lettering on these two CDs, *Pure Pleasure Seeker* and *Indigo*, for Moloko. Each handmade component is quaint, and, overall, this is a spot-on parody of conventional crafts.

Designer, letterer, illustrator: Lizzie Fin Photographer: Barnaby & Scott Client: The Echo Label

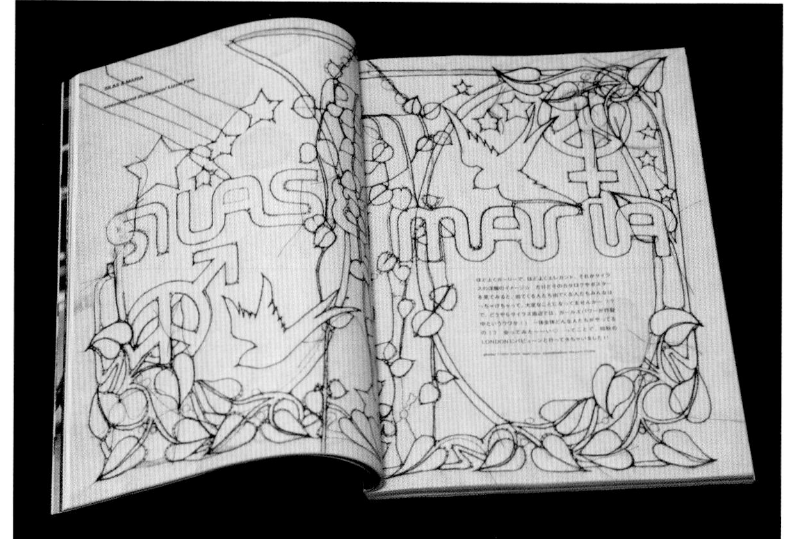

RIGHT **Naturalistic Art Nouveau idiosyncrasy** and 1960s-style lettering eccentricity are stitched together in the most literal sense of the word for the opening spread of an article on Silas, the UK clothing label.

Designer, letterer, illustrator: Lizzie Fin Client: *Relax Magazine*, Tokyo

LEFT **Sewing is not usually considered as graffiti**, but this illustration, showing the stitching used on Silas garments in the spring 2003 collection, is a combination of precisely rendered patterns and ad-hoc signatures that form a kind of unique urban scrawl.

Designer, letterer, illustrator: Lizzie Fin Client: Silas

RIGHT **This imitation of a classic sampler** is based on the grid developed in the early-nineteenth century and has been used on a poster called '1001 Nachmittag'.

Art directors: Josef Perndl, Nina Pavicsits Designer, letterer, illustrator: Nina Pavicsits Client: Mak

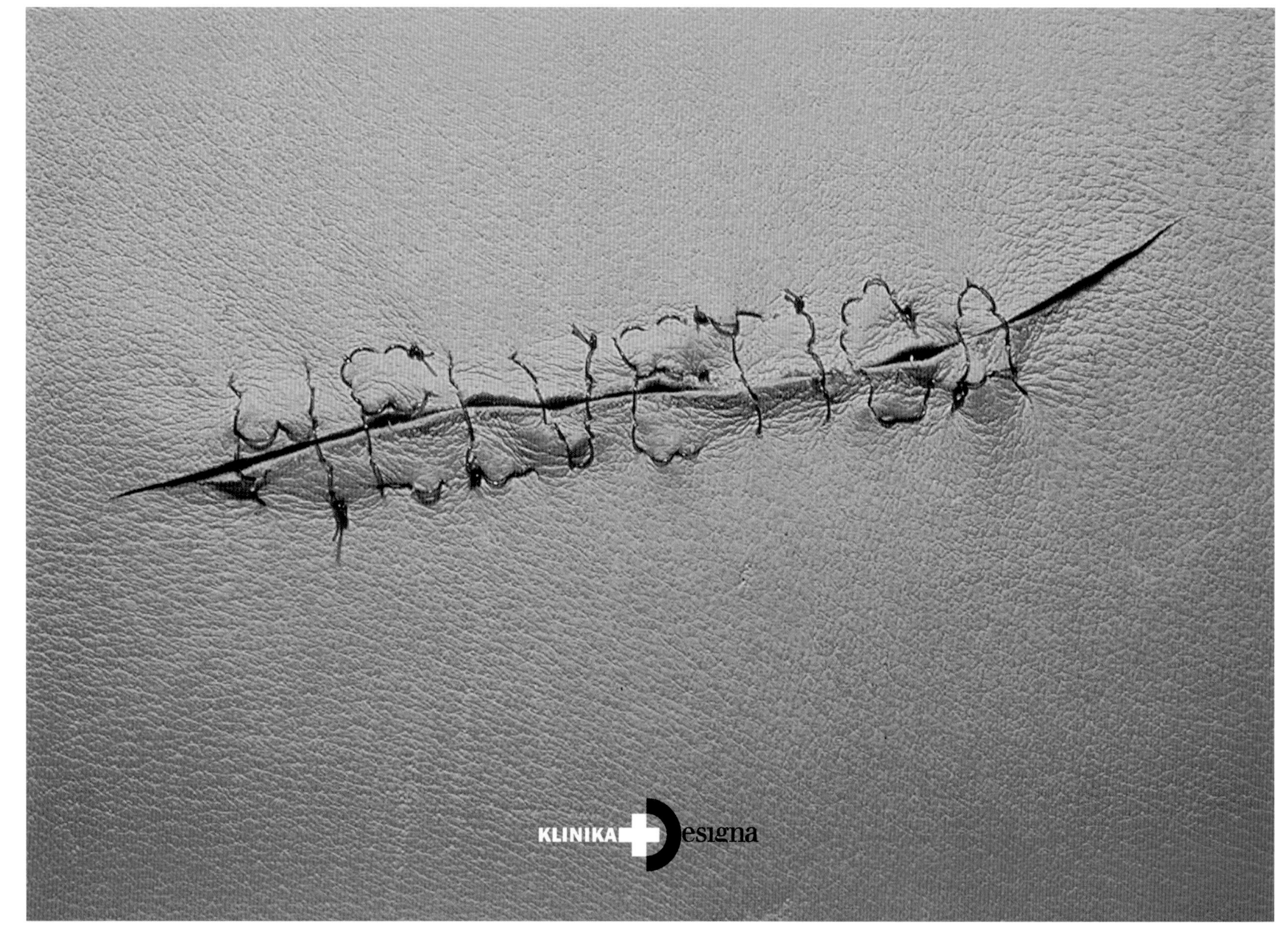

This is not the perfect cut of Helvetica, but the poster is a witty commentary on the universal typeface using what can best be described as sutured-style lettering to make the sardonic point.
Designer, letterer, illustrator, photographer: Tomato Kosir Client: Klinika + Designa

Stitching yarn onto cardboard is not easy, which accounts for the purposeful sloppiness of this composition. The resulting raw quality gives this promotional material for the group Lyrical Cru its playful allure.
Designer, letterer, illustrator: Sarah Doyle Client: *This Is A Magazine*, www.thisisamagazine.com

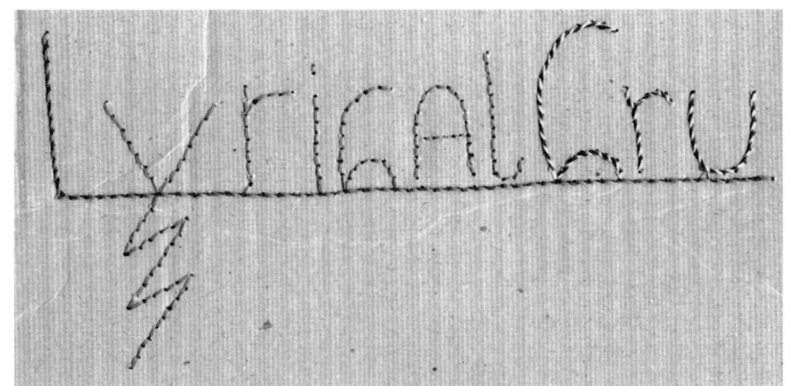

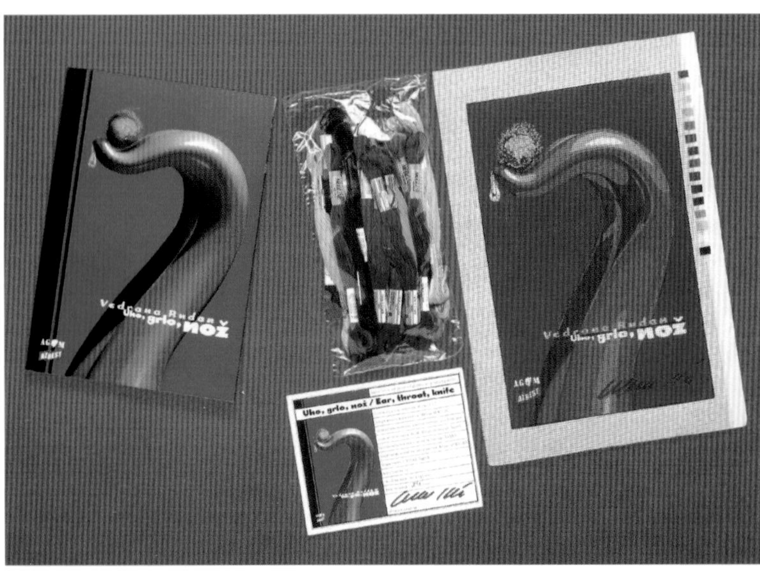

THIS PAGE **It takes wit, humour and a little hubris** to transform a typical computer-rendered image, in this case a mockingly erotic one, into an actual needlepoint sampler (with real yarn and a pattern included). This book promotion for *Uho, Grlo, Noz* (*Ear, Throat, Knife*) works very well.
Art director: Kruno Lokotar Designer: Melina Mikulić Illustrator: Mirko Ilić Client: AGM

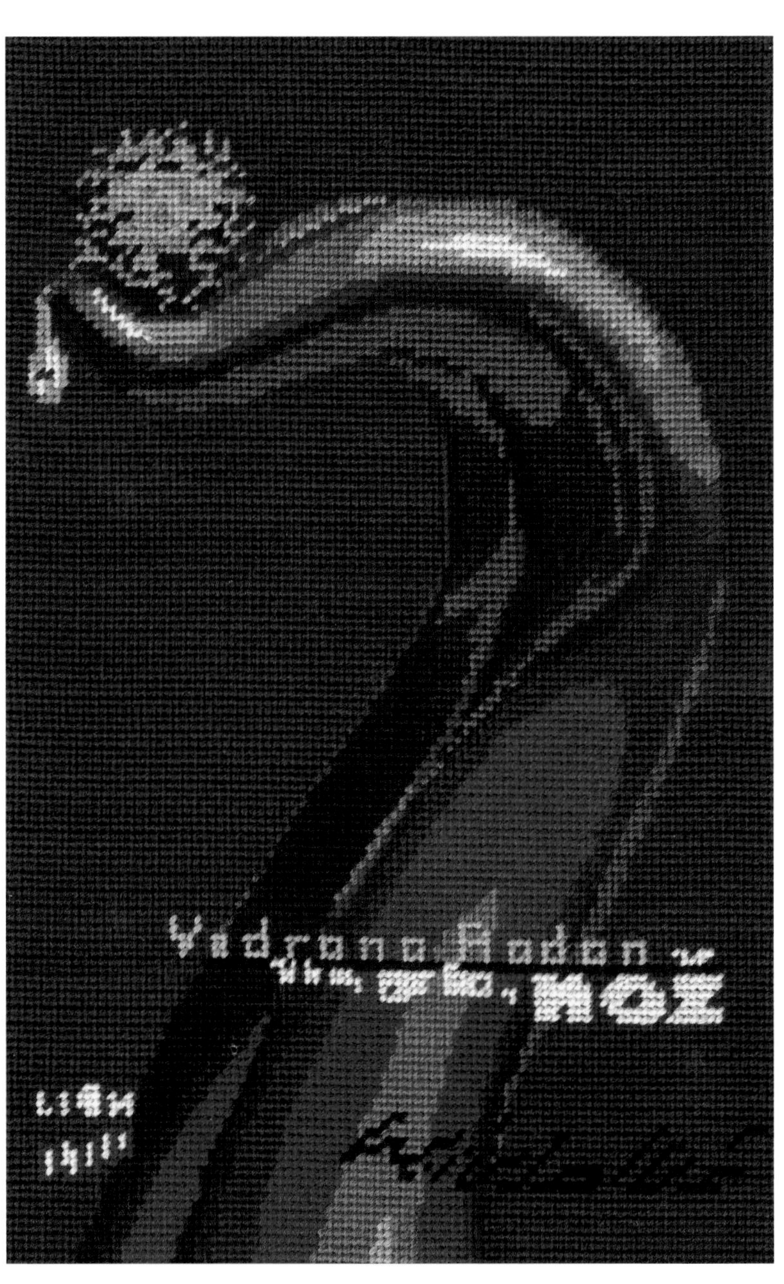

OPPOSITE **Only a master craftsperson can turn the sampler cliché** into an acerbic satire. Everything on this magazine cover is rendered with exactitude and loyalty to the original sampler form.
Art director: Min Uong Letterer, illustrator: Margaret Cusack Client: *The Village Voice*

Silicon Alley Top 10 p.38 | Making HIV a Crime p.46
the village
VOICE
WPS 35860 NO. 45 ©VV PUBLISHING CORPORATION
Whip Me, Honey!
S/M Goes Mainstream
BY GUY TREBAY p.32
CUSACK

sim

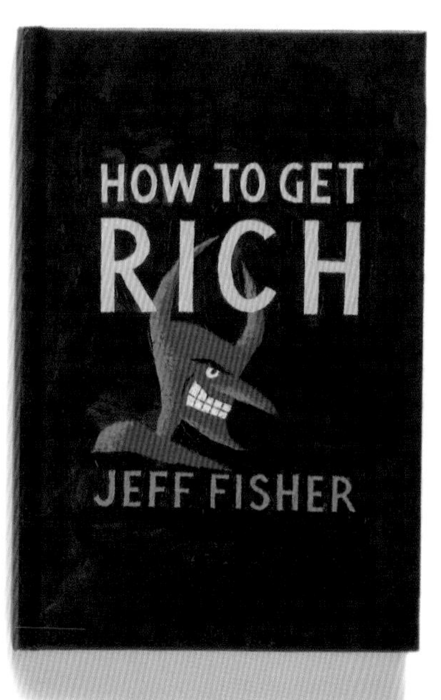

There was a time when everyone worthy of the name graphic designer knew how to precisely comp (or simulate) actual typefaces. Like a painter or sculptor who copies perfectly from life, the designer rendered exact letterforms as a formal and linguistic necessity. Since type is the language of design, what better way to achieve fluency than to construct the basic forms by hand? This was a very sound theory and still is. Furthermore, professionally speaking, during the era before photostat machines, the hand was one of the major tools in the creation of typography, along with the t-square drafting instrument, pen and ink. While lazy designers used a lucy (a bulky light box with enlarging and reducing functions) to trace letters, true artisans eschewed such easy short cuts as a matter of pride. The meticulous replication of type, making it look as though it were set by machine, was a very coveted skill that separated novice from master and typographer from commercial artist.

Many formerly arduous design processes are now taken for granted thanks to the speed of the computer. Clients and designers alike expect no less than exact mock-ups (often showing many variations) with type and image unerringly in place and just as they will appear when printed. There are countless fonts digitally available to meet all formal and expressive needs, but back in the pre-cold-type days, not to mention BC (before computer), not only were many standard typefaces re-created by hand but invented ones that echoed recognized originals were commonly used. William Addison Dwiggins, who coined the term graphic designer in the early 1920s and designed

scores of book spines, title pages and jackets, worked almost exclusively with precisionist drawings of classically based, custom-made lettering (some of which later became the basis for complete hot-metal type fonts). To look at his flawless finished renderings, in pen and ink on illustration board, the reader is easily deceived into believing they were produced by machine. Dwiggins was both a master calligrapher and a typeface designer (Metro, Electra and Caledonia are among his most popular commercial faces), so he understood balance, colour and harmony better than most. Less accomplished letterers still managed to achieve perfection, however, simply as a result of their basic training. The profession was filled with highly skilled designers who contributed style and flair to the typographic lexicon. Lucian Bernhard (1883–1972) – the early-twentieth-century pioneer of German poster design who produced over thirty standard typefaces, including Bernhard Gothic, for the American Type Founders Company (ATF) in the 1920s and 1930s after emigrating to New York City – said that he could not draw straight lines. Yet his Modern typefaces are as geometrically pure as the human hand can accomplish.

In Dwiggins's seminal design handbook *Layout in Advertising* (Harper & Brothers, NY, 1928), handlettering is celebrated in its own section because it is endemic to all design. 'The expression "hand-lettering" is used to designate lettering drawn by a designer for the specific job', he writes. 'The virtues to be looked for in handlettering are, generally, the virtues to be looked for in type.' Dwiggins goes on to say that 'drawn-to-order' lettering must follow closely the style and nuances of the type that it is simulating, but he also argues that since lettering is not type it should be apparent that it is not type. The first stipulation provides unity for the overall design, the second 'furnishes more liveliness'. He explains that liberty and licence are endemic to handlettering: 'Drawn lettering is not subject to the rigidities that restrain type,' but, he warns, this freedom can be a temptation to stray in dangerous ways 'unless the draughtsman ... has due regard for legibility and other calligraphic virtues'. In other words, the merit of a simulated concoction depends on personal taste and knowledge of the anatomy of letterforms.

Typeface rendering was once an everyday requirement in all design schools. A student could not graduate without knowing how to make with ease serif and sans-serif letters, ampersands, capitals and minuscules at various sizes and weights. Likewise, the old learn-by-mail schools, of which there were many and through which a high percentage of graphic artists from the 1910s to the 1950s were trained, emphasized that custom-made handlettering and realistic type rendering were endemic to the production of commercial signs and Shocards. Since it was incumbent on designers to create novel display typefaces, they had to be adept at altering existing letterforms in convincing and agreeable ways. Record albums, book covers, posters and even magazine mastheads required uniquely tailored letterforms, and, while calligraphy was prevalent, classic Roman typefaces were the primary inspirations for customized letters. Therefore, designers had to be well versed in the essence of type and lettering history.

Since this early epoch of graphic design much has changed stylistically, technologically and philosophically. What was once a most virtuous craft – the exact simulation of real type – is today considered fairly archaic, if not unnecessary. While professional typeface designers must know how to flawlessly and schematically draw alphabets, the average graphic designer need only be proficient at using a software program. Tedious comping is a thing of the past – today's equivalent can be done instantaneously in QuarkXPress or InDesign, and such swift technology has further altered the designer's fundamental attitude toward type design. Standardization, once the loftiest of modern ideals, has turned into the hobgoblin of expressive design. Type, long revered purely for its graceful elegance, has become a fluid form ripe for morphing, sculpting and transforming. The classic ideals of beauty, like balance and harmony, which have been common denominators of design, are no longer the supreme virtues. Lettering has become a vessel in which all these changes are manifest, wherein anything is possible and readability and legibility are no longer the first qualities on a designer's checklist.

During the postmodern 1990s intrepid young designers often appropriated classic typefaces for purposes of distortion. The computer not only gave them licence it appeared virtually to command that they digitally contort, distort and abort revered typographies to snub the past and establish dominion over the present. Some of these letterforms were bastardizations of existing Bodonis, Garamonds and Didots in which digital 'noise' and visual gobbledegook obliterated all but a remnant of the original iteration. Weird postmodern typefaces were toyed with; for example, Jeffery Keedy's Lushus was based on a Victorian slab-serif woodtype that was adulterated and abused in such a curious way that it retained enough of its original characteristics to suggest a Victorian element but was also absurdly imbued with enough graphic junk to make it something else. Lushus was definitely a fake Victorian face but, at the same time, it was a unique contemporary one. This and other quirky bastardizations were mostly based on digital interventions (some of them at the behest of *FUSE*, the experimental digital type magazine). However, as computer typesetting became more refined, digital play became less adventuresome and more commonplace. As a greater number of designers played around with Fontographer, high jinks became more expected and more routine. There was an insatiable urge to feed the culture of the new, and the collective obsession to push to the next level of invention was so profound that computer manipulation fell out of favour and the hand emerged again as the new digital tool.

Of all handlettering produced today, the latest genre of simulated type (shown in this section) is one of the quirkiest, not necessarily the most beautiful but definitely the most curious. These replications are deliberately designed to resemble existing alphabets but, unlike the comps of yore, have a postmodern, self-referential twist. Like Keedy's digitally constructed Lushus, the hand letters on the following pages are meant to be, in part, commentaries on past and present alphabets, critiques on the sanctity of alphabet design.

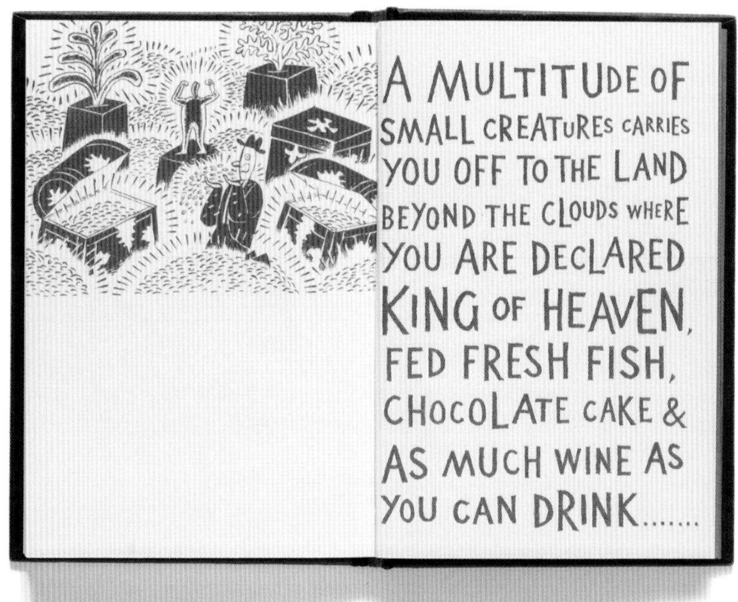

pp 116–19 **The easiest way to simulate a standard typeface** by hand is to draw sans-serif capital letters. Jeff Fisher uses the venerable Trade Gothic typeface as his model and mixes the sizes for the book *How to Get Rich*. Letterer, illustrator: Jeff Fisher, personal work

YOU CONSTRUCT AN
ELABORATE PERSONA,
INVOLVING DUTCH
ROYALTY, VINTAGE
CARS AND ADOPTED
MANNERISMS, PURELY
FROM FOUND OBJECTS
YOU CHARM, YOU
POLO TILL DAWN

On a less academic note, they are also pleasurable ways of making type that is not type at all, rather the illusion of typefaces. They are cagey deceptions. They are doodles. And, what designer has not casually copied Bodoni, Garamond, Didot and Bembo, or any number of beautiful faces, as they are doodling on a pad? The pencil and pen have become such a novelty in the computer design environment that designers amuse themselves by scribbling letterforms, which, rather than toss in the garbage, they more often than not scan in and use in layouts. In short, in the postmodern age what was once considered rough is now accepted as finished.

The variety of simulated letters around today is as extensive as the number of formally designed alphabets. Furthermore, not all simulated letters are based on existing forms: some are exact replicas while others are improvisations that carry on the formal attributes of specific typefaces or are generalizations of all typefaces. Simulating the formal aspects of letters holds some strange appeal for designers, almost like the artist's attraction to painting a bowl of fruit in an abstract manner. Sometimes, the more outlandish the original letter, the more appealing the rendering. Such is the case on Angus Hyland's book jacket for *Arsenal on the Double* (see p. 128), which combines various eclectic styles into one pseudo-Victorian composition, at once a nod to the past and a salute to the present. Hyland's lettering is in perfect harmony with his illustration style, which is knowingly primitive. Likewise, illustrator L.K. Hanson employs a handlettering approach in 'Hand in Your Thoughts' (see p. 134) that is both consistent with his raw style and yet attempts to re-create real typefaces in a naive manner.

On occasion, simulated lettering has a vague resemblance to something we have all seen before, but this sensation of déjà-vu is based on our collective understanding of typographic form. James McMullen's poster for *An American Daughter* (see p. 121) pays homage to standard type but it is really ersatz type. Similarly, Dutchman Max Kisman's letters for *Typ/Typografisch Papier* (see p. 132) are entirely expressive but each letter is based on (and exaggerates) common knowledge of sans-serif letterforms. In the same vein, Monika Starowicz's poster for *Hamlet* (see p. 133) cleverly transforms the 'M' in the damned Danish prince's name into a crown and also builds upon a common perception of Gothic letters.

Then, there are the simulations that come as close to original alphabets as possible yet purposely retain the hand-hewn quality to, as Dwiggins wrote, make the forms even more lively than in their perfect, original state. The Bodoni-like lettering for illustrator Dusan Petricic's children's book *On Tumbledown Hill* (see p. 122) is a concession to traditional books that are often set in similar Roman faces. Yet, these are jazzed-up, jumpy letters used to add a more exciting voice to the story and to bring life to the phrase 'Yes, leaving seems prudent, sensible, good, and I doubt they would notice, but maybe they would.' On a less exuberant but no less witty note Chika Azuma's book jacket for *The Dangerous Husband* (see p. 128) is a sublimely understated comp-like rendering of a Roman typeface void of flair or flourish but imbued with a charming informality. Stephen Doyle's lettering for the brochure *The End of Communism is a Message to the Human Race* (see p. 127, and part of the 'Subjective Reasoning' series, Khiwer Academic Publishers, 1976) is so finely and precisely sketched to resemble the actual lettering that one has to ask, why bother? However, the fact that it was so carefully rendered simply to deceive gives it charm and value. Likewise, Steven Brower's logo and headline type for *Print* magazine (see p. 129), drawn on a human body as if a tattoo, is designed to be something of a double take, at once a collection of cover headlines and a simulation of body art. At first glance the viewer is deceived into believing the type is real, but a second more careful glance shows it is clearly drawn, with small imperfections, onto the skin.

Finally, this chapter looks at simulated letters that are souped up versions of the basic forms. In James Lacey's poster for the Ballet Folklorico (see p. 120), a customized serif face (with swashes) is goosed and tweaked to exude a formal and informal aura, the purpose of which is to toe the line between imaginative lettering and formal typography. In all cases, the hand-drawn simulation shows an understanding, or at least an acknowledgment, of type's form and function. The best of these add a sense of surprise to a page, while retaining at least one toe (if not an entire foot) in the formal world of typefaces.

RIGHT **The lettering is curiously classic** but ornamented in the style of the Latino-inspired drawing on this colouring poster for the Anita N. Martinez Ballet Folklorico.

Designer, Letterer, illustrator: James Lacey Client: Anita N. Martinez Ballet Folklorico

ABOVE **Why should a designer draw exact copies of type** when it is easier to typeset them? Easy: the handmade adds an expressive component, as shown in this book, *Genie Wahnsinn*.

Designers, letterers, illustrators: Christoph Niemann, Thomas Fuchs, Titus Ackermann, personal work

RIGHT **Engraving-style illustrations are set off** by the faux traditional lettering on this vintage-looking book cover for *Ale i Bauci* (*Ogres and Bogeys*).

Designer, letterer: Rastko Ciric Client: Naucna Knjiga, Belgrade

BELOW **The colourful scrawled and tightly constructed lettering** on this poster is carefully conceived to test the eye and create an unmistakable identity for the play *Family Time Productions*, which takes place in the past and present.

Designer, letterer, illustrator: Steven Brower Photographer: Jellybean Client: The First Avenue Playhouse

RIGHT **Adhering to the nineteenth-century theatrical poster tradition** in France, Germany and Italy, James McMullen includes hand-rendered simulations of real type, in this case a News Gothic face, on his poster for the play *An American Daughter*.

Designer, letterer, illustrator: James McMullen Client: Lincoln Center Theater

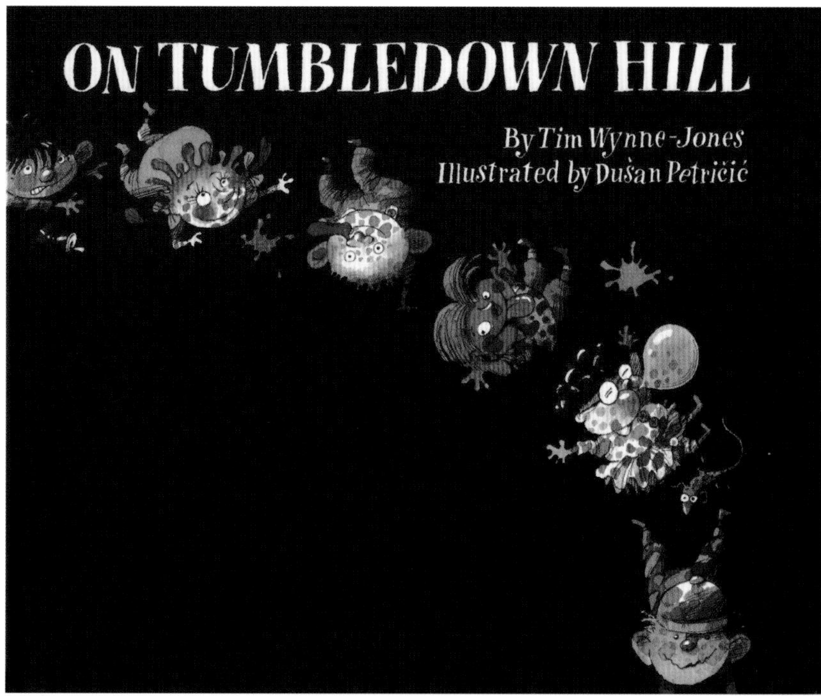

These huge words are not merely captions for the pictures but are seamlessly interrelated texts that become an alternative form of illustration in the book *On Tumbledown Hill.*
Letterer, illustrator: Dusan Petricic Client: Red Deer Press

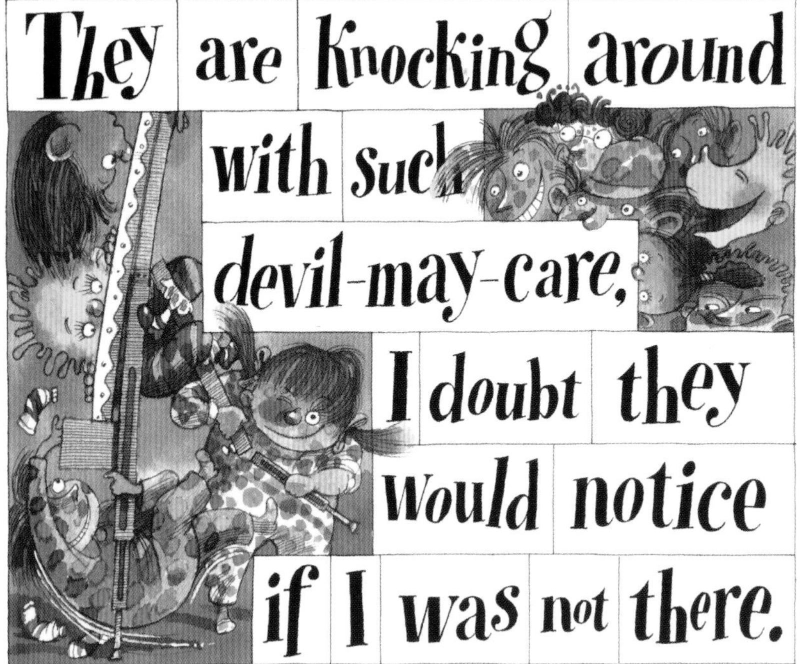

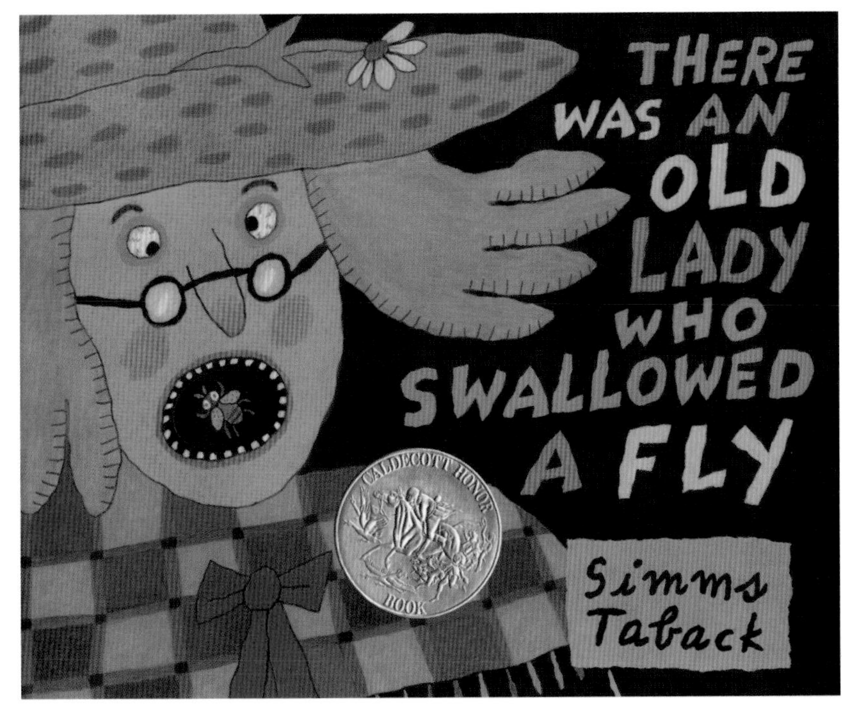

Basing his letters on actual Gothics to produce a unique alphabet, Simms Taback does not rely on impersonal typefaces to complement his raucous pictures in the book *There Was an Old Lady Who Swallowed a Fly*.
Letterer, illustrator: Simms Taback Client: Viking Children's Books

Poster artists of the 1920s and 1930s painted type onto their illustrations; likewise, Richard McGuire's lettering fully conforms to his artwork on the book cover for *The Handbook for Pricing and Ethical Guidelines.*
Art director: Sara Love Designer, illustrator: Richard McGuire
Client: Graphic Artist Guild

It is sometimes difficult to find the exact cut of a new or old typeface to suit a particular drawing style. This lettering, however, is made for the picture on the book cover of *La Méridienne.*
Designer, illustrator: Richard McGuire Client: Éditions Robert Laffont

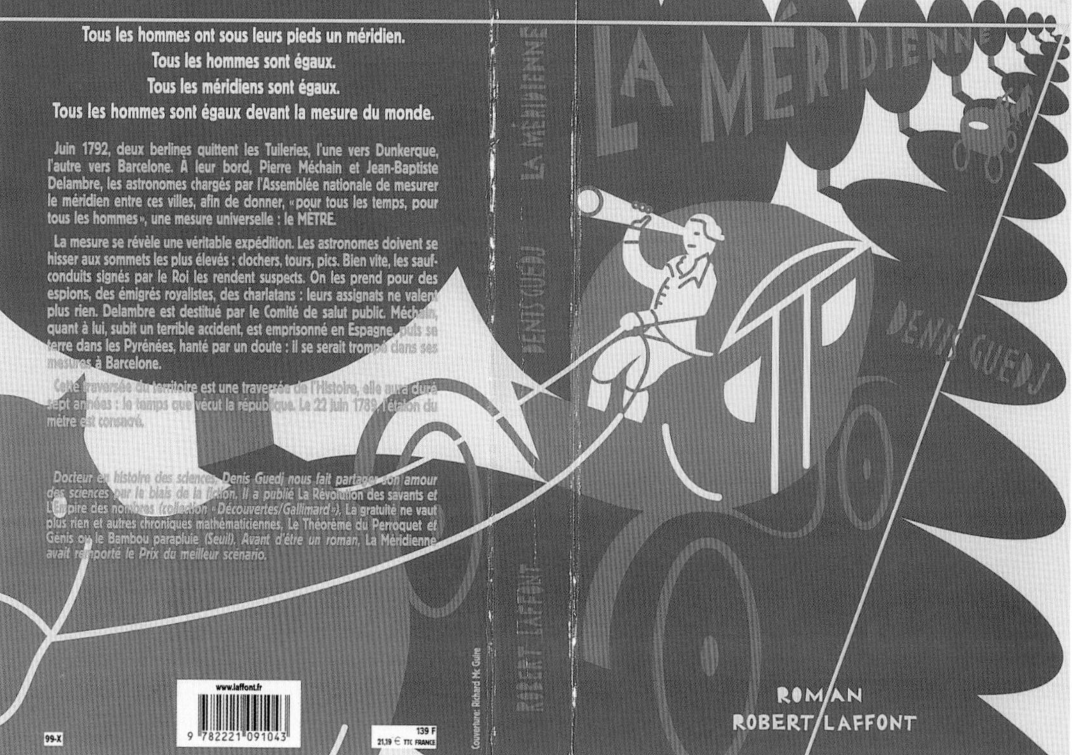

LEFT **This comic transformation of the letter 'R'** on a poster for the magazine *Rough* could only have been accomplished by a smoothly moving hand. The rest of the word is also wittily and smartly rendered.
Art director: Scott Ray Letterer, illustrator: Noah Woods Client: Dallas Society of Visual Communications

ABOVE **Drawn letterforms are brought alive** by clever ideas and not simply by leaving them as readable compositions; these letters on the book cover for *ABC* take the form of a dancer with a strange affectation.
Designer: Rodrigo Corral Letterer, illustrator: Brian Cronin Client: Farrar, Straus and Giroux

This would have been much simpler as a typesetting job, but headline and body text in this calendar book was painstakingly drawn by hand because it was a challenge to do so.

Creative director: Stanislav Sharp Art director, design: Mirko Ilić Illustrator: Slavimir Stojanović

Letterers: Mirko Ilić , Ringo Takahashi, Jelena Camba Djordjević Client: Publikum

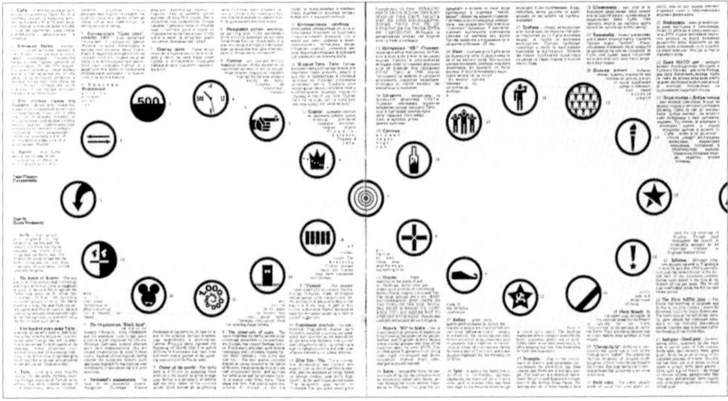

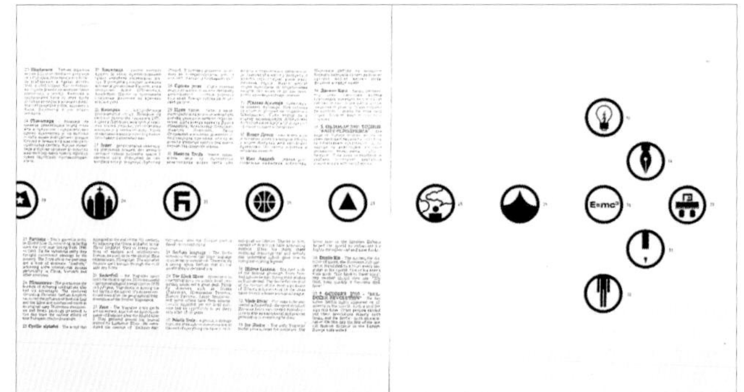

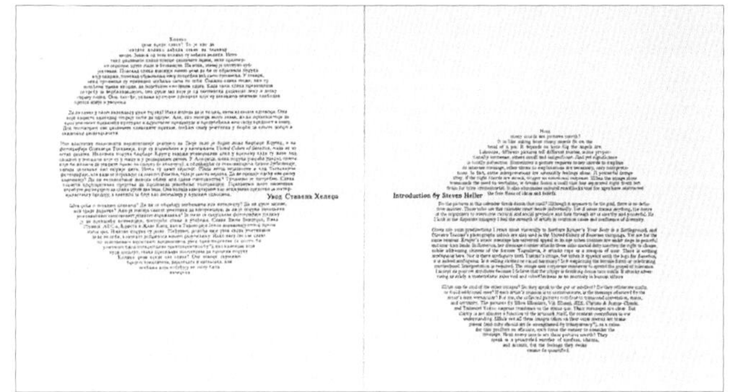

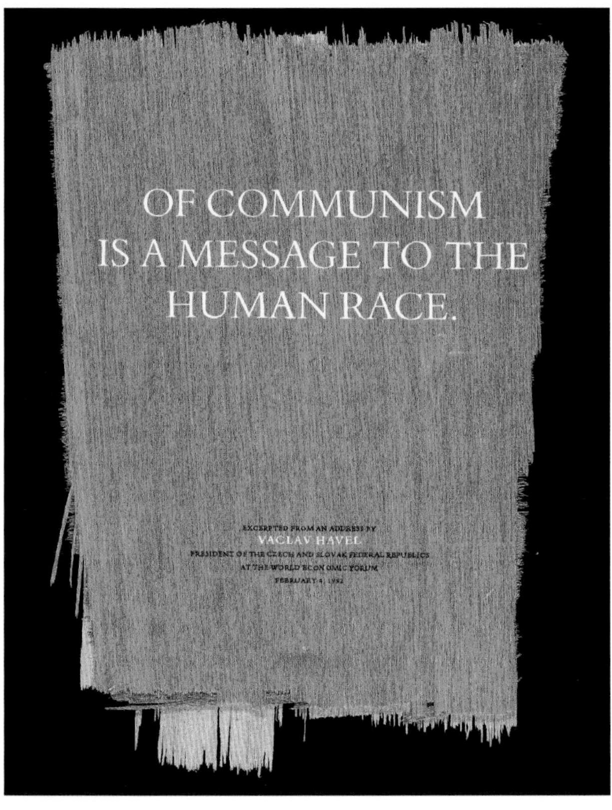

It is a message we have not yet fully deciphered and comprehended. In its deepest sense, the end of Communism has brought a major era in human history to an end. It has brought an end not just to the 19th and 20th centuries, but to the modern age as a whole.

The modern era has been dominated by the culminating belief, expressed in different forms, that the world—and Being as such—is a wholly knowable system governed by a finite number of universal laws that man can grasp and rationally direct for his own benefit. This era, beginning in the Renaissance and developing from the Enlightenment to socialism, from positivism to scientism, from the Industrial Revolution to the information revolution, was characterized by rapid advances in rational, cognitive thinking.

This, in turn, gave rise to the proud belief that man, as the pinnacle of everything that exists, was capable of objectively describing, explaining and controlling everything that exists, and of possessing the one and only truth about the world. It was an era in which there was a cult of depersonalized objectivity, an era in which objective knowledge was amassed and technologically exploited, an era of belief in automatic progress brokered by the scientific method. It was an era of systems, institutions, mechanisms and statistical averages. It was an era of ideologies, doctrines, interpretations of reality, an era in which the goal was to find a universal theory of the world, and thus a universal

Disciplined attention to detail and a dedication that indicates almost obsessive or compulsive behaviour are demanded when drawing every letter in a block of text by hand, as done here. It is hardly possible to tell that this brochure, *The End of Communism is a Message to the Human Race*, uses a non-standard typeface. Designer, letterer: Stephen Doyle Client: Champion International

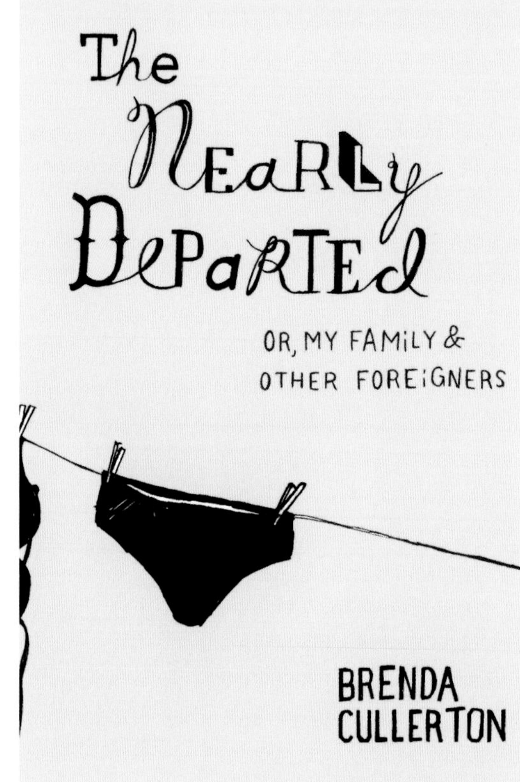
The Nearly Departed
OR, MY FAMILY & OTHER FOREIGNERS
BRENDA CULLERTON

ABOVE **A personal signature is inherent** in the hand-drawn title of this book, *The Dangerous Husband*, but it would have been lost had the title been set by computer.
Designer, letterer, illustrator: Chika Azuma Client: Little, Brown & Company

ABOVE RIGHT **As time-consuming as rendering** the letters for the cover of *The Nearly Departed* by hand may have been, the result is much more eye-catching and amusing than black-letter type.
Designer: Kelly Blair Letterer, illustrator: Joel Holland Client: Little, Brown & Company

RIGHT **Bringing together various Gothic**, serif and script types traced from specimen books produces a delightfully comic innovation on the cover of *Arsenal on the Double*.
Designer: Angus Hyland Design assistant: Sharon Hwang Client: Mainstream Sport

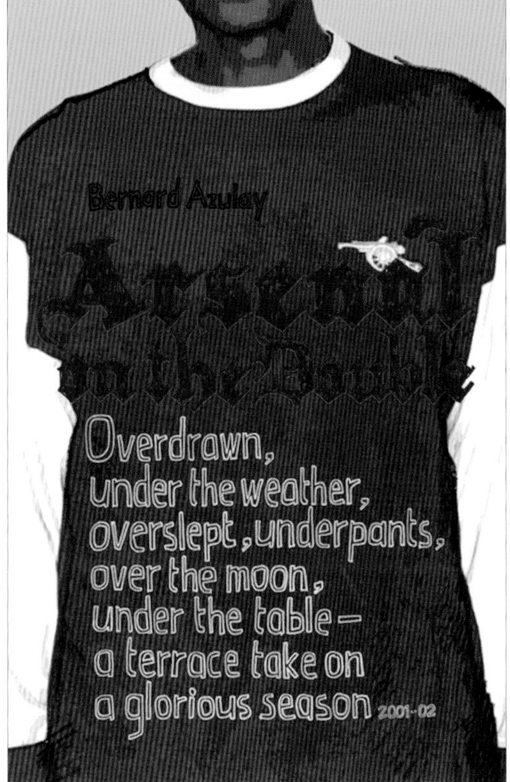
Bernard Azulay
Overdrawn,
under the weather,
overslept, underpants,
over the moon,
under the table –
a terrace take on
a glorious season 2001-02

LEFT **A fairly bland logo** for *The Progressive* is afforded more character through its handlettered presentation – and it complements the illustration, too.
Designer: Nick Jehlen Letterer, illustrator: Seymour Chwast Client: *The Progressive Magazine*

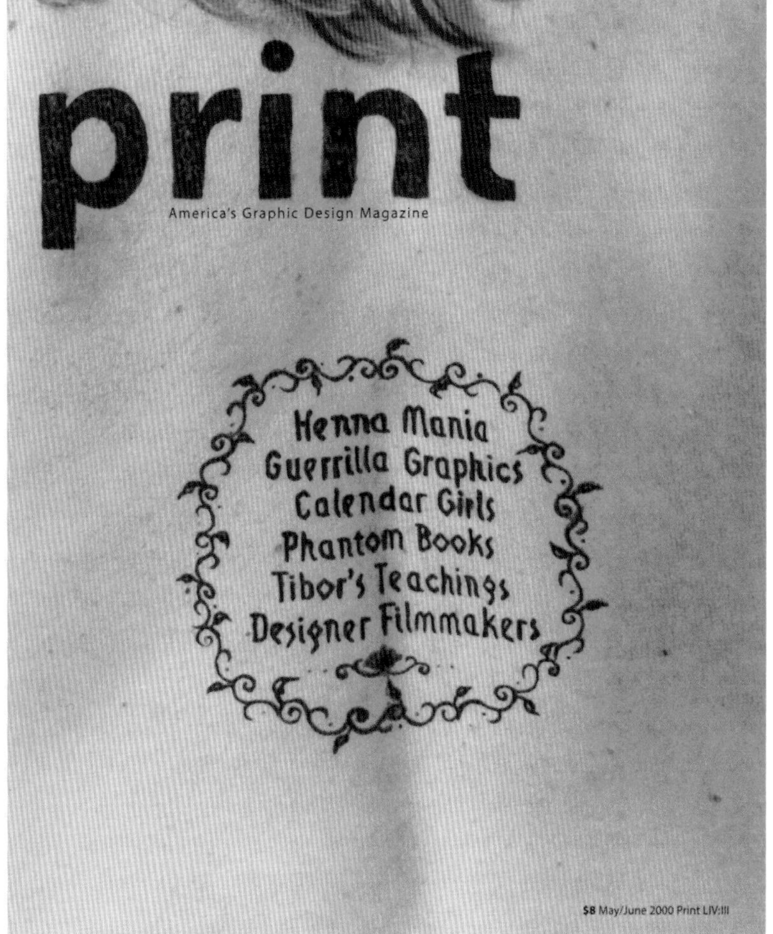

RIGHT **Designed to give the impression** of having been tattooed onto a body, the magazine name, *Print*, and headlines set the tone for a piece on Henna body writing.
Art director, designer: Steven Brower Letterer: Makiko Yoshimura Photographer: Barnaby Hall Client: *Print*

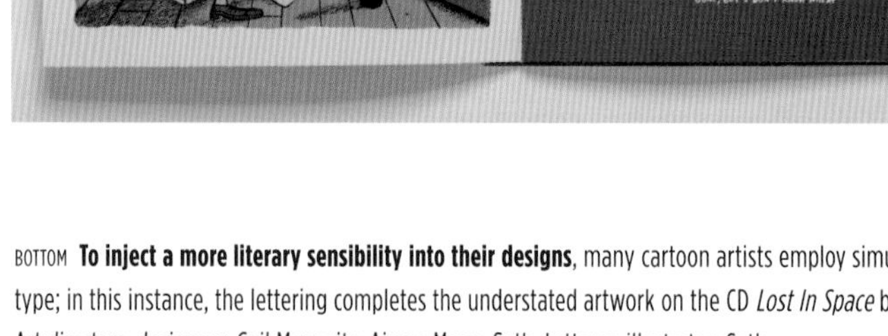

TOP **Quotidian concert and prize-fight posters** are the inspiration behind the design of this Nike sneaker campaign. Imitating the standard lettering by hand imbues it with more character than mechanically setting the type.
Art director: Danielle Flagg Designers, letterers: Joshua Berger, Pete McCracken, Lotus Child, Jon Steinhorst
Copywriter: Jimmy Smith Client: Nike

BOTTOM **To inject a more literary sensibility into their designs**, many cartoon artists employ simulations of real type; in this instance, the lettering completes the understated artwork on the CD *Lost In Space* by Aimee Mann.
Art directors, designers: Gail Marowitz, Aimee Mann, Seth Letterer, illustrator: Seth
Clients: Superego Records, United Musicians

RIGHT **There is something paradoxical about having body art** that looks like it came from a type specimen book, yet this CD design for Brian Setzer recognizes that tattoo artists are known for their attempts to re-create real typefaces in their work.
Art director: Darren Wong Designers: Michael Strassburger, Vittorio Costarella Letterer: Michael Strassburger
Client: EMI Records

BELOW **Decorative in a quirky and disturbing manner**, the simulated lettering fits the weird storybook feeling created through the drawings on this fantastical CD packaging and book for *How We Quit the Forest*.
Art director: Kiku Yamaguchi Designer, letterer, illustrator: Melora Creager Client: Sony Music Entertainment

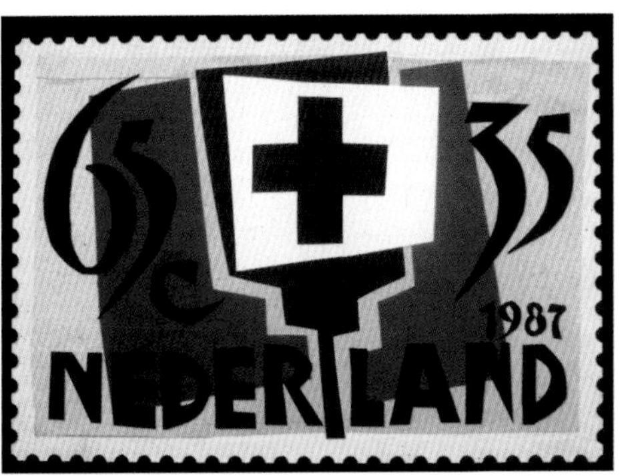

TOP **A commentary on traditional book composition**, this book, *Typ/Typografisch Papier*, has cut-out, bold, sans-serif letters that convey immediacy and demand the reader's undivided attention.
Designer, letterer, illustrator: Max Kisman Client: Typ/Typografisch Papier

BOTTOM **Postage stamps require simplicity**; the seamless marriage of letterform, colour and image gives these stamps for the Red Cross the impact of posters twenty times their size.
Designer, letterer, illustrator: Max Kisman Client: Royal PTT Postal Service, the Netherlands

RIGHT **Suggesting a second reality**, every element of this calendar poster is cleverly conceived to create the perfect graphic concept to announce the year of the tiger.
Designer, letterer: Wang Xu Client: Guangdong Fu Tak Fine Paper Co., Ltd.

BOTTOM RIGHT **The designer's loyalty to formal alphabets**, which have been used here as models, is the only difference between the lettering on this exhibition poster and a pure scrawl.
Designer, letterer, illustrator: Sebastian Kubica Client: Gallery Lincoln Center, New York

BELOW **Not only revolving around the 'M' as Hamlet's crown**, the virtues of this theatre poster are also determined by the oddities of the expressive lettering that has been created in a woodcut style.
Designer, letterer, illustrator: Monika Starowicz Client: City Hall, Zabki

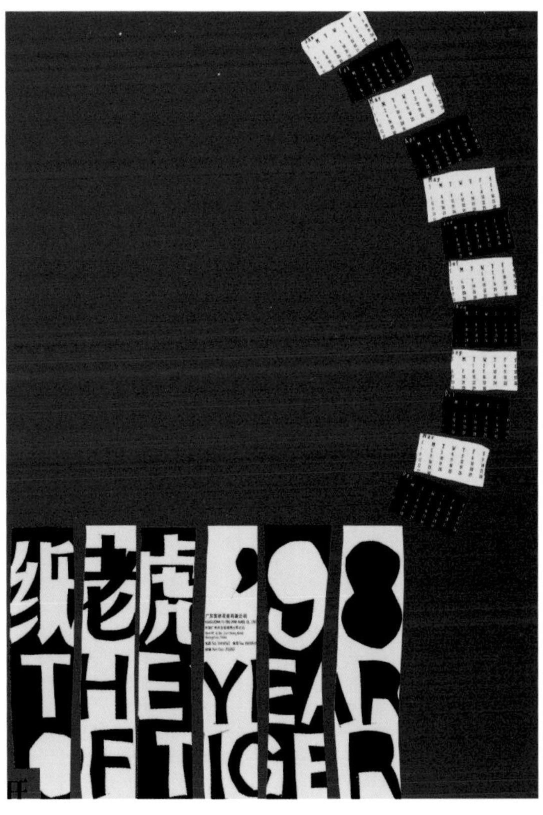

133

RIGHT **Using numerous kinds of Gothic type**, each composed to look ad hoc, Paula Scher produced many variations of this theatre poster advertising *Bring in 'Da Noise, Bring in 'Da Funk.* This version simulates the sketch on the original poster.
Designer, letterer: Paula Scher Client: The Ambassador Theater

BOTTOM RIGHT **Hybrid approaches coalesce into one overall style** in this densely packed design for a voter registration card, which shows lettering that is not a pure replica of type.
Art director: Soonduk Krebs Designer: Jeremy Holmes Client: Rock the Vote

BELOW **The obsessive, art brut quality of this lettering**, on a poster entitled 'Hand in Your Thoughts', draws the reader directly to the message, like a bee is attracted to a flower.
Creative director: Timothy Sumption Art directors: Judy Sell, Laura Stanke Copywriter: Beth Wolfe
Illustrator: L.K. Hanson Client: *Star Tribune*

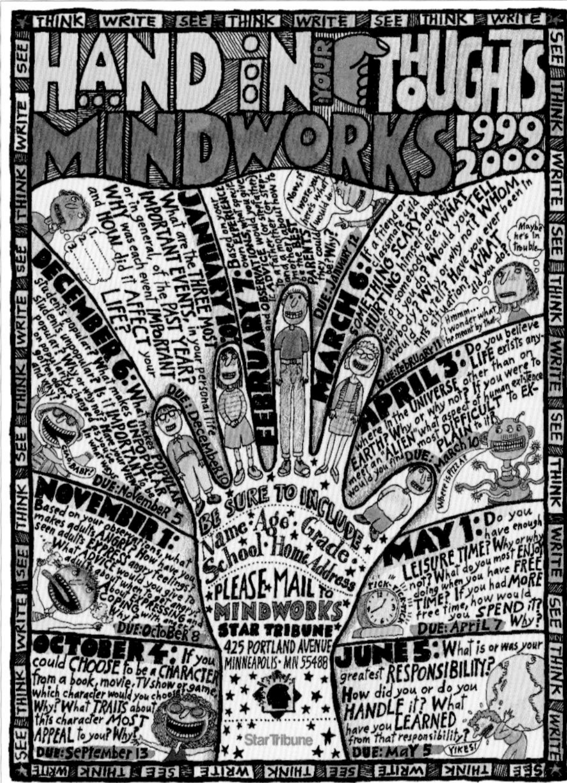

LEFT **Incorporating unique handmade idiosyncrasies**, the Japanese writing on this poster, called 'Secret Palace', also echoes conventional hot-type and cold-type characters.
Designer, letterer, illustrator: Tadanori Yokoo Client: Laforet Museum, Harajuku

ABOVE AND LEFT **Pseudo Art Nouveau lettering was common in 1960s psychedelic graphics.** In these two posters, 'The Legend of Tenko' and 'Yaesu Book Center', the combination of the drawing style and the Roman letters results in a strange marriage of the weird and the classic.
Designer, letterer, illustrator: Tadanori Yokoo Clients: Mori Enterprise Co., Ltd, Yaesu Book Center Co., Ltd

dimensional, voluminous, monumental

From their inception as commercial lettering in the nineteenth century, shadowed characters have been toying pleasurably with viewers' perceptions. Few typeforms are more dramatic. Whether a subtle tint or a bold silhouette, the shadow gives dimension, allowing words to rise monumentally and voluminously from an otherwise flat surface.

Shadowed letters began as hand-drawn renderings of both classic and invented type. They were introduced as metal typefaces as early as 1815 and were popularized by such type founders as Vincent Figgins, William Thorowgood and Blake Garnett. Most shadowed type began as fat faces with typically thin stems and hair serifs that proved, at times, difficult to reproduce. Out of necessity, type founders compensated by adding shadows to the more troublesome cuts. They revelled in the surprising results, 'It is as if the designers were absorbed in enjoying the ingenuity of their own invention', observed type historian Nicolete Gray in her book *Nineteenth-Century Ornamented Typefaces* (University of California Press, CA, 1976). Job printers quickly adopted the resulting faces because, regardless of size, they exploded off the page. In response to this surge in popularity, foundries issued wide selections of styles and sizes, including some quite awkward ones and other curiously elegant options. Even French literary giant Honoré de Balzac, the proprietor of a Parisian type foundry, issued a lavish specimen catalogue that offered an assortment of Lettres Egyptiennes Ombrées – slab-serif types with linear dimensional shading. Shadowed wood type was also in demand during the late-nineteenth century, mostly on posters designed to catch the eye of frantic passersby.

G
GARY PANTER
VISITING LECTURER
APR. TEN
THREE PM
SVA MFA DESIGN

Shadow faces are illusions, typographic trompes l'oeils that pique and flirt with the viewer's understanding. They are based on the real three-dimensional letters found on buildings, which are made dramatic by the ways light falls upon them, increasing or decreasing the depth of the shadow as the sun rises and sets, and thus altering the letter shape and proportion. This sculptural essence adds immensely not only to the visibility of the letters but also to their aesthetic appeal: shadowed letters bring intrigue and spectacle to otherwise mundane words.

Commercial sign painters long ago mimicked these sculpted letterforms in hand-painted facsimiles on glass, wood and enamelled metal. Although shadowed typefaces were most frequently used on small printed pages and posters, the finest – indeed most colourful – examples were to be found on late-nineteenth- and early-to-mid-twentieth-century store windows and glass or enamel merchant's signs, all of which were created by hand with uncommon precision. Before the explosion of neon in the early-twentieth century, and even afterward, shadowed letters served as virtual illumination. Depending on the intensity of the artificial light source, the hue of the silhouette and the colour of the background on which they sat, the letters were often radiant. Designers underwent years of hard practice before becoming skilled enough to make shadow letters work, because when ineptly used they could look unpleasantly grotesque.

Sign makers drew inspiration from a common vocabulary of shaded formats and a vast, ever-increasing number of lettering examples. The models were routinely reproduced in sign-painting manuals, which also included various stylish alphabets in bright hues. These were especially designed for copying and were then customized by hand for individual clients. The streets of Paris, London, Florence, Barcelona and countless other European cities still retain store fronts with original shadowed signs from the late-nineteenth and early-twentieth centuries. This fundamental time-honoured practice continues today in sign-painting, truck lettering and restaurant and boutique awnings.

Handmade shadowed letters were also frequently seen on theatrical posters and sheet music, but their most common application in printed matter – in fact, the key publishing area in which the vocabulary became a typographic language – was on mastheads for vintage pulp magazines. Pulps, which started around 1900 and continued until the 1940s, were printed in black and white on cheap rag paper while the covers were a slightly better grade of paper and were usually illustrated in full colour. The torrid cover images were mesmerizing realist paintings of melodramatically composed fantasy scenes featuring herculean heroes and defenceless dames. At the top of each full-page image a bold and colourful drop-shadow title (such as 'Gangster Stories', 'Weird Tales', 'Love Story' and, coincidentally, 'The Shadow') had the same visual impact on the viewer as a striking store or truck sign. These mastheads helped to define the typography of mass culture and ultimately influenced the look of comic books that, in turn,

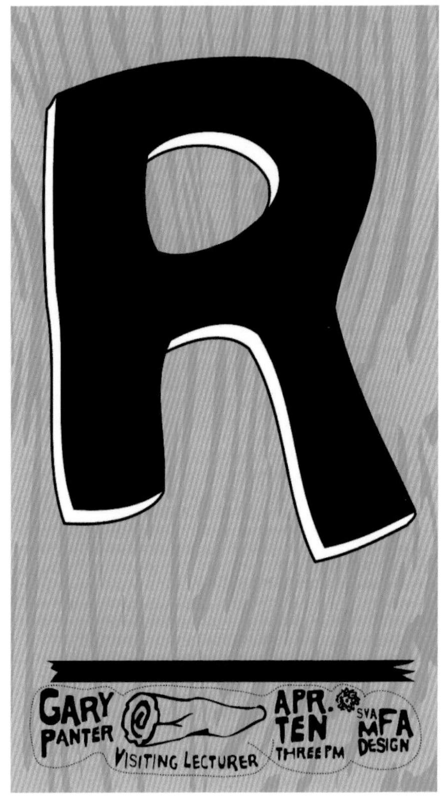

had an impact on the look of movie posters and film title cards. All were created by hand as custom-made shadowed letters and, eventually, this form was adopted for other emblematic purposes, as well: in the USA, the traditional school varsity letter and, for that matter, most shadowed, blocky and script letterforms used on athletic uniforms are among the most ubiquitous uses. Referring to these varied applications in commercial printing, Nicolete Gray wrote in her book that these faces 'are enjoyable without being particularly characteristic of either a mood or a period'.

The shadowed letter evokes many moods and many periods, but, and Gray is absolutely right, never one in particular. The shadowed form represents the nineteenth century if a designer so chooses (by employing a Victorian lettering style), but it can as easily give the feel of the 1950s, 1990s or 2010s, depending on the context in which the forms are used. A shadow alone cannot date a letterform because light is timeless; any letterform from any period can be given a shadow. These letterforms are less about style (which is always locked in time) and more about adding dimensionality to flatness and drama to that which is static.

A well-composed stack of luminescent shadowed letters on a poster can be as aesthetically satisfying as any beautifully designed object. To flawlessly draw these kinds of letters requires keen drafting skill. Before the computer, designers could – figuratively speaking – render such letters with their eyes closed. Today, such draftsmanship is less valued and little required, so those lacking the twin virtues of patience and expertise have adopted alternative methods to achieve shadow effects.

Given the postmodern penchant for vernacular or untutored applied art, perfection is no longer mandatory. In fact, imperfection – the absence of that which is impeccable – is valued as highly, if not higher, in the search for expression whatever the formal consequences. One proven method of achieving pure expression in this particular lettering genre is the simple act of doodling.

Since making shadowed doodles is an enjoyable pastime (everyone has spent many an hour in this way), a sizeable number of designers and illustrators represented in this book have imbedded their own improvised letterforms in illustrations and designs as an efficient if not also aesthetically pleasing way of integrating type and image. While the artless scrawl (see pp 10–55) has a more makeshift look, the doodled shadow letter, though no less ad lib, provides a more colossal aura: the shadow letter may be just as informal, but the extra strokes and the voluminous mass suggest something immense.

During the era of Modernism, this immensity in shadowed lettering was synonymous with ornament, which was rejected as bourgeois. Minimalism reigned and the shadowed letter played little, if any, role in modernist graphic design. But the shadow is not definitively ornamental; it can be functional and can increase visibility. So, in addition to the pure pleasure of making the forms, the current trend for shadows is also rooted in its inherent utility – even informal or crude shadowed letters do a phenomenal job of capturing interest.

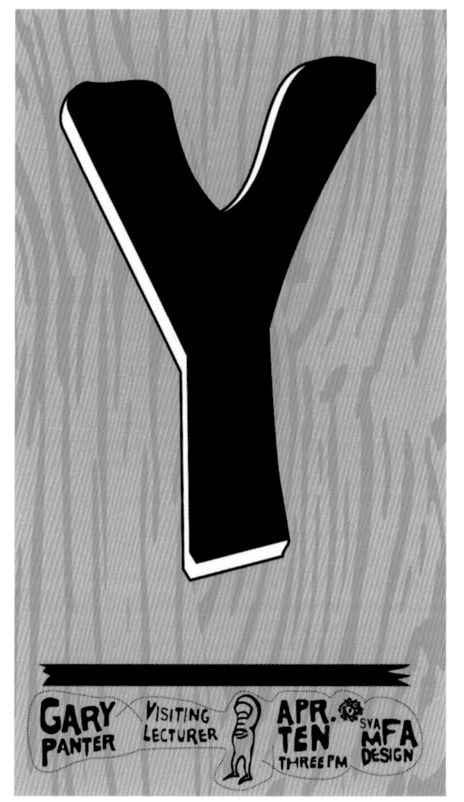

Rousing interest is the exact purpose of Japanese-born Junko Fuwa's shadowed doodles on the cover of *Blueprint* magazine (see p. 152), which continue as headlines throughout the interior spreads. The letters play with the viewer's equilibrium, and, in a magazine known for traditional typography, the ad-hoc style provides shock and awe. In an issue devoted to 'The New Communicators', the shadowed letters (and a few hand-drawn outlined headlines, too) are a witty counterpoint to the straight photography and the more official typography in the main text. Fuwa's lettering forces the reader to question the nature of new communicators.

Fuwa's approach is also a send-up of generic lettering rendered in a distinctly personal manner. Similarly, Kelly Blair's book jacket for *Fearless Jones* (see p. 149) exemplifies how shadowed lettering can replace conventional typography to provide a personal and eclectic visual point of view, in much the same way that a handmade sign gives personality to a barber's shop or general store. Increasingly, then, contemporary graphic designs might be seen as vociferous rejections of standardization, and that means anything not made by hand.

The exaggerated shadow is a fixture in comic-book lettering and has had a considerable influence on much of the work in this section even if it is not specifically comics related. Posters for silent films and early talkies also drew on the comic-book sensibility. For example, Thomas Matthaeus Müller borrows from these older genres in his poster for the 1993 documentary *Making of Ben Hur* (see p. 147). He creates a delightful, comic parody of the monumental fortress of shadowed letters that appeared in the titles for the actual 1959 film *Ben Hur*. Also in the comic-strip tradition, Steven Guarnaccia's cover for the comics magazine *Drawn & Quarterly* (see p. 148) pays homage to the classic comics splash panel with shadow letters dramatically rendered at a sharp angle.

The pure joy of handlettering is evident in Jonny Hannah's work (see p. 154), which is replete with unusual styles of shadowed letter, both invented and simulated. In his seamless marriage of letter and image, the mélange of quirky and discordant visual approaches draws the eye to the message and adds textural patterns to the entire composition. The shadow is also used as pattern and text in the 'Nashville Modern Dog' poster (see p. 144) in which the letterforms are framed by colourful shadows, giving the poster an abstract vibrancy that pure type could not achieve.

The letter as abstract art is an undercurrent in some of the work collected in this section. As a means of heightening expression, the shadow adds a level of spectacle: depending on the peculiarities of the letterforms themselves, the shadow contributes to an eccentric air. In Joel Elrod's surrealistic David Byrne poster (see p. 141), for example, shadowed lettering sits alongside other hand-created letters in a zany ballet of dimensionality.

Some of the letters here are predictably zany, others possess an unforeseen humour. Shadowed lettering simulates three dimensions, so it is fitting if surprising that the lettering by Sara Schwartz on the jacket for the children's book *A Leaf Named Bud* (see p. 149) is made from three-dimensional materials that have then been photographed so that even more shadows add to the multilevel illusion. Furthermore, shadows are used to enhance the tactility of the illustrative materials inside the book.

There is also a shadow language that has emerged since the advent of the computer, and this blocky random construction method is perhaps the most typical and the most common genre of anti-digital shadowed handlettering. For instance, Slovenian-born Mina Zabnikar's 'Vsi Na Zur!' ('Everybody to the Party!', see p. 156) combines a variety of letters with left-side, right-side, top and drop shadows, regardless of logic. Many designers simply throw shadows around without worrying about uniformity or rationality. Exactitude is on holiday and randomness reigns in this realm of handlettering. Why not?

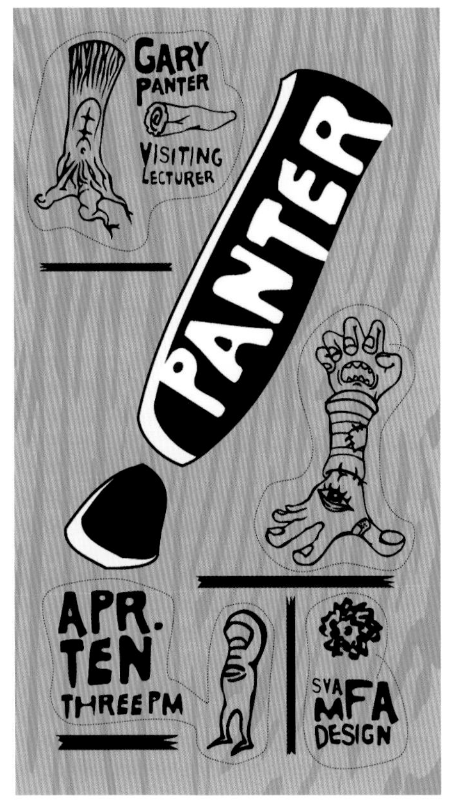

pp 136–39 **Large, imperfect letters** with reverse shadows (black letters with white shadows) spell out the name Gary Panter on five separate posters advertising his lecture series. They are as attention grabbing as a stop sign.
Art director, designer, illustrator: Melvin de los Santos
Client: School of Visual Arts, MFA Design

Only shadow letters, influenced here by the fancy faces of the nineteenth century, have a chance of standing out in paintings that are as densely packed as these advertisements.
Creative directors: Jeffrey Goodby, Rich Silverstein
Art director: Paul Hirsch Copywriter: Josh Denberg
Illustrator: The Clayton Brothers
Client: Specialized Bicycle Components

ABOVE **Enhancing textual visibility**, the subtly applied shadow motif also offers an alternative focal point to the eye-catching surrealist image on this concert poster for Ryan Adams.
Designer, letterer, illustrator: Joel Elrod Client: The Fillmore

ABOVE LEFT **Creating letters as crude as these** on the David Byrne poster would have been unacceptable in the modernist 1950s; today, this kind of approach is acknowledged as the design ethos of the twenty-first century.
Designer, letterer, illustrator: Joel Elrod Client: The Fillmore

LEFT **Drawing on the traditions of the illuminated manuscript** and the fancy face, this kind of shadow lettering, on a concert poster for Tift Merritt, still manages not to slavishly mimic either.
Designer, letterer, illustrator: Joel Elrod Client: Lost Highway Records

AMERICAN ILLUSTRATION 22
CALL FOR ENTRIES
THE MOST EXCITING GALLERY IN PRINT
CAPTURING THE SPIRIT OF THE YEAR

2 WAYS TO WIN AND BE SEEN:
SELECTED IMAGES WILL APPEAR
IN THE PRESTIGIOUS AMERICAN ILLUSTRATION ANNUAL.
SELECTED IMAGES, TOGETHER WITH CHOSEN IMAGES
WILL APPEAR ON OUR WEB SITE IN NOVEMBER 2003.
SEE THE CURRENT WINNING IMAGES FROM BOTH AI21 AND AP18 NOW AT →
AI-AP.COM

AMERICAN
ILL.
AMERICAN
AMERICAN
ILLUSTRATION
KING COBRA
JUST DONT KILL ME
13
TEEN
BEAT
I CAN
RIP YOU
APART
13
ILLUSTRATION
USED
NUMBER THIRTEEN
ILL

OPPOSITE, TOP **As if to prove that illustration is every bit as demonstrative** as PhotoShop-aided graphic design, all aspects of this call-for-entries booklet have been produced by hand.
Designer, letterer: Stefan G. Bucher Illustrators: various Client: American Illustration

OPPOSITE, BOTTOM **The aesthetic values of psychotic artists** and the ad-hoc quality of folk-art signs are brought together in this cover for *American Illustration 13*. Nothing is fine-tuned but the mélange works well overall.
Designer: David Armario Letterer, illustrator: Christian Northeast Client: American Illustration

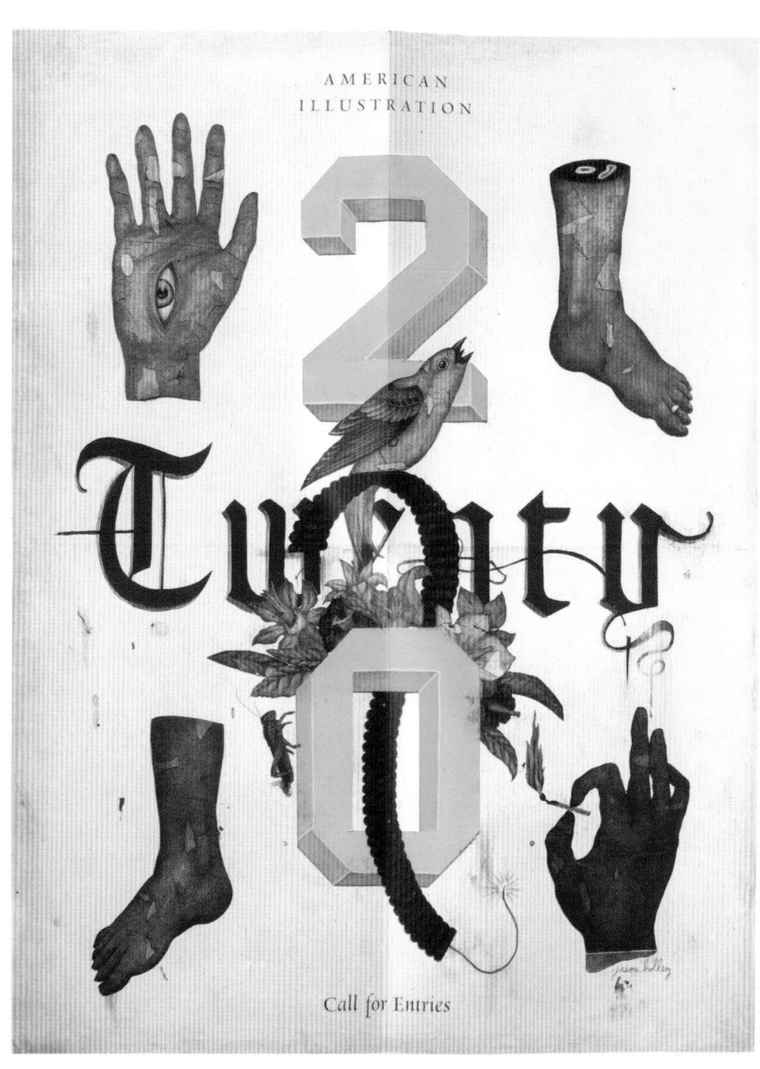

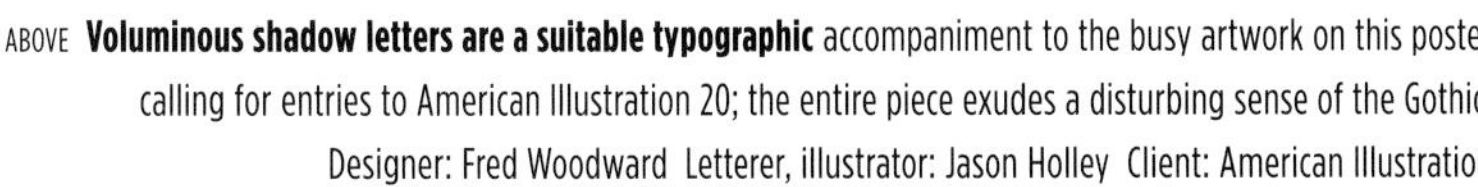
ABOVE **Voluminous shadow letters are a suitable typographic** accompaniment to the busy artwork on this poster calling for entries to American Illustration 20; the entire piece exudes a disturbing sense of the Gothic.
Designer: Fred Woodward Letterer, illustrator: Jason Holley Client: American Illustration

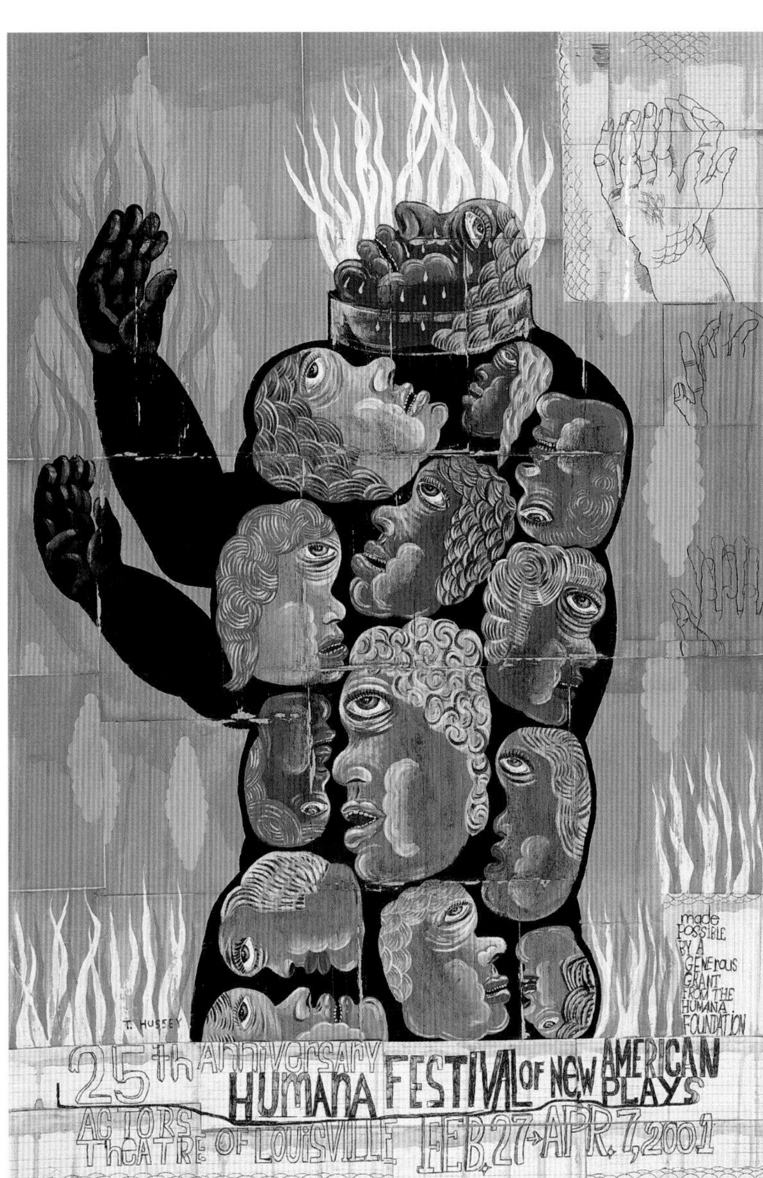

ABOVE **In keeping with the unmistakably grotesque apparition** that is the central focus of this poster for the 25th Annual Humana Festival of New American Plays, the lettering is reminiscent of mental-patient art.
Designer, letterer, illustrator: Tim Hussey Client: Actors Theatre of Louisville

The drop shadows in this jazz-like lettering improvisation form a grid of colour that intensifies the wording on this poster for the lecture 'Nashville Modern Dog'.
Designer, letterer, illustrator: Vittorio Costarella Client: Creative Forum Nashville

There is perhaps no better way to scream out the word 'freak' on this theatre poster than to print it in yellow with a black drop shadow.
Designer: Kevin Brainard Letterer, illustrator: Ward Sutton Client: *Freak* (The Broadway Show)

OPPOSITE **As a way to trip out on pure graphic form**, psychedelic poster artists of the 1960s would interminably play with shadows as an optical illusion, as shown in these poster advertisements for *High Times Magazine*.
Creative director: Sal De Vito Art director: Anthony DeCarolis Copywriter: Erik Fahrenkopf
Type designers: Erik Fahrenkopf, Anthony DeCarolis Client: *High Times Magazine*

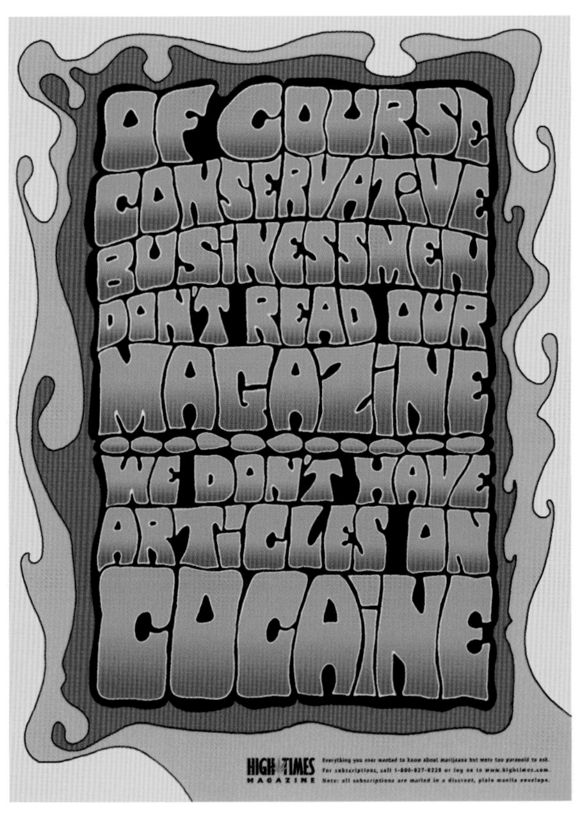
OF COURSE CONSERVATIVE BUSINESSMEN DON'T READ OUR MAGAZINE
WE DON'T HAVE ARTICLES ON COCAINE
HIGH TIMES MAGAZINE
Everything you ever wanted to know about marijuana but were too paranoid to ask.
For subscriptions, call 1-800-827-0228 or log on to www.hightimes.com.
Note: all subscriptions are mailed in a discreet, plain manila envelope.

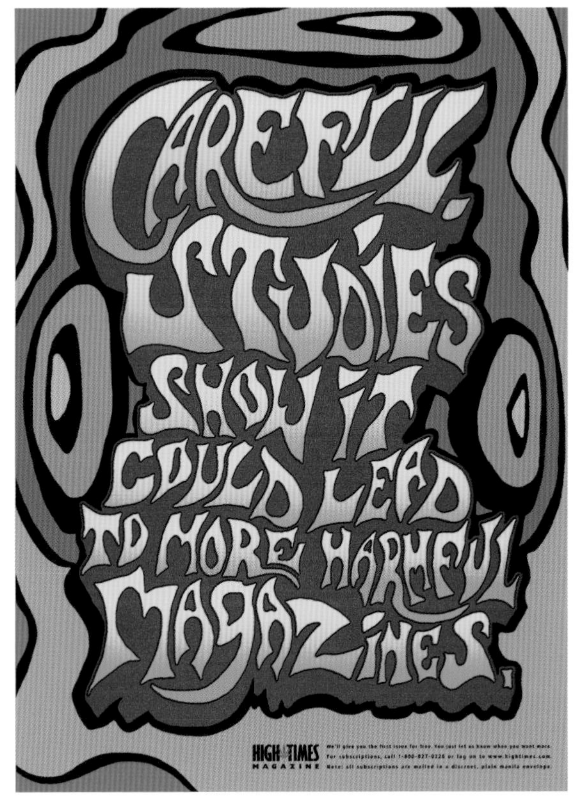
CAREFUL STUDIES SHOW IT COULD LEAD TO MORE HARMFUL MAGAZINES.
HIGH TIMES MAGAZINE
We'll give you the first issue for free. You just let us know when you want more.
Note: all subscriptions are mailed in a discreet, plain manila envelope.

TWO WORDS
SUBSCRIBE TO OUR MAGAZINE
HIGH TIMES MAGAZINE
Give your brain cells some intellectual stimulation. Right before you kill them.
For subscriptions, call 1-800-827-0228 or log on to www.hightimes.com.
Note: all subscriptions are mailed in a discreet, plain manila envelope.

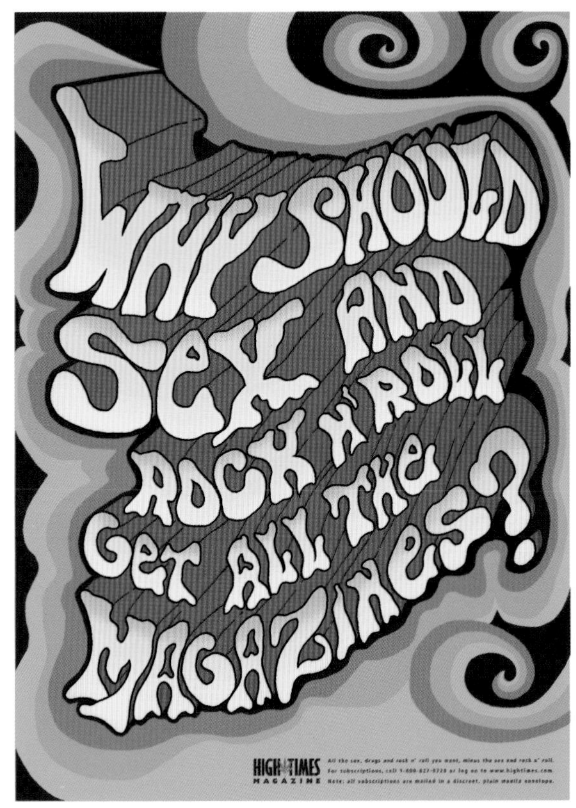
WHY SHOULD SEX AND ROCK N' ROLL GET ALL THE MAGAZINES?
HIGH TIMES MAGAZINE
All the sex, drugs and rock n' roll you want, minus the sex and rock n' roll.
Note: all subscriptions are mailed in a discreet, plain manila envelope.

ABOVE and ABOVE LEFT **There are various kinds of shadows** and these two book covers – for *Einstein's Dreams* and *The Dork of Cork* – reveal many of them; for example, the ghost shadows apparent on *Einstein's Dreams*. Designer, letterer, illustrator: Richard Beards Client: Bloomsbury Publishing

LEFT **The top shadow is as prominent** as the body of the lettering on this book cover for *La Spirale de L'Escargot*. Designer, letterer, illustrator: Richard Beards Client: Editions du Seuil

OPPOSITE **In the original Ben Hur movie (1959)**, the title was shown as a stone monument; this jumble of rocks on the poster advertising the documentary *Making of Ben Hur* is a comic parody. Designer, letterer, illustrator: Thomas Matthaeus Müller Client: INSELbühne

Die INSELbühne zeigt
Making of
BEN HUR
SOMMERTHEATER DER MORITZBASTEI
EINE PRODUKTION DER INSELbühne UND DES MORITZBASTEI e.V.
PREMIERE AM 2. AUGUST • WEITERE VORSTELLUNGEN VOM 3. BIS ZUM 18. AUGUST
KARTEN UNTER 0341-702590
MIT FREUNDLICHER UNTERSTÜTZUNG DER KULTURSTIFTUNG DES FREISTAATES SACHSEN, DES REGIERUNGSPRÄSIDIUMS LEIPZIG,
DES KULTURAMTES DER STADT LEIPZIG, DER UR-KROSTITZER BRAUEREI, SCHÖFFERHOFER, CORONA
Ur-Krostitzer

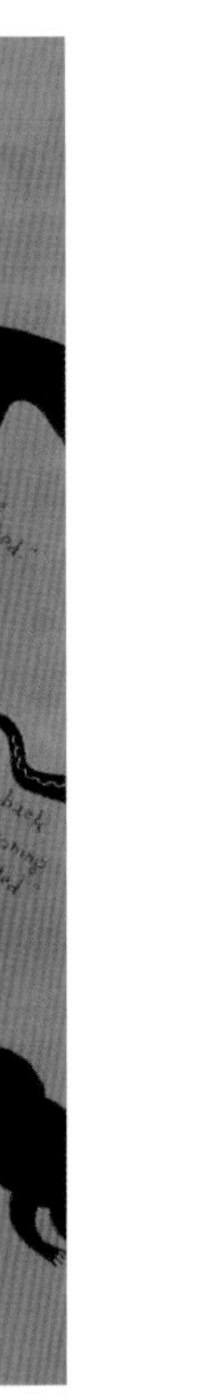

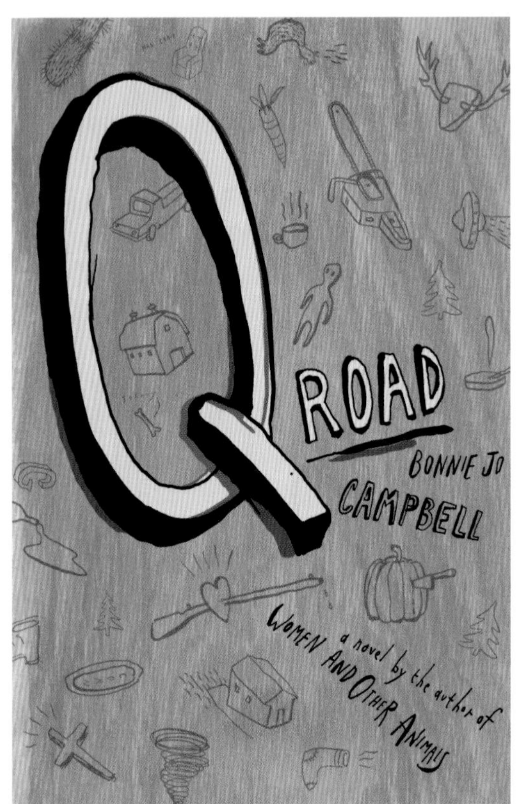

ABOVE **Angular shadowed lettering for the progressive comics magazine** *Drawn & Quarterly* reprises, with a slight twist, the traditional comics splash panel in its colourful dramatic dimensionality.
Designer, letterer, illustrator: Steven Guarnaccia Client: *Drawn & Quarterly*

TOP RIGHT **The 'Q' resembles a face with a cigarette dangling** from the mouth on this book cover for *Q Road*. The shadow offers the designer the chance to create many different illusions.
Art director, designer: John Fulbrook III Letterer, illustrator: Brian Rea Client: Scribner

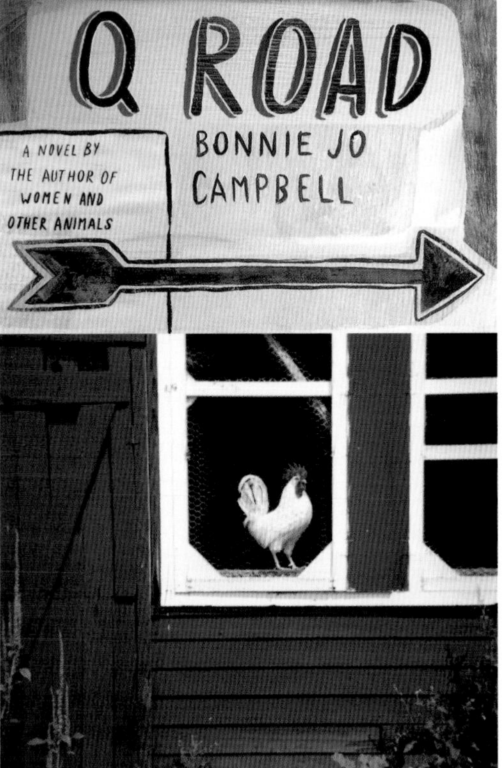

RIGHT **Store and farm signs throughout rural America** have been the inspiration for a number of vernacular designers. The shadow is a common trope on many of these signs because it increases visibility, as proved on this book cover for *Q Road*.
Art director, designer: John Fulbrook III Letterer, illustrator: Brian Rea Photographer: Michael Kelley Client: Scribner

LEFT **Looking as if it has been painted directly onto the picture**, this colour inline and outline shadow lettering style presents a beautiful contrast to the black-and-white photograph on the book *Fearless Jones.*
Designer: Kelly Blair Letterer: Brian Rea Photographer: Patrick Farrell Client: Little, Brown & Company

BOTTOM LEFT **Words and phrases float in thin air like clouds**; at least, that is the impression given by this semi-transparent shadow lettering on the book cover for *Cuba on My Mind.*
Designer, letterer, illustrator: Brian Rea Client: Verso UK

BELOW **Made from the same clay used to fashion** the characters in the children's book *A Leaf Named Bud,* the crude lettering has been photographed as a three-dimensional object to create a dramatic impact on the cover.
Letterer, illustrator: Sara Schwartz Client: Rizzoli

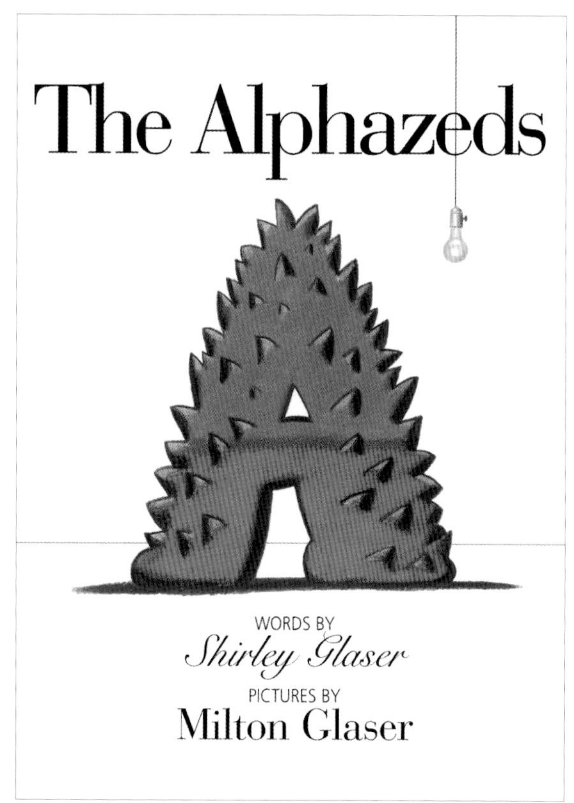

To bring this quirky and obstreperous alphabet to life, Milton Glaser created an engrossing typographic menagerie filled with all kinds of shadowy creatures for the book *The Alphazeds*.
Letterer, illustrator: Milton Glaser Client: Hyperion Books

WHAT IS THAT THING?
MY WORD!
HELP!
GASP!
HOW WOULD I KNOW— I JUST GOT HERE.
TA-DA!

HOP, HOP, HOP, HOP, YA KNOW WHAT I'M SAYIN'?
TALL PEOPLE NEED MORE ROOM THAN OTHERS!
I-I-I-C-C-CAN'T BREATHE!
DON'T LET ANYONE ELSE IN!
HOW LONG HAS THIS BEEN GOING ON?
IF YOU DON'T GET OFF MY FOOT I'LL KNOCK YOU OFF!
THINGS HAVE NEVER BEEN WORSE!
IS THERE A WAY OUT OF HERE?
THIS CAN'T GO ON!
STOP PUSHING!
AIR!
WHAT A MESS!
I CANNOT BELIEVE THAT THIS IS HAPPENING!
GASP
CLOSE THAT DOOR!
THIS HAS BECOME MOST UNCOMFORTABLE!
STOP YELLING!
THIS IS A SQUEEZE THAT DOES NOT PLEASE.
THIS IS NOT A VERY NICE CROWD.
WHY ARE WE HERE?
HOW MANY OTHERS ARE COMING?
THIS SITUATION IS INTOLERABLE
OPEN THAT DOOR!
I WISH EVERYONE WOULD QUIET DOWN.
IN OR OUT? IN OR OUT? WHATEVER.
I'M GOING TO SCREAM!
I THINK I'M GOING TO PERISH!
JE SUIS DESOLÉ.
I'M OUTA HERE.
IT'S NOT MY FAULT I'M SO BEAUTIFUL.
I WISH I HAD A BETTER SPOT.
SHHH!
TA-DA!
I HATE THIS PLACE!
NO!
IS ANYONE IN CHARGE?
FOOEY ON EVERYBODY!
HELP!

151

THIS PAGE **The drama of this lettering** in *Blueprint* becomes apparent in the contrast between the crude headlines and the conventional magazine layout.
Art director: Junko Fuwa Illustrator, photographer: Billie Jean Client: *Blueprint*

OPPOSITE, TOP **Shadow lettering is common** in the more ambitious kinds of street graffiti, which is doubtless the primary inspiration behind this layout in *RollingStone*.
Art director: Fred Woodward Designer, letterer: Siung Tjia Photographer: Albert Watson Client: *RollingStone*

OPPOSITE, BOTTOM LEFT **Magazine covers are not usually** so typographically casual, but this shadowed brush and pen lettering sets *Metropoli* apart from more mainstream journals.
Designer, letterer: Rodrigo Sanchez Client: Unidad Editorial S.A.

OPPOSITE, BOTTOM RIGHT **The original masthead** for *The New York Times Book Review* had never been tampered with before this brush-drawn design with its dramatic back-shadow marks.
Art director: Steven Heller Letterer, illustrator: Christoph Niemann Client: *The New York Times*

NEW COMMUNICATORS

THE BOOKKEEPERS

Not so long ago, the "design section" in a bookstore equated to two or three books sandwiched unceremoniously somewhere between Delia and Nigella. Then design became "cool" – bringing with it a flood of new titles covering everything from chairs to concrete. But while most were happy to jump aboard the proverbial bandwagon, there is a select group of publishers for whom the subject of design is about a lot more than a quick feel down the back of a Starck sofa.

All are distinguishable not only by the common agenda that unites them but by the individual focus that sets them apart. Together, they have a collective aim: to publish fresh, innovative material that doesn't look to the past, but anticipates the future, asking the questions as well as providing the answers. Apart, each offers a unique approach to a subject that all of us need, but only a few really care about.

August counts itself as one of the few publishing houses which actively treats images and words in equal measure, but it is the quality of the thinking – whether radical or controversial – that attracts publisher Nick Barley to a subject. "We're not really into celebrating great careers," he says. "We're into people who are asking difficult questions."

Thames & Hudson combines originality and editorial vigour with a touch of eccentricity. Commissioning editor Lucas Dietrich sees design "not just as a style that improves our lives, but as a human construct that everyone needs to exist". He hopes to "continue looking for ways to commission books that will be as meaningful in a generation as they were exciting and unexpected when they were first published".

Aidan Walker's self-confessed talent for "matching the way readers like to have their information put across with the information they actually want or need" has brought him great success in the past and is a skill he intends to put to good use in his current role of publisher at Rotovision. "Complex and difficult subjects can be presented, both visually and intellectually, in an attractive and seductive way," he says. "That's my aim."

Booth-Clibborn, represented here by commissioning editor Liz Farrelly, is happy to focus all its energy on a niche market in which it clearly excels. The company's books on the fine, media and decorative arts are a physical representation of its approach to publishing: "to commission first-class, creative work from the best of today's designers – whether they are renowned book specialists or innovative younger groups".

For Laurence King, design brings with it an excitement of working in the present that is reflected in his company's books. "We are keen to show people things that are new, but we approach it with an edge of seriousness that people can either ignore or benefit from, as they wish." *Lakshmi Bhaskaran*

DMX
REIGNS AS THE DARK PRINCE OF HIP-HOP
PHOTOGRAPHS BY ALBERT WATSON
WHOSE TALES OF HELL ON EARTH COME FROM HIS OWN HARROWING PAST
BY TOURÉ
82 · Rolling Stone, April 13, 2000
Rolling Stone, April 13, 2000 · 83

EL MUNDO
METROPOLI
A REVISTA DE MADRID. N°527. DEL 30 DE JUNIO AL 6 DE JULIO DE 2000
NUESTRO INFORME ANUAL
TERRAZAS
2000
BARES DE COPAS HELADERIAS
RESTAURANTES

Book Review
Summer Reading

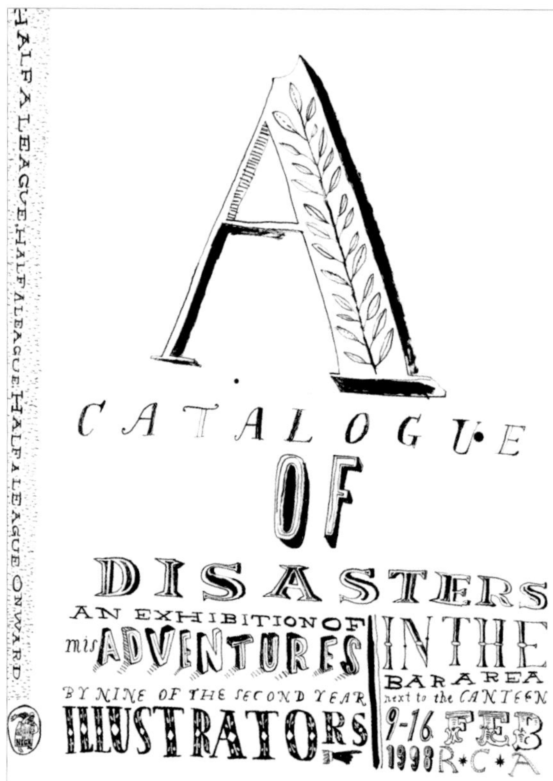

RIGHT **Paying homage to vintage county fair** and circus posters, Jonny Hannah uses every kind of shadowed letter he can think of for this exhibition poster.
Letterer, illustrator: Jonny Hannah Client: Royal College of Art, London

BOTTOM RIGHT **Kinetic excitement is created** in Hannah's work through the addition of transparent colour and numerous shadowed letters in the book *Introducing the Unquiet Grave*.
Letterer, illustrator: Jonny Hannah Client: Ruskin Press

BELOW **The letters in this composition** are seemingly composed without a care for the adjacent styles in the book *Notes from the Unquiet Grave No.6*.
Letterer, illustrator: Jonny Hannah Client: Ruskin Press

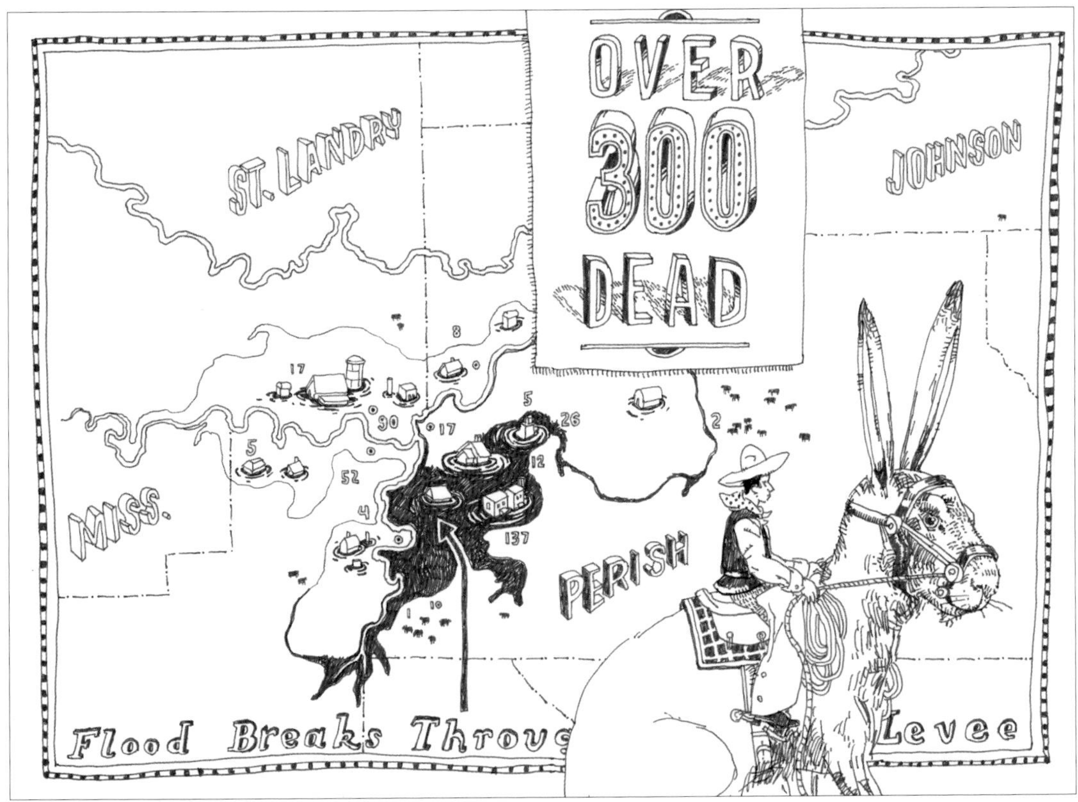

LEFT **Shadow letters suggest a historical aesthetic** while expressing a contemporary event in the illustration 'Over 300 Dead'.
Letterer, illustrator: John Hendrix, personal work

BOTTOM LEFT **This virtual sampler of dimensional** possibilities, for the announcement 'Order by Number', is composed in the style of an old sign painter's manual.
Designer, letterer, illustrator: George Hardie
Clients: Trickett & Webb, Augustus Martin

BELOW **Vintage old wood and steel engraving** methods of producing type are shown in this collection of variegated shadings for the announcement 'Typopress'.
Designer, letterer, illustrator: George Hardie Client: Roland Scotoni

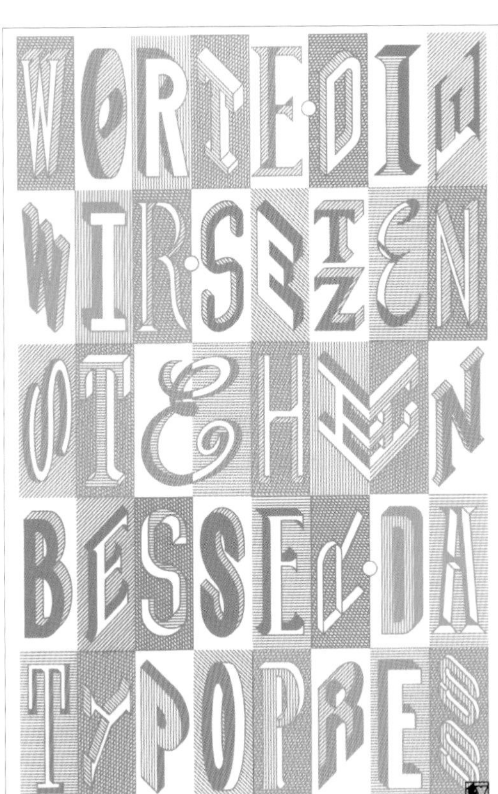

THIS PAGE **This design is reminiscent of informal doodles** of three-dimensional letters on scraps of paper, which are then coloured in using waterproof markers. Whatever the music on this CD compilation, the lettering is melodic.
Designer, letterer: So Takahashi Photographer: Julie Meinich Jacobsen Client: Carpark Records

OPPOSITE, TOP **Deliberately ignoring the fall of any natural light source**, the designer mixed different kinds of dark and light shadows into one big stew to create a frenetic look on this record for Meterman.
Designer, letterer, illustrator: Justin Fines Client: Someoddpilot Record

01. greg davis - "brocade"
(from upcoming full length)
02. kit clayton vs. safety scissors - "17-11"
(from "the ping pong ep")
03. marumari - "saka"
(from their out-of-print first cd "story of the heavens")
04. so takahashi - "blue, blue, electronic blue"
(exclusive track)
05. ogurusu norihide - "5:00"
(from "modern")
06. dinky - "no love"
(from "black cabaret")
07. freescha - "live and learn me"
(exclusive track)
08. casino versus japan "aquarium"
(from "whole numbers play the basics")
09. kid606 - "if my heart ever ran away it would be looking for the day when right beside you it could forever stay"
10. takagi masakatsu - "golden town with sunglasses"
hrvatski - "equinox"
signer - "interior dub"
jake mandell - "beartrap!"
©2003 carpark records usa
photo: julie meinich jacobsen
masayo kishi

OPPOSITE, BOTTOM LEFT **In the taxonomy of lettering** there are categories for maximal and minimal shadows. Mance practises the latter on this CD, *Covjek iz Katange*Plavi Bar* (*Man from Katanga*Blue Bar*) – a simple form of sculpted lettering that seems to rise gently off the surface.
Designers: Dejan Krsic, Dejan Dragosavac Rutta Letterer: Dejan Dragosavac Rutta
Illustrator: Milan Manojlovic Mance Client: Carnival Tunes

OPPOSITE, BOTTOM RIGHT **The shadowed lettering is anarchic** but it reveals a strong sense of the formal balance between light and dark on this party flyer, 'Vsi Na Zur!' ('Everybody to the Party!').
Designer, letterer, illustrator: Mina Zabnikar Client: Student Organization

čovjek iz katange ✦ plavi bar
mance

VSI NA ŽUR!
ŽUR! ALU AGRFT
MESTNA ŠOLA
RISANJA 18.10
SREDA OB 21:00
DJ! MUSIKA PIJČKA
V TEATRU GROMKI
METELKOVA MESTO
VSTOPNINE NI!
STOPNICE AIRWAY

Suggestive lettering metaphorically looks like the idea or entity it represents. It is also known as typography *parlant*, the most common example of which is the word 'ice' (as seen on ice-cube vending machines), where the tops of the otherwise Gothic letters are capped with – surprise – icicles. Incidentally, this particular typeface is called Icicle. Then there is the word 'fire' (as seen on displays for USA 'fire sales', big sales after a disaster), where the letterforms are consumed in flames. This typeface is predictably named Fire. Of course, menus for Chinese restaurants with type in the shape of chopsticks or bamboo are also common. These typefaces are called Chopstick and Bamboo, respectively. There are also those letters used to advertize horror movies or vampire products that look like dripping blood. This face has a few names, but Blood is the most common.

Over a century ago, these kinds of novelty alphabets were referred to as fancy faces, the most famous being Rustic (in the UK) or Log Cabin (in the USA), for which the letters were comprised of suggestively cut logs and twigs. Originally designed and engraved in 1845 at the Vincent Figgins Foundry, this typeface is still used today for such things as rest-room signs at park campsites or as building markers at Frontier Land in Disney World.

Novelties like these are considered anti-modern, proto-postmodern, crass and goofy, and, therefore, widespread interest in them today ebbs and flows depending on how crass or goofy a designer may be or how ironic a design is supposed to be. Suggestive letters must be used carefully and always with a wink and a nod because when used in an overly serious way the results can be disastrous. Stylistically speaking, these faces are always crude and gawky; humorously speaking, they are the lowest form of gag or visual pun. However, semiotically speaking (if one is so linguistically inclined), Log Cabin, for example, is perfect for imparting an essence of the great outdoors because it immediately allows the reader to conjure up an unambiguous mental picture. Likewise, another face in this *parlant* genre, Lariat, composed of knotted ropes, vividly suggests Western themes – and could the brand name for a line of cowboy clothing ever be set in Helvetica? While most type for reading matter is designed to be relatively neutral, these novelty faces were intended to take the guesswork out of communicating messages. Clearly, they are a gift to any nuance-challenged designer.

When fancy faces began in the early-nineteenth century, each one was originally hand drawn for specific projects. Only later, when it was apparent that they were successful in attracting attention to handbills and posters, were they made into metal casts and used as formal alphabets. By the late-nineteenth century, commercial job printers could not have run a viable business without a few of these much-used novelty fonts readily to hand. Even during the 1920s and 1930s (the era of Modernism), these fonts were used in appropriate and inappropriate mass-market advertising and on packaging. During the 1950s and 1960s, they were among the most popular Letraset (press-down, adhesive-backed letters) and Photo Typositor alphabets for advertisements and even the occasional editorial layout. As silly and as anachronistic

metaphorical, symbolic, surreal

as they are, they have inherent charm in the computer era. Moreover, lest anyone think suggestive letterforms are mere trifles, they do derive from serious historical beginnings.

The hand-carved inscription on Trajan's column in Rome (c. 113 AD) is considered the paradigm (or Holy Grail) of Roman letterforms. Perhaps the archetype of suggestive handlettering is the Sacramentarium of Gellone (dating from between 755 and 787 AD). In the Sacramentarium, the 'T' of the prayer *Te igitur* in folio 36 v° is a typographic portrayal of Christ on the cross. This ancient document is one of the finest examples of how illuminators transformed the figures of man and beast into expressive letters. And, it was not only men and animals: women, fruit, vegetables, buildings and many more fanciful and functional things were also subjects for letterform construction in ancient times. These letters served as sacred metaphors and allegories, communicating either complex tales or simple lessons. From this evidence alone, it is clear that the suggestive letter is one of the most venerable forms of handlettering to marry illustration and alphabet.

Suggestive lettering, therefore, is also referred to as illustrative lettering because the essence of the letter depends entirely on a sublime combination of image and letterform (or type as image). Unconstrained by the tenets of pure typography, the possibilities are limitless. Furthermore, it does not require an orthodox type designer to accomplish a degree of perfection in this area; a good imagination and the ability to create acute metaphoric associations are the prime skills. Of course, a talent for drawing is also useful.

Many of the most common suggestive letters are developed from the traditional illuminated initial – the entry point on many a manuscript – which provides readers with a pictorial cue as to the content of the paragraph or story to follow. During the early-nineteenth century, when faithful image reproduction was still something of a costly novelty, the wood- or steel-engraved illuminated capital was a way of not only adding to the narrative but also including illustration material in otherwise grey columns of text. These initials were often expanded into cleverly designed pictorial alphabets used as teaser images for books and lengthy stories.

Initial capitals are second nature today as in years past. Arguably, there is something inherently archaic about them, but they are still used in a variety of media in different contexts. Suggestive lettering in the digital age has a quirkier look and is not excessively representational; rather, abstraction is more in tune with the times. These letters today have symbolic and metaphoric roles and establish moods that add dimension to the storytelling process. Indeed, occasionally, they may not push a narrative but instead give the reader something else to ponder over, a respite from routine.

Ed Fella's work (see p. 178) typifies the kind of playful abstraction that suggests concreteness but is still illusory. He draws letters that seem to be more about pure form than physical depiction but that are also suggestive of something quite real. Fella's work is all about the intensity and expressive powers of colour, shape and elasticity. He moulds letterforms in his coloured pencil renderings, stretching them to their most absurd, yet they remain decidedly discernable. Fella's lettering stands at the nonfigurative end of the suggestive spectrum, while most other designers stay rooted in realistic representation.

Typical of the realistic genre is a contemporary Broadway musical poster art-directed by Gail Anderson of SpotCo and designed with lettering and illustration by Ward Schumaker and James Victore, respectively (see p. 176). The title, *Man of La Mancha,* is twisted into the shape of a horse on which the aging knight of La Mancha rides to do battle with the fabled windmills. Making the words fit the image is not as easy as it looks, but it certainly solves the problem of creating an illustrated 'trademark' that also includes the title. It is immediately evident that this particular integration of lettering and image is the perfect result, and the design is even workable in various sizes and formats. However, not all suggestive lettering solutions are so obvious.

Why Not Associates' letters for Dodgy's single (see p. 174) are a more strained yet no less appealing solution. The metaphoric letters are made from pieces of found and natural materials that evoke the improvisational nature of the music. The serendipity of the found materials presents a rawness that is endemic to the sound. Conversely, Paul Buckley's book cover for *Last Things* (see p. 163), while surprising, is more conceptually to the point; using real bones to form the letters is a humorous albeit grisly way of conveying elements of the plot. As with Log Cabin, the bones neatly provide the allegorical weight that real type might not be able to offer.

It is hard not to look back to the past when making suggestive lettering, after all, it has probably been done before in some fashion. Indeed, following in the tradition of the eccentric medieval illuminators, L.K. Hanson uses scads of odd imaginative forms to alter each letter in the headlines of the *Minneapolis Star Tribune's Book Review*. He combines a floriated 'P' with a jewel-encrusted 'O', swashed 'E', spiked 'T', cloudlike 'R', and indescribably kooky 'Y' to make the word 'poetry' (see p. 177). In a similar vein, Richard Beards's words for the signs of the zodiac (see p. 177) are made up of letters that visually become the shape of the scorpion, lion and archer (in which the 'A' is a visual pun on the legs).

Lettering of this kind derives from many traditional and unconventional sources, but for today's designers the latter is perhaps more compelling. The makeshift lettering for Charlotte Strick's *The Mercy Seat* and David Garcia's 'Don't You Wish You Were in Miami Now?' (see p. 172), drawn with a finger in the snow accumulated on car windscreens, is more than suggestive. It could suggest the lack of any type budget, but it is the most efficient use of natural materials to symbolically send a message about moving to warmer climes.

These lettering techniques are fairly straightforward in so far as they are unambiguously drawn from common forms. The suggestive letter as pun, on the other hand, requires more forethought. For a poster entitled 'Creative Hot Dog of the Month' (see p. 165), letterer Scott Ray uses the real food item itself, very nicely decorated with various garnishes, to form the word 'hot'. Another conceptual *tour de force* creates Japanese characters from water drops to spell out 'Shinmura Fisheries', an elegant yet difficult metaphorical conceit. The same is true of the transformation of a common fishing net into letterforms for the same company, which is both smartly allegorical and efficiently utilitarian (see p. 173).

The 'Scrawl' section (see pp 10–55) contains letters strung together in phrases that sound like what they mean. Although suggestive letterforms could definitely be considered onomatopoeic, just as some also have a sarcastic tenor, the lettering in this section has integral strength of its own regardless of meaning. In the case of suggestive lettering, the form enriches and is more important than the content.

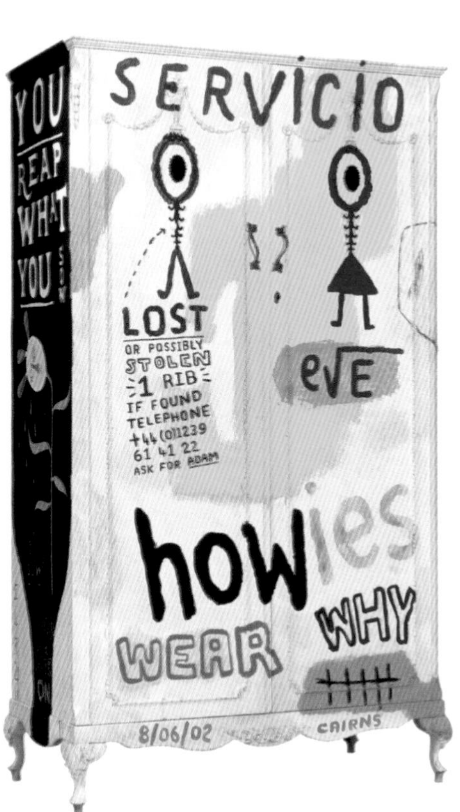

pp 158–61 **Drawing, painting and even carving letters** onto a wardrobe is an act of creating something monumental, as shown in this art project for recycled wardrobes. The letterforms become the furniture, allowing the pieces to be transformed into ideas that transcend their original function.
Creative director: Phil Carter Designers: Phil Carter, Neil Hedger Photographer: John Miller
Illustrators: Andrew Mockett, Jeff Fisher, Richard Beards, Marion Deuchars, Billie Jean, Brian Cairns
Client: Howies

LEFT **Made from wood and steel**, these letters on the book cover of *Kill Bill* form a striking dimensional illusion that frames the illustration.
Art director: Chuck Robinson Designer: Jia Hwang Letterer: Stephen Doyle Photographer: Timothy Saccenti
Client: Miramax Books

BOTTOM LEFT **Carving letters from old pieces of wood** is an age-old way of making type, while making wood into letters is a way of achieving dimension, as shown on the book cover for *The Regulators*.
Designer: Paul Buckley Letterers: Mark Ryden, Shasti O'leary, Paul Buckley Illustrator: Mark Ryden
Clients: Penguin USA, Paul Buckley

BELOW **The name Stephen King is synonymous** with all things weird and scary and those feelings are heightened by the suggestive letters on the book cover for *Desperation*.
Designer: Paul Buckley Letterer, illustrator: Mark Ryden Clients: Penguin USA, Paul Buckley

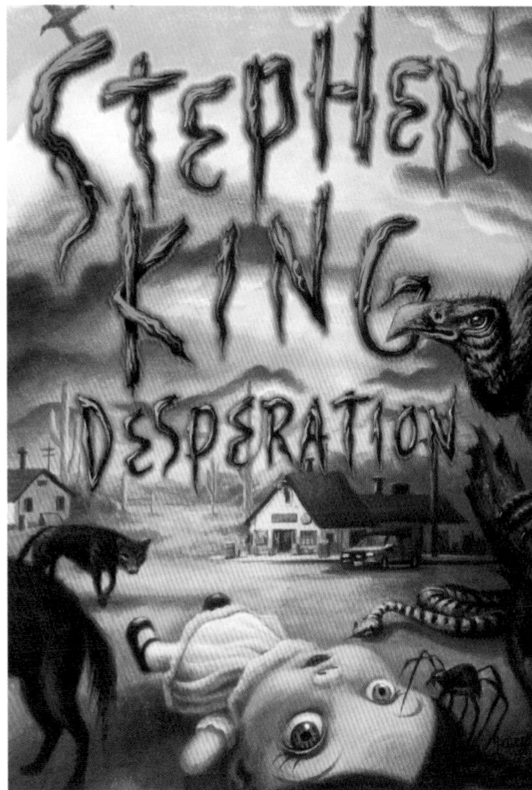

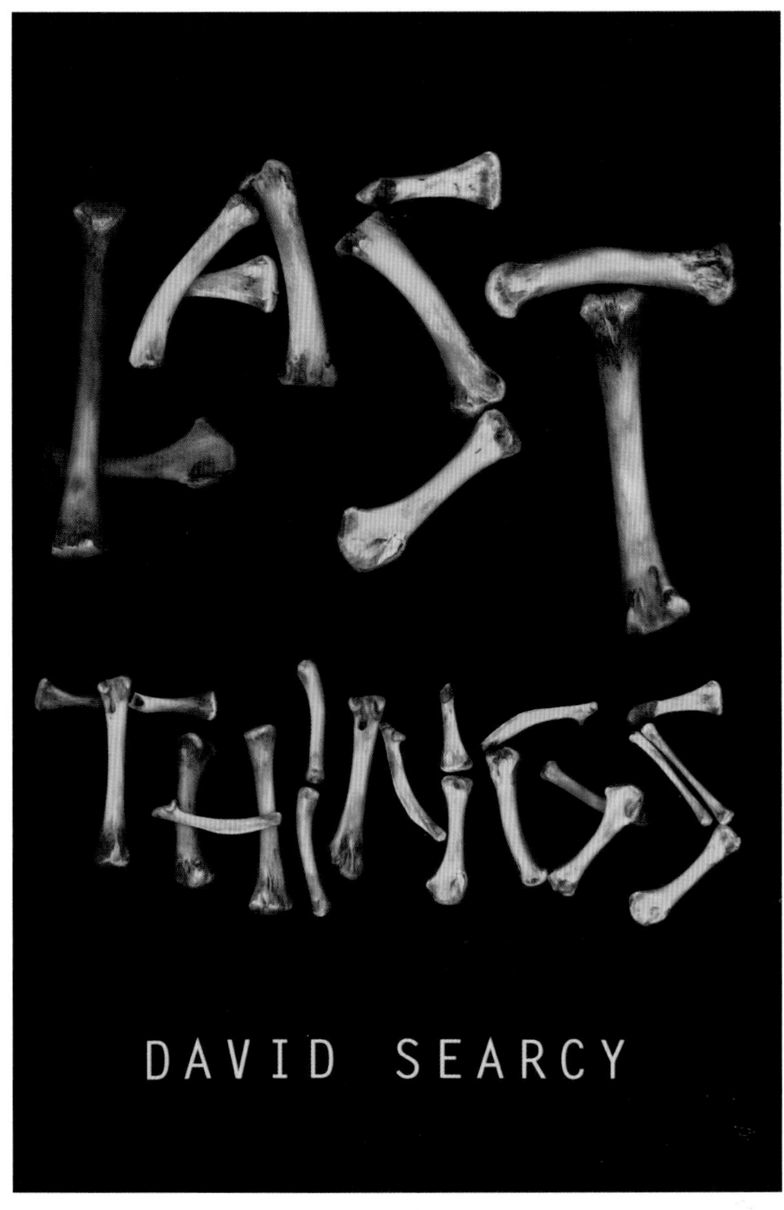

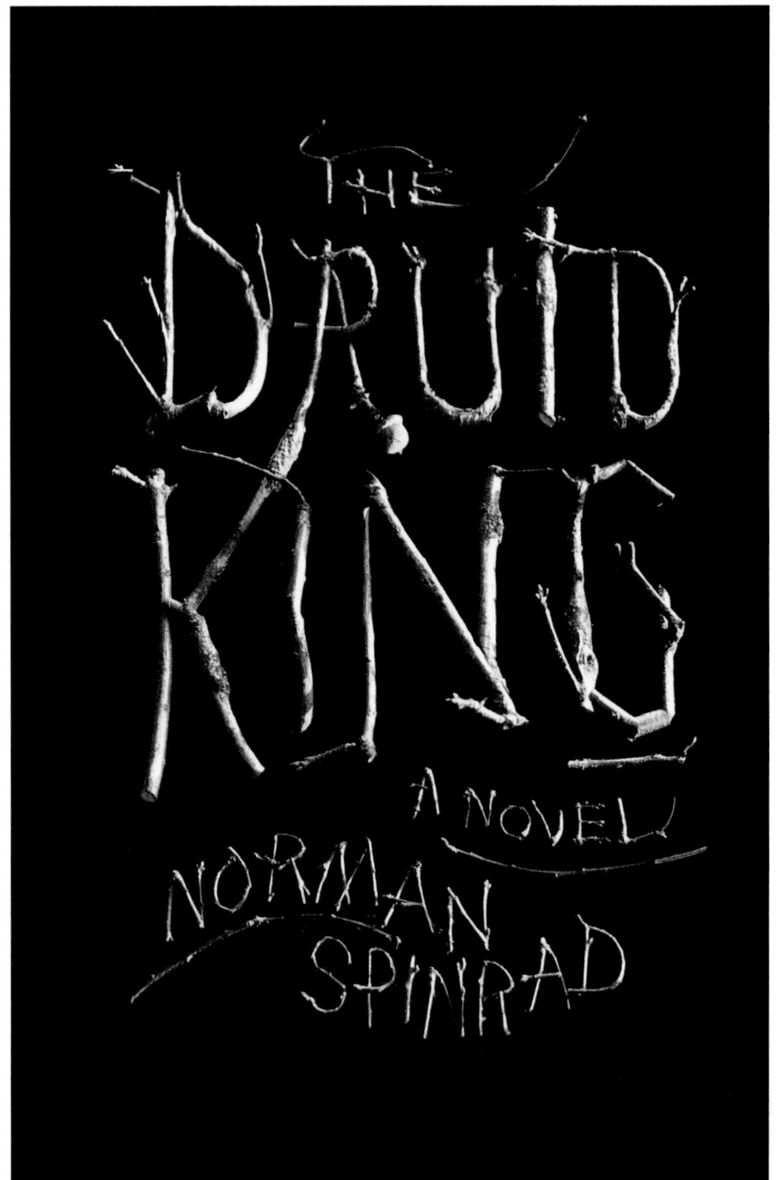

Bones in art and design suggest death, or something equally as bad. These letters on the book cover for *Last Things*, made from real bones, project an aura of doom, danger and decay yet also impart an element of fun.
Designer, letterer, photographer: Tom Brown Clients: Penguin USA, Paul Buckley

One of the first suggestive faces ever made, the nineteenth-century, hand-drawn typeface Log Cabin continues to have quaint appeal. Real twigs have been positioned to form a witty lettering style on the book cover for *The Druid King*.
Designer, letterer, photographer: Stephen Doyle Client: Knopf

Writing greetings or congratulations with icing on cakes and pastries derives from a sweet and ancient practice and is used frequently as a typographic conceit. Here, it works well on the packaging for Mud Honey's CD single.
Designer: Art Chantry Letterers: Mark Arm, Art Chantry Illustrator, photographer: Tannas Root
Clients: Reprise, Warner Bros. Records

The decorative sugar squiggle is the most famous and common addition to appear on confection, especially cupcakes. Transforming it into words exploits this universal familiarity on the poster 'Got Milk?'.
Creative directors: Jeffrey Goodby, Rich Silverstein Art director: Sean Ehringer Photographer: Dan Escobar
Client: California Milk Processors Advisory Board

Never failing to whet the reader's appetite, making words from food is a very common design concept, but it does not always manage to create such an appetizing display as on this poster for a design competition.
Designer, letterer: Scott Ray Photographer: John Messina Client: Dallas Society of Visual Communications

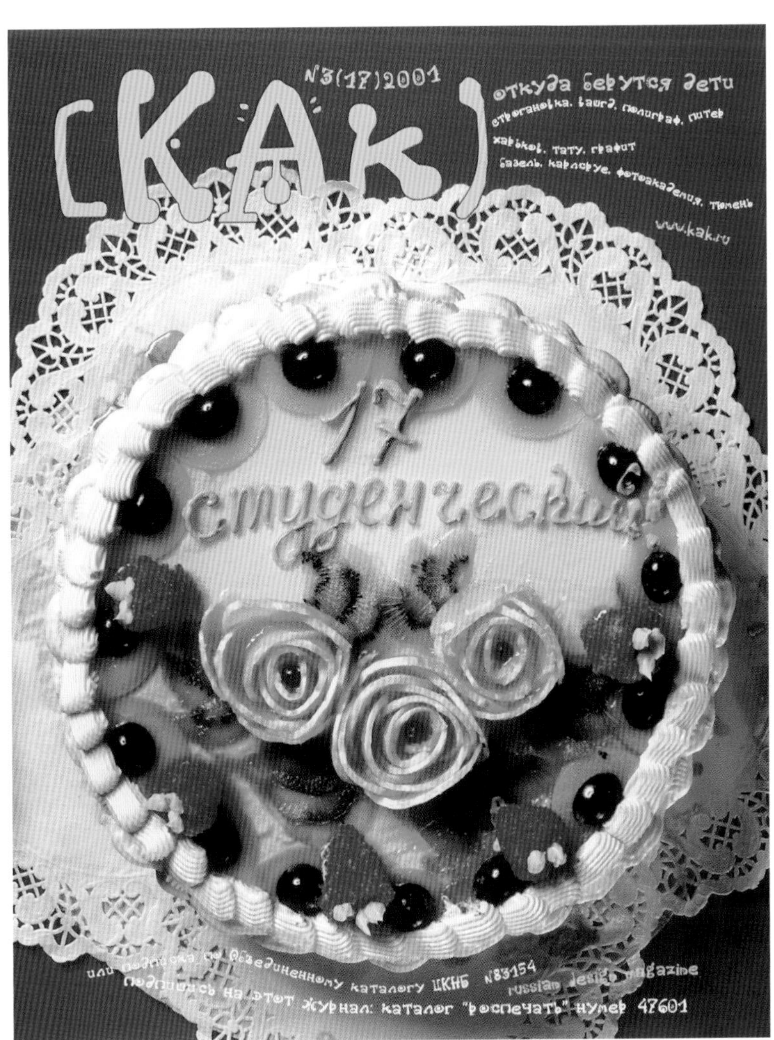

Decorating cakes requires a real knack, a steady hand and the ability to avoid typos at all costs – the designer only has one chance in this do-or-die context.
Designer: Petr Bankov Letterer: Vlad Vasilyez Photographer: Boris Bendikov Client: *[KAK] Graphic Design Magazine*

Paper currency takes on another valuable role when folded into sans-serif letters and photographed from above, as on this poster.
Art director, designer: Masayuki Terashima Client: Day by Day

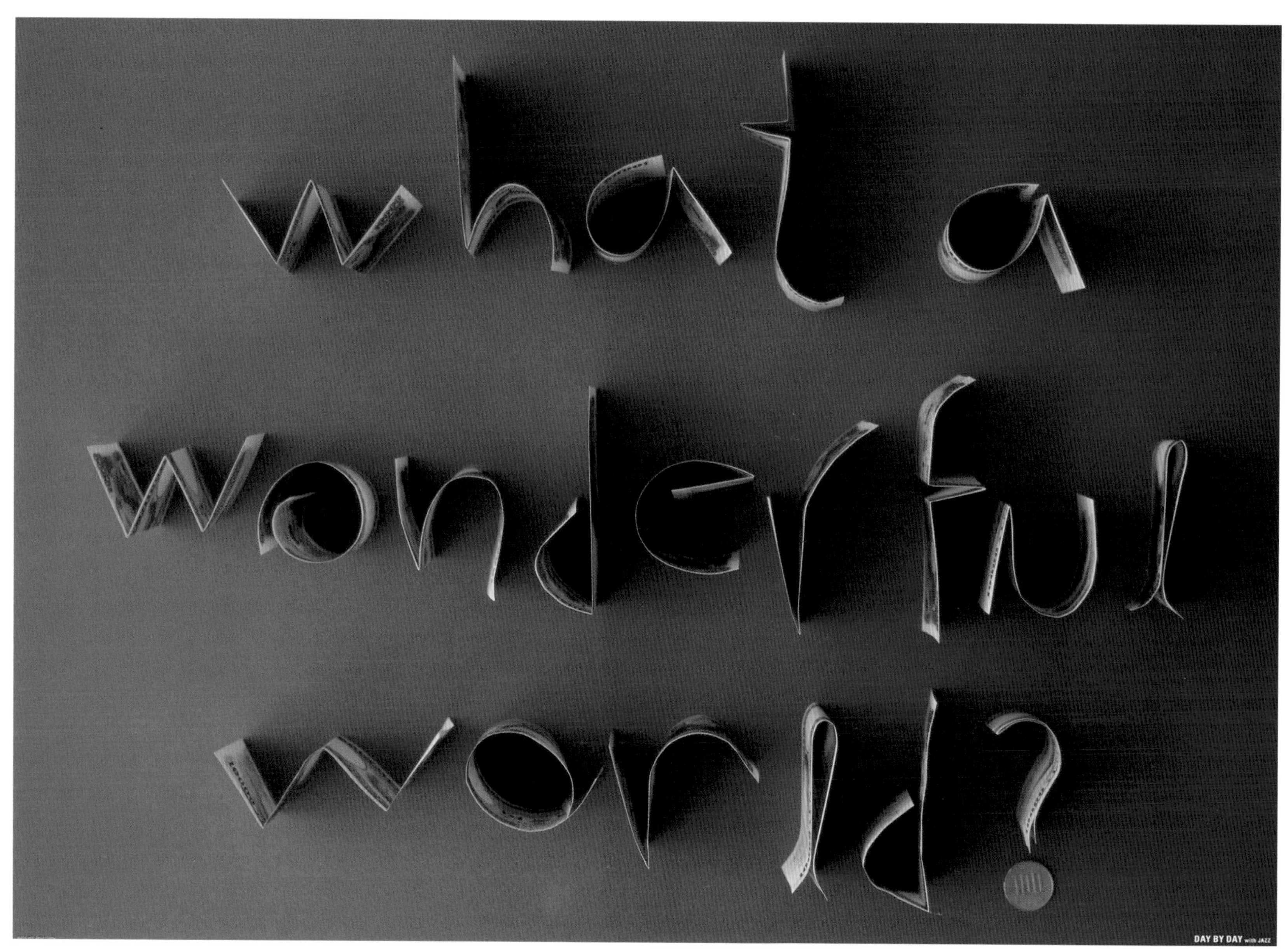

OPPOSITE **Letters made from wax drips, water droplets, bird feathers and glass shards** are clever visual puns that give character to the meaning of the words and phrases on this CD series.
Designer, illustrator, photographer: Michal Batory Client: Radio France

Bernard Cavanna
MESSE un jour ordinaire

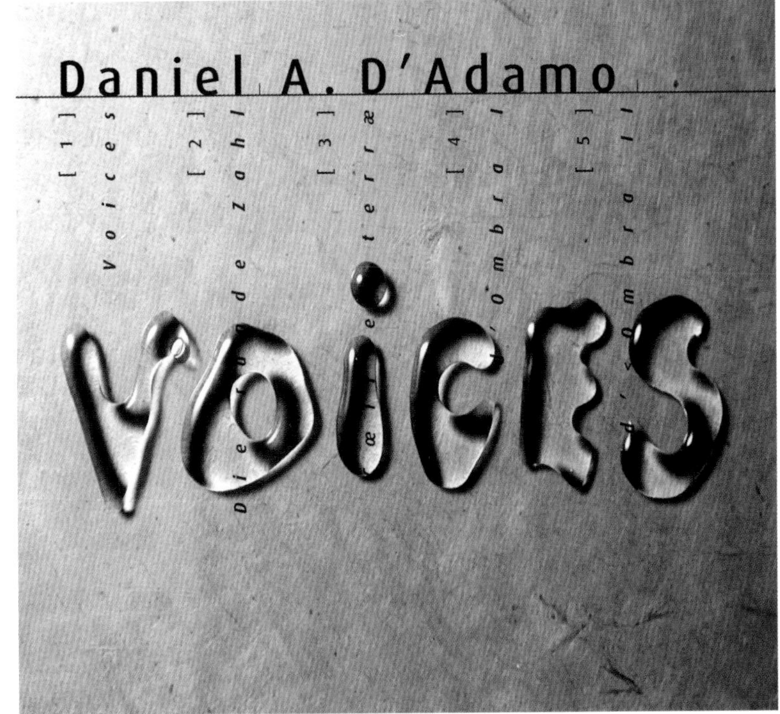
Daniel A. D'Adamo
VOICES

Olivier Messiaen
3e LIVRE du CATALOGUE d'OISEAUX

Pascal Dusapin
TO BE SUNG

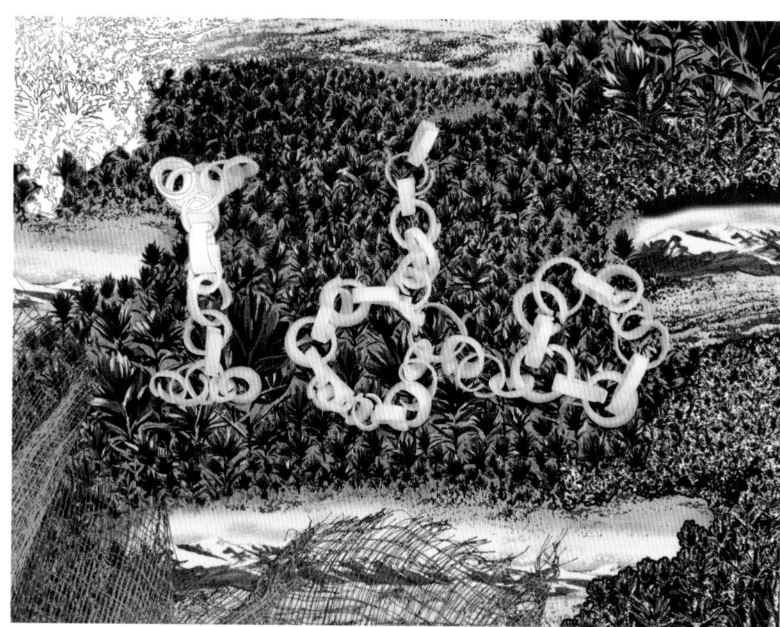

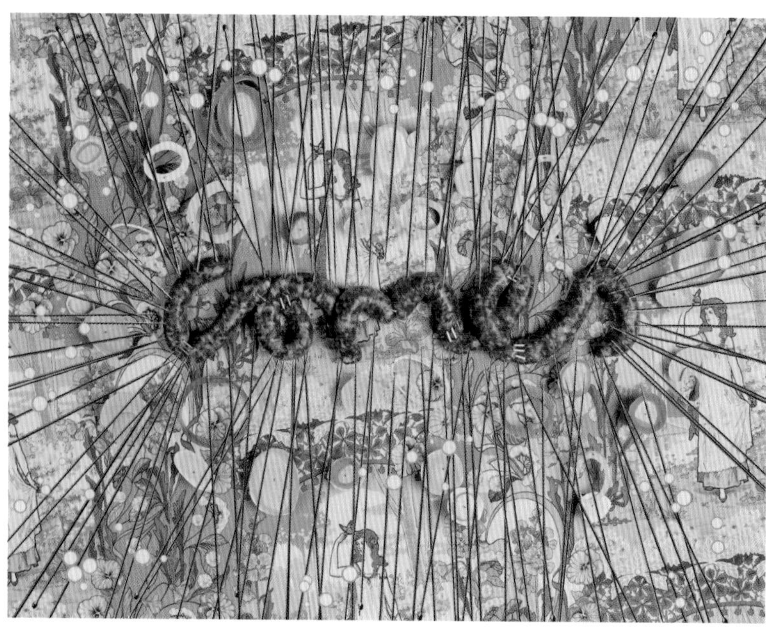

OPPOSITE **Contorted objects, such as sausages and toys**, form the words in these interconnected images on the magazine spreads 'Everything', 'I Do', 'Comes', 'Back'.
Art director: Stefan Sagmeister Photographer: Matthias Ernstberger Model maker: Eva Hueckmann
Designers, letterers: Eva Hueckmann, Matthias Ernstberger, Doris Pendorfer, Stefan Sagmeister
Background: (everything) Wolf-Gorden Inc. Client: *Copy Magazine*

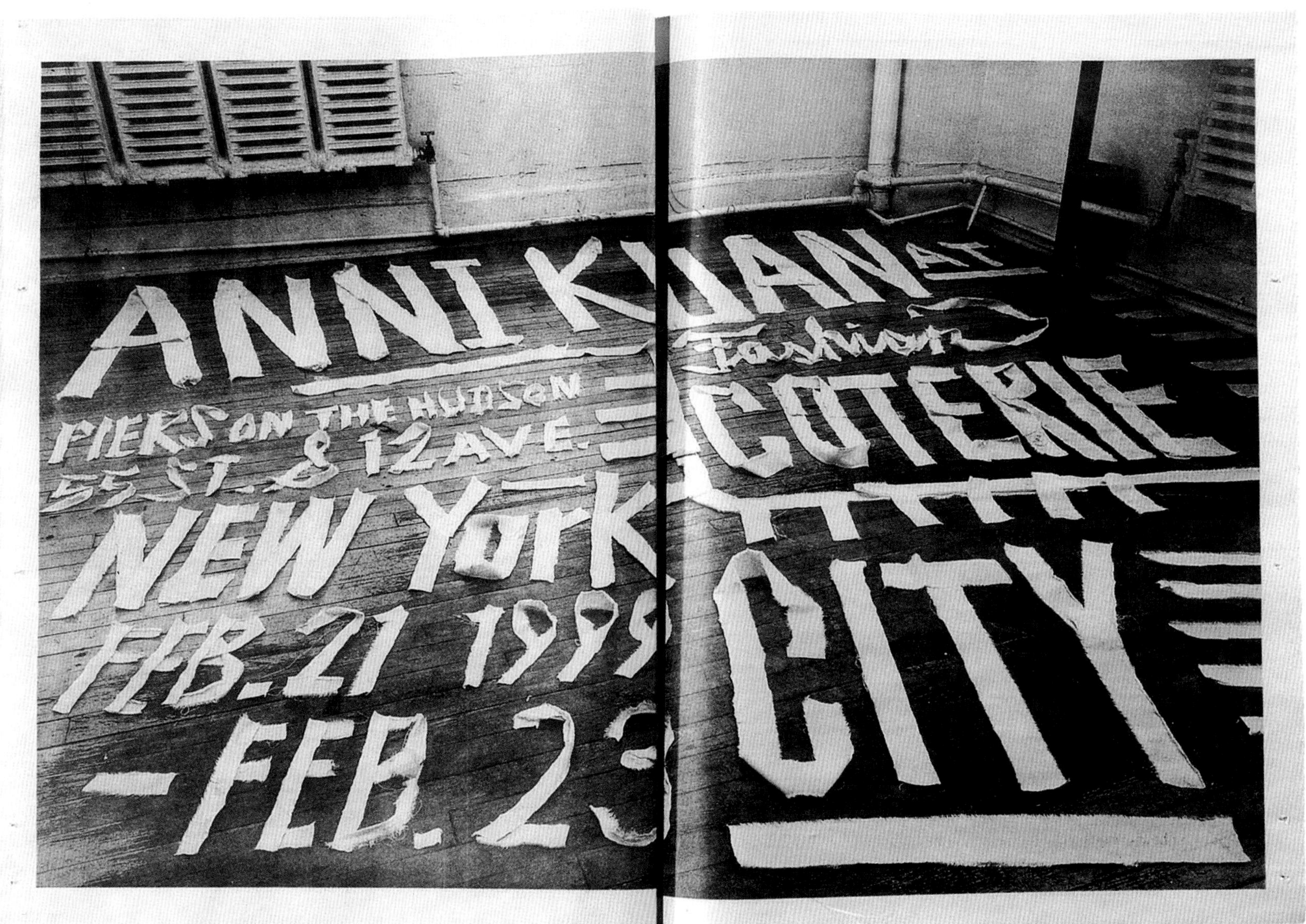

This brochure for the New York fashion designer Anni Kuan is printed on newspaper. The large letters are made from pieces of cut-out fabric, which were then photographed in black and white.
Art director, copywriter, designer: Stefan Sagmeister Client: Anni Kuan Design

Hand-drawn numerals, meticulously composed as texture on these stark landscapes, symbolize the focus of this international business periodical.
Creative directors: Tomás Lorente, Carlos Domingos
Art director: Tomás Lorente Copywriter: Carlos Domingos
Illustrator: Tobia Ravà Client: *Valor Financial Newspaper*

Don't get lost in the world of numbers. Subscribe and get your bearings.
Valor
Financial Newspaper

Don't get lost in the world of numbers. Subscribe and get your bearings.
Valor
Financial Newspaper

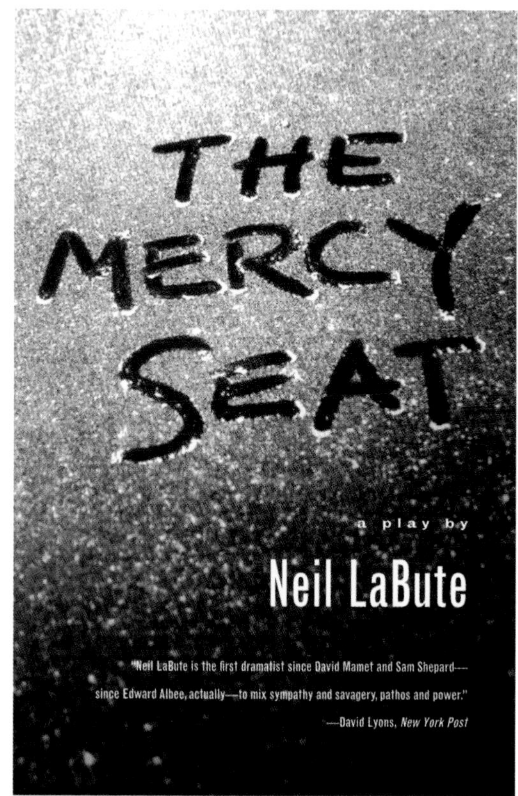

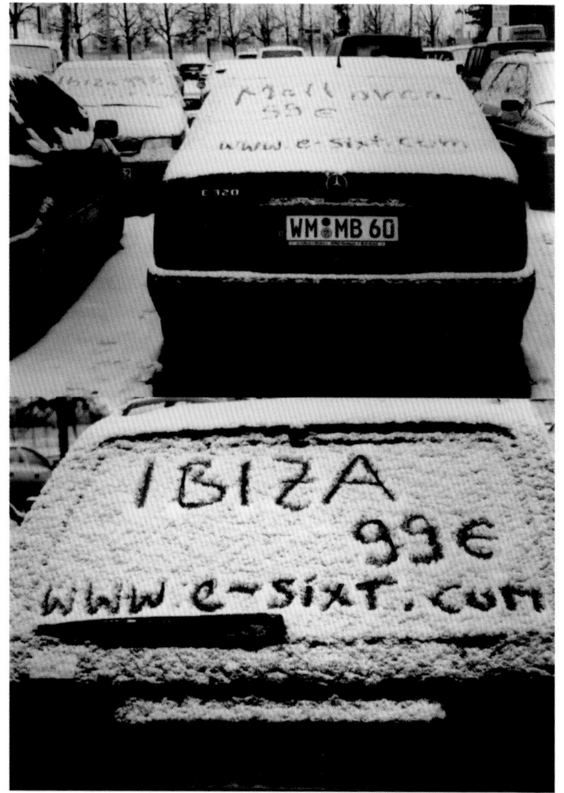

ABOVE **When dramatically photographed even the most informal lettering** can create a striking message; on this book cover for *The Mercy Seat*, the characters clearly evoke the idea of freezing temperatures.
Art director: Lynn Buckley Designer, letterer: Charlotte Strick Photographer: Jeff Williams Client: Faber and Faber

ABOVE LEFT **Who has not casually written words and phrases** onto frozen windows or windscreens with their fingers? It is as common as making snowballs. The feeling of cold is the operative sensation in the poster 'Don't You Wish You Were in Miami Now?'.
Designer, letterer: David Garcia Copywriter: Bruce Turkel Client: Greater Miami Convention/Visitors Bureau

LEFT **Making the perfect typeface in snow is a definite challenge**, but it is nonetheless a speedy and very inexpensive way of producing noticeable messages.
Creative directors: Thim Wagner, Niels Alzen Art director: Hans Weishaupl Designer: Alexandra Marzoll Copywriter: Peter Kirchhoff Client: Sixt AG

OPPOSITE **The Roman lettering and Japanese characters** on the top row of posters – [left] 'Waterdrops', [right] 'Octopus' – are formed by drops of water, while the Japanese script on the bottom row – [left] 'Fishing Net "Ray"', [right] 'Fishing Net' – is designed to look like it is made from fishing nets.
Art director, designer: Norito Shinmura Copywriter: Kazutaka Sato Client: Shinmura Fisheries
[opposite, top] Photographer: Kiyofusa Nozu [opposite, bottom] Artist: Masashi Shinmura
Photographer: Kogo Inoue

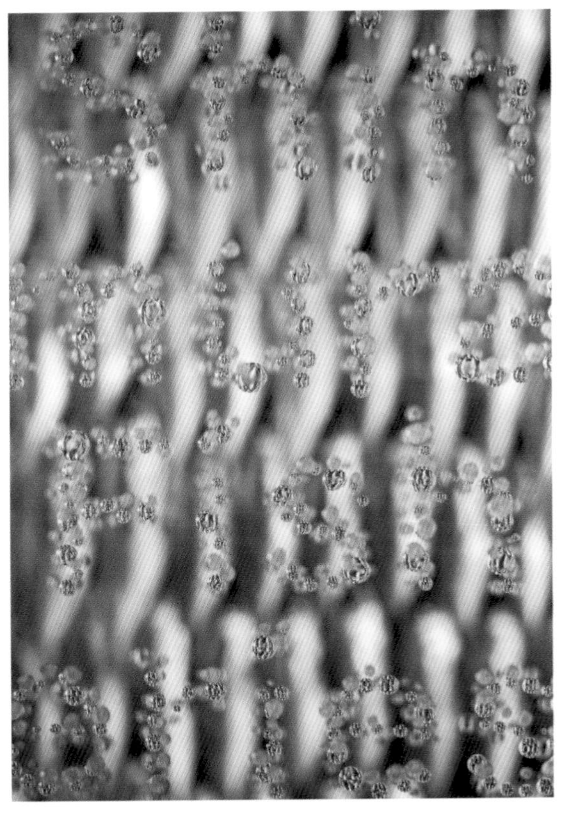

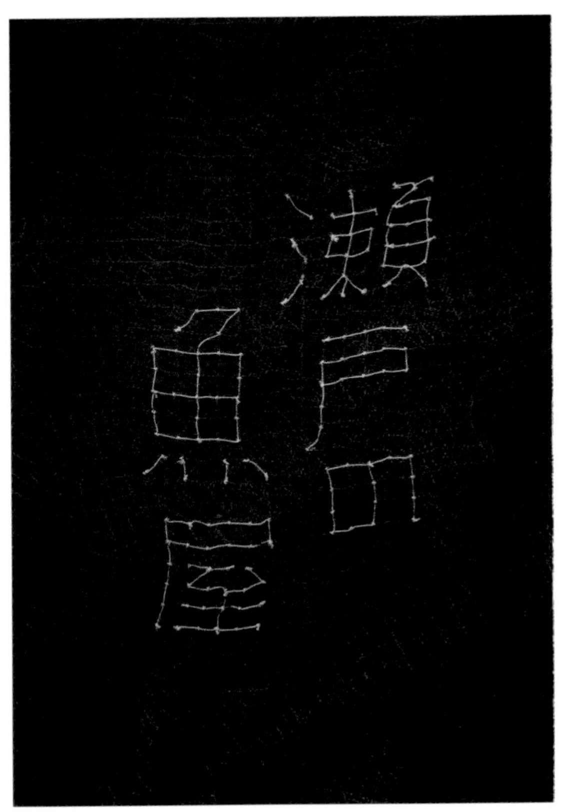
瀬戸
魚屋

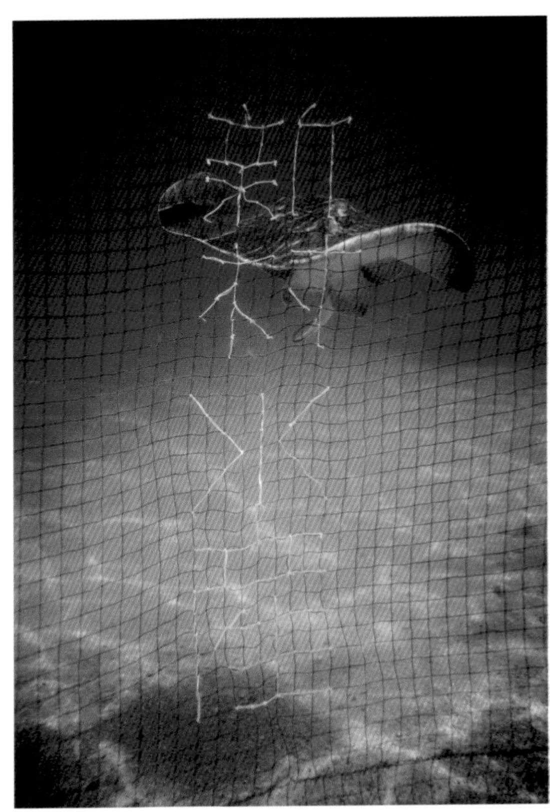

In animated cartoons, bullet holes are a common way of making words or signs. This cover for *The Village Voice* uses the technique effectively to criticize a murder carried out by NYC police.
Art directors: Minh Uong, Ted Keller Artist: Jeff Crosby Client: *The Village Voice*

Found objects are often used to create unique and clever letterforms. On this poster advertising the single 'Water Under the Bridge', the word 'dodgy' is made from various bits and pieces, most notably the sloppily tied together branches.
Designer: Why Not Associates Letterer: Chris Priest Photographer: Rocco Redondo Client: A and M Records

OPPOSITE, TOP **Selecting and using found objects is not always easy**; and when the poster is advertising an exhibition on a sculptor who works with such materials, the choice really has to be a perfect conceptual fit.
Designer, letterer, illustrator: Radovan Jenko Photographers: Dragan Arrigler, Radovan Jenko
Client: Modern Gallery, Ljubljana

OPPOSITE, BOTTOM **All the headlines used in this annual have musty vernacular references**, from old restaurant signs to mechanical parts, from nineteenth-century engravings to twig lettering. The spread is taken from *Typography 22*.
Designer, letterer, illustrator: Gail Anderson Photographer: Bob Grant Client: Type Directors Club

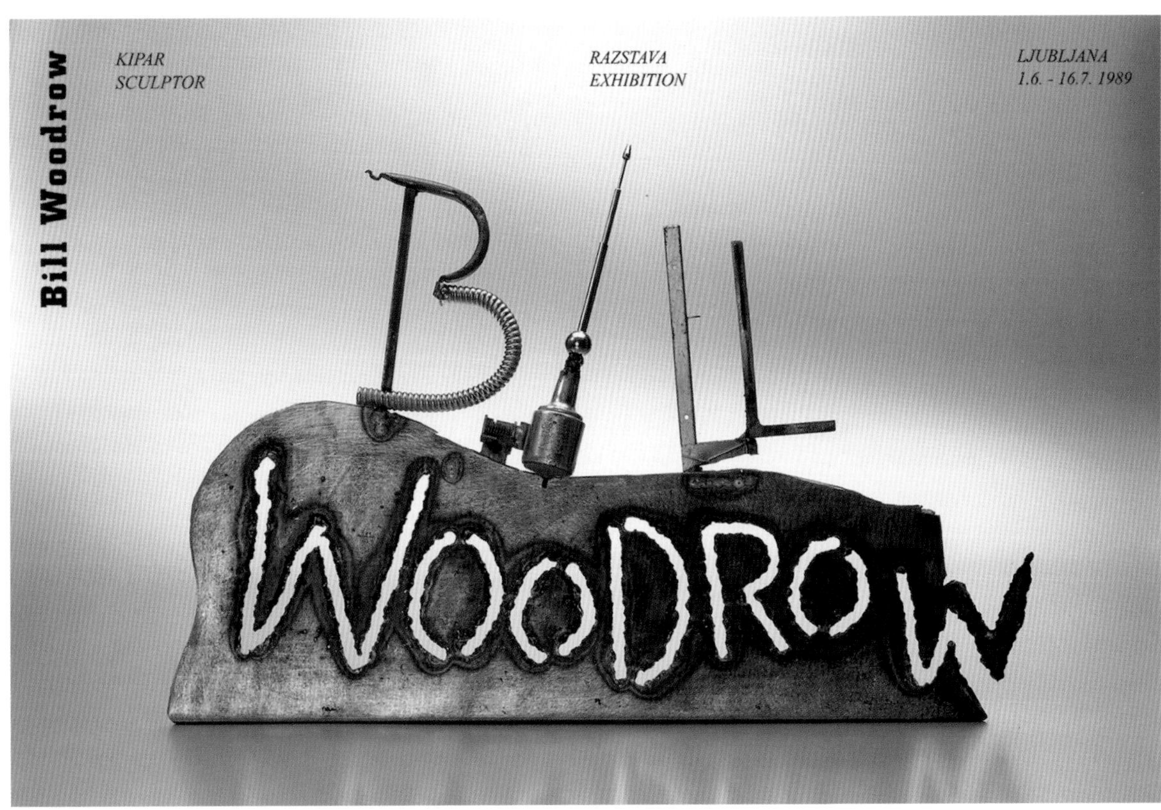

BY KLAUS SCHMIDT

DURING THE 1940s letterpress was the norm for quality printing, while rotogravure was used predominately for mass circulation periodicals. If one could not afford the best, there was always offset lithography – a bit flat and gray but great on uncoated paper and tight budgets. Art directors worked with new typefaces, such as Bernhard Modern, Fairfield, and Lydian. For commercial design and advertising, type was set by hand or on quality machinery like Monotype but less frequently on linecasters in specialized typesetting plants. In the 40s more than 50 advertising typography shops in America belonged to the Advertising Typographers Association. Many of them were centered on East 45th Street in New York, which was nicknamed Ad Type Alley.

07

BELOW **This lettering is a metaphor for nature and natural things** in the nineteenth-century tradition. The title of the magazine spread is made from tiny twigs and great care is given to each letter.
Designer: Scott Farestad Letterer: David Butler Photographer: Martha Madigan Client: *Photo Insider*

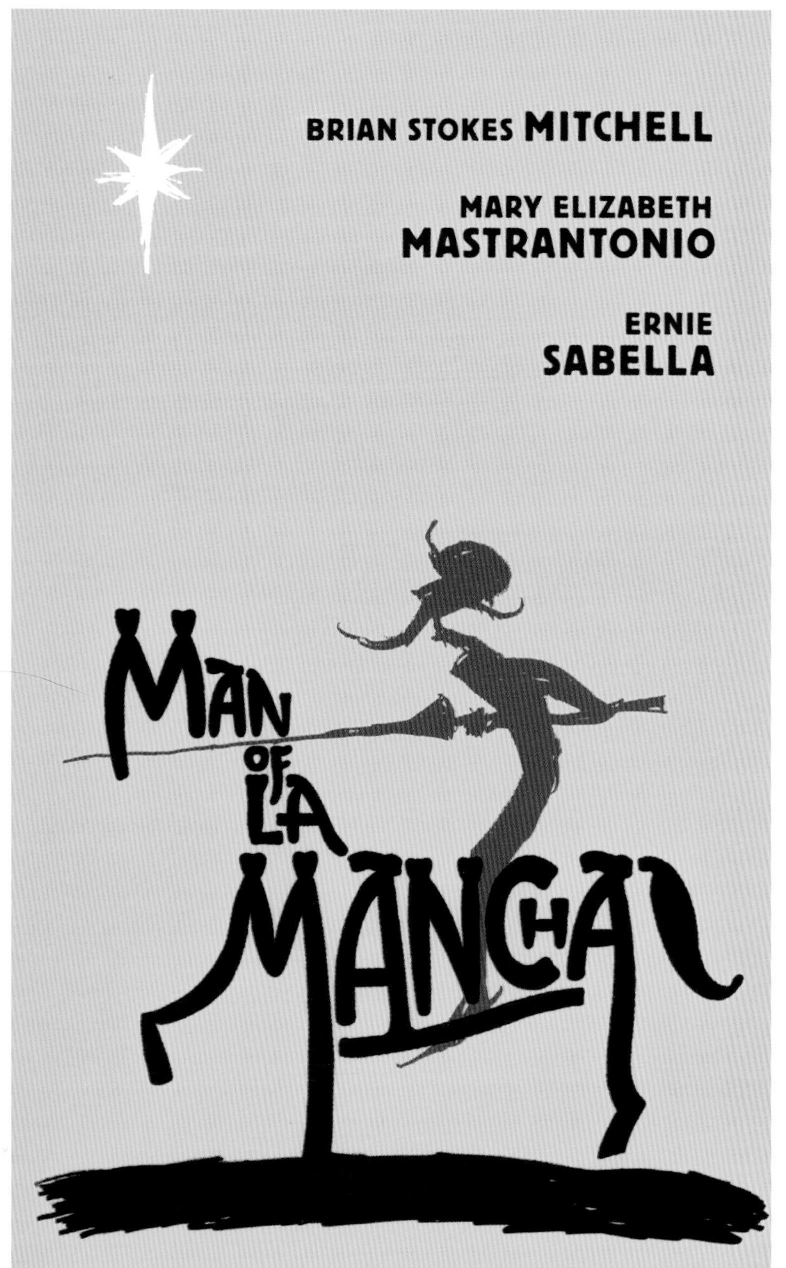

LEFT **Using a very free-form lettering style to suggest Don Quixote's horse**, the designer creates a title for this poster promoting the musical *Man of La Mancha* that is also a smartly integrated illustration.
Creative director: Drew Hodges Letterer: Ward Schumaker Art director, designer: Gail Anderson
Illustrator: James Victore Client: SpotCo

OPPOSITE, TOP LEFT **Mixing weird and discordant objects** with otherwise fairly standard letters is commonplace among illuminators and doodlers. In this theatre poster, the approach has comic appeal.
Designer, letterer, illustrator: Marian Oslislo Client: Teatr Nowy W Zabrzu

OPPOSITE, TOP RIGHT **The quintessential suggestive letter** is one that has been transformed into the thing it represents. This series of astrological signs emphasizes the meaning of the familiar words.
Designer, letterer, illustrator: Richard Beards Client: *Cosmopolitan*

ABOVE **Combining funny and surreal objects** and transforming them into common letterforms creates symbolic and expressive appeal in these illustrations entitled 'Poetry' and 'Love'.
Letterer, illustrator: L.K. Hanson Client: *Minneapolis Star Tribune*

RIGHT **Comic, metaphoric capital letters**, especially those incorporating representations of animals, date back to the medieval illuminators and show no sign of becoming obsolete.
Designer, letterer, illustrator: Boris Lisjak, personal work

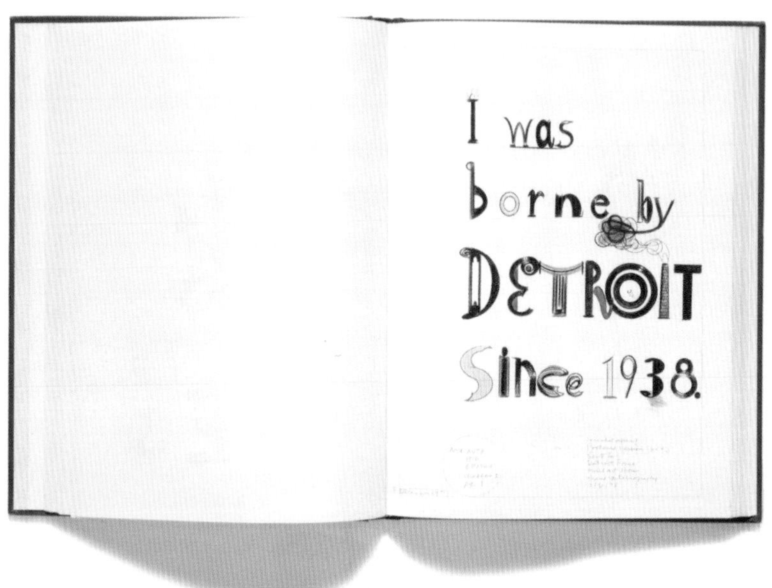

Ed Fella evolves these abstract coloured-pencil doodles into quirky words and phrases that tell a uniquely eccentric autobiographical tale in his sketchbook.
Designer, letterer, illustrator: Ed Fella, personal work

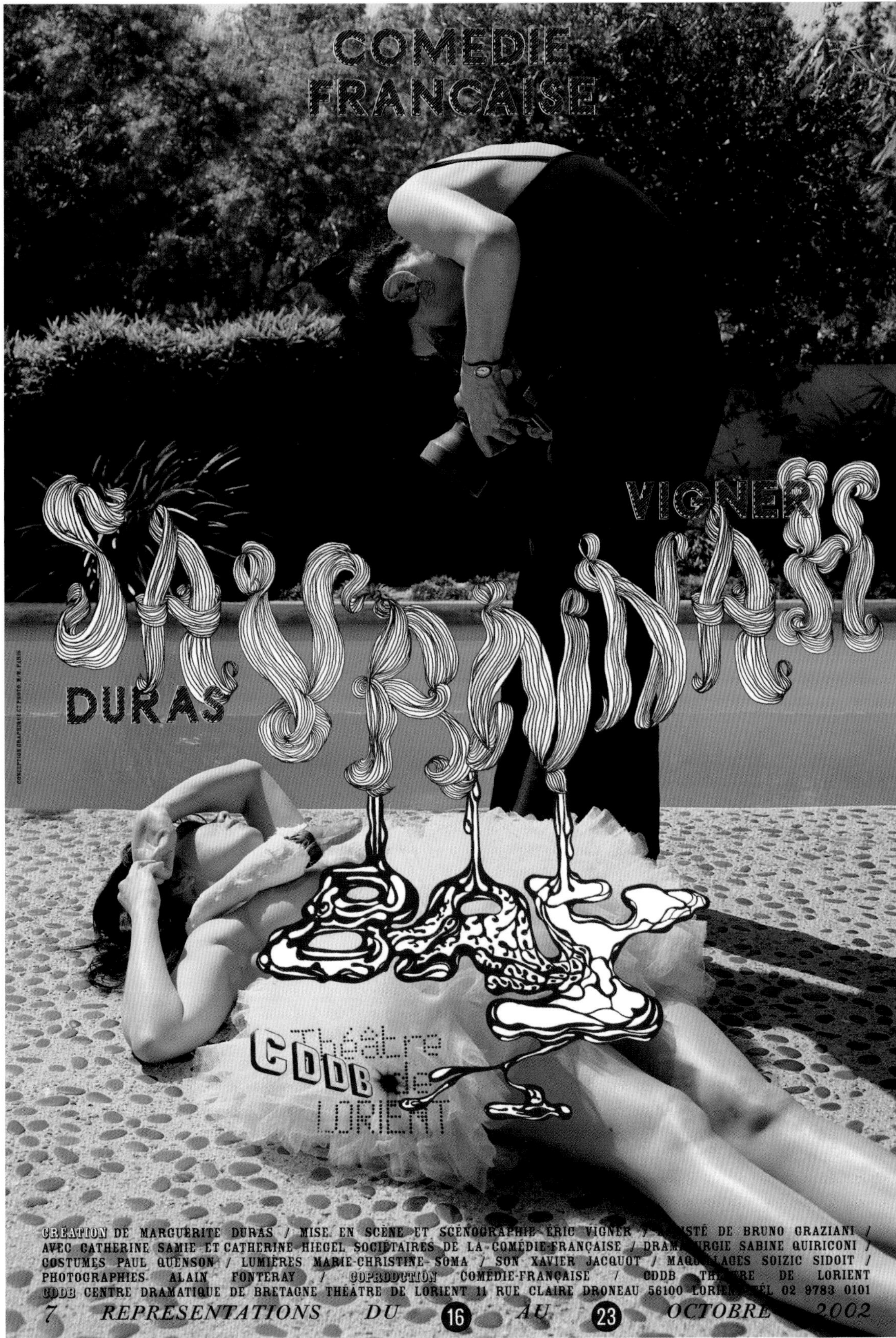

Juicy, greasy, oily letters: what could be more suggestive than these forms that ooze like streams of lava into a gluttonous headline on a theatre poster advertising the production *Savannah Bay*?
Designer, letterer, photographer: M/M (Paris)
Client: CDDB Théâtre de Lorient

comical, ironical, satirical

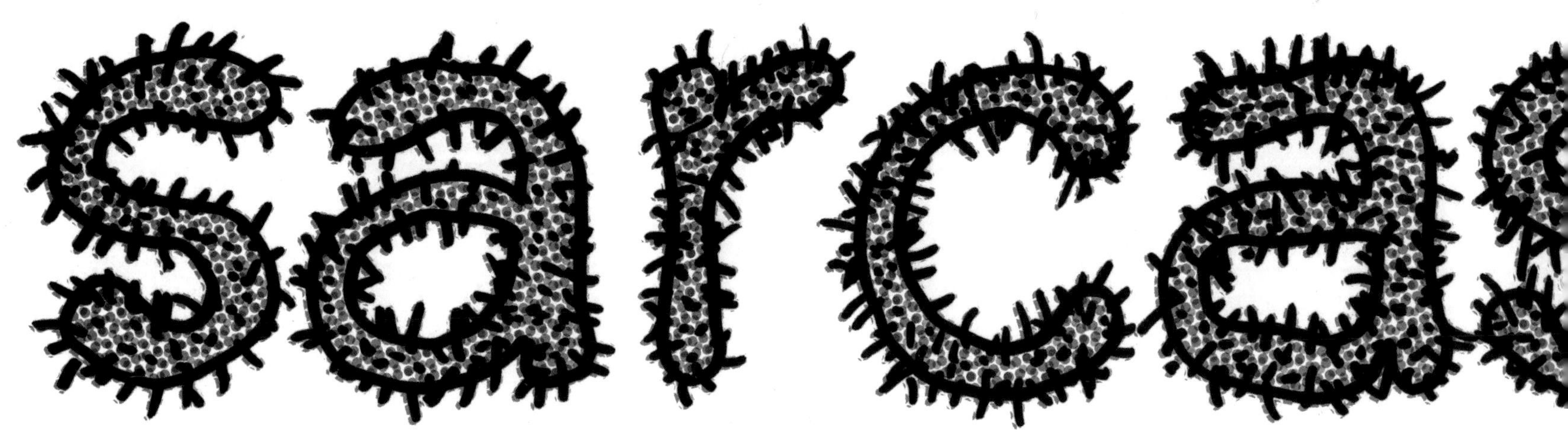

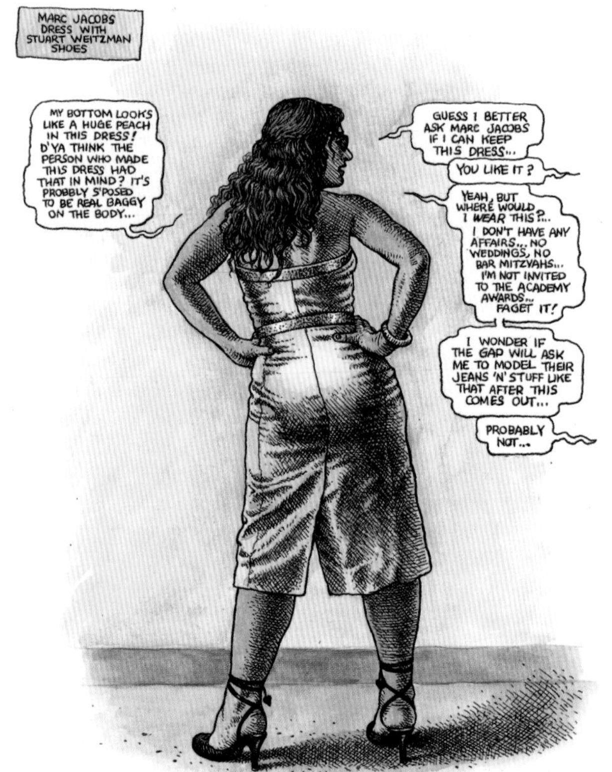

Culture snobs bifurcate art into high and low, creating polar opposites within everything from literature to graphic design. High design is given classic or modernist pedigrees, while low design is crass and populist, and comics are normally associated with the latter grouping. Even within the hierarchies of art schools and professional circles, designers are considered saints and, with few exceptions, comics artists are merely a notch above greeting-card illustrators. Although graphic novels have earned serious critical attention thanks in large part to Art Spiegelman's Pulitzer Prize-winning book *Maus*, Joe Sacco's visual journalism and Chris Ware's stunning epics (and even Gary Panter was awarded the Chrysler Award for Design in 2000 for design excellence), they are still seen in design culture's pecking order as the bastard offspring of a sordid *ménage à trois* between art, literature and design. In reality, comics are the first real multimedia, a mix of these three disciplines and something more: comics are founts of typographic and lettering innovation.

More than mere 'Wham', 'Bang', 'Boom', comic-strip lettering has been inspired by, and is the inspiration for, numerous visual artifacts from billboards to tattoos. Yet, the lettering's origins go back to illuminated manuscripts, the first incarnation of official handlettering. A comic strip is a kind of sequential manuscript in which word and picture have equal weight. This style of lettering also has roots in the nineteenth-century sign or Sho-card painting, known for its bold, brash and bulbous contoured letters with colourful dramatic drop shadows and circus-poster alphabets made from ornamented Tuscans

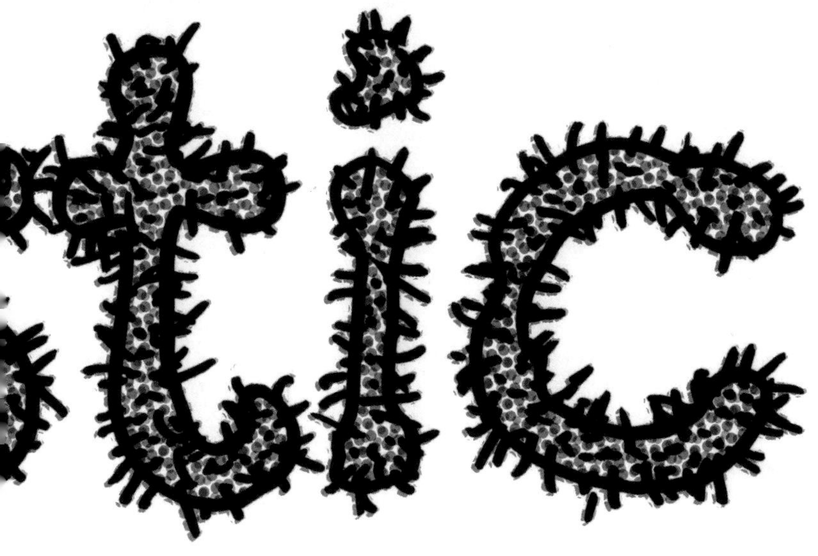

and Egyptians. Vintage twentieth-century film title cards and movie foyer posters are also among comic-strip lettering's forebears. Today, with such easy access to digital typefaces, comics-style handlettering offers more than a historical grounding, it is a quirky alternative to rote typography.

The introductory frame of a comic strip, known as the splash panel, is designed to dramatically announce the visual narrative and is invested with more graphic bravado than a common book title page. Nonetheless, there is an exaggerated bookishness in comics lettering in so far as it establishes a visual tone and a dramatic aura. Comic-book lettering is usually designed to echo either the drawing style or thematic thrust of a particular strip and is intentionally composed to cue the reader into the overall tone of the piece. In fact, what to some may seem like generic lettering is to others filled with the personality, character and nuance endemic to all fine typography, if not more so because it is so uniquely individual. It is certainly possible to tell who lettered the more distinctive comics.

The lettering in comics evokes mood, sends signals, tickles the funny bone. While splashy words illuminate the stage on which a comic-strip drama, comedy or fantasy takes place, speech balloon lettering underscores the narrative's timbre and verbal identity. Like other traditional forms of typesetting, comic-book lettering has a very particular task that it would not be possible to accomplish by traditional typographic means. Balloons demand an incredibly specific form of typography that has become an integral part of the comic. Originally, the old-fashioned Leroy Lettering kit was used, which influenced the feel and impact of the comics. Comic-book typography is not secondary to the image in the way that it is in most graphic design.

In the world of traditional strips, super-hero comics have a style suited to the subject matter – demonstrative, masculine and loud. The same approach is true for war, horror and sci-fi titles, while romantic comics use feminine letters with swashes and curlicues. Certain lettering styles are emblematic of the comic's themes, but since the advent of Underground Comix in the late 1960s, the lettering has expressed even more than the obvious metaphoric relationships. The lettering is indeed art.

Harking back to antique typographic sources, the 1960s San Francisco Underground Comix artists – among them R. Crumb, Rick Griffin, Stanley Mouse and Victor Moscoso – appropriated slab-serif Victorian wood type and curvilinear Art Nouveau letters. This sampling of the old is apparent in many examples in this section, as well as on 1910s and 1920s Sho-card lettering and on the kind of letters that feature in the 'Simulate' section (see pp 116–35). However, the applications in this section were not simply copied verbatim, instead they were massaged into a comics form. Rick Griffin (1944–91) was one of the most innovative and visionary of these underground letterers. In addition to designing the original nineteenth-century, psychedelic curlicue swash logo for *RollingStone* magazine in 1968 (no longer in use), he developed hand-drawn typography that was more beautifully eccentric than, dare it be said, most of the recent crop of expressive digital alphabets. The intricately inked meandering words and phrases, virtually sewn into a complex mélange of inline and outline alphabetic forms, are artworks as much as type works. His typography is a veritable commentary on the function and abstraction of letterforms. Griffin was a true master of what might be called the Roarshock school of calligraphy, where page after page of letter drawings have mysterious, multiple meanings.

Comic-book lettering comes in two varieties: straight and sarcastic or, stated differently, subtle and slapstick. Subtle, however, is something of a misnomer because no comics lettering is without an inherently ironic side, but some forms are more low-key than others. As defined and shown here, certain kinds of handlettering are produced with less artifice or double entendre than others. Brandt Botes and Conrad Botes's application kit for Brightest Young Minds (see p. 188) is produced in the classic comics style, but is comparatively quiet insofar as the lettering is not an exaggeration of the basic comic-book idea. Sometimes going overboard is the desired effect, but often simply the hint of a cartoon style is all that is required to give a particular design the necessary mood.

The stylistic range of lettering for comics is as diverse as the artists' idiosyncrasies. There is the light-hearted lettering of Pascal Lemaitre, the understated neutrality of Anton Kannemeyer for 'The Pursuit of Perverse Thoughts' (*BitterKomix*, no. 13, see p. 188) and the bravado of Móuvara's fiery 'Gonebald', which owes a debt to the Devil Girl Choco-Bar (see p. 185) by R. Crumb, the greatest contemporary comic-book letterer of them all.

It could be said that Crumb's mighty loins (or at least his ink-filled pen) have produced all the styles of comics lettering (sarcastic and otherwise) used today. Crumb is such a master draughtsman that everything he touches is imbued with wit, even the anomalous fashion drawings originally done for *The New York Times* (see pp 180–83), which are as straight-on representational as they come. For these pieces, Crumb's matter-of-fact comic-style lettering gives voice to the otherwise sensual but static images. Without the speech balloons the art would still be unconventional as typical fashion illustration, but with them the overall composition becomes excitedly animated. Crumb is known for his animated strips featuring quirky and sometimes disturbing characters; he captures every range of emotion with his keen mastery of gesture. Likewise, the key to his lettering – from his own candy-bar, soda-pop-styled signature to the splash panels on his comics and the burning, teasing logotype for the Devil Girl Choco-Bar – is found in totally convincing, unmitigated, kinetic and emotive gesture.

Crumb's gestural letters, like his drawings, come as naturally to him as breathing. For other comics artists, their drawings and letterings are more strained, perhaps more affected, yet no less effective. The covers by Caroline Sury for *Vagina Mushroom* (see p. 186) are grotesquely angst-ridden with different kinds of metamorphic letters, which are perfectly suited and symbolically appropriate. These are not the traditional, dispassionate letters found in the 1930s and 1940s comics, but they reflect the intensely autobiographical nature of today's comics. In fact, the lettering is akin to a personal logo, another clue to the power of sarcastic lettering.

A sage – or maybe a curmudgeon – once said that comics artists who cannot letter should not draw comics. Lettering is endemic to the art form, and the lettering-challenged have no business in the business. The comics of Ward Sutton, a poster artist and cartoonist, exhibit the total integration of picture and letter. He draws on a number of historical references, including album covers, book covers and old comics, 'I often look at these examples and create my own hand-drawn version of the type or a composite of different type styles combined into one. And, of course, I also just make up type styles as well.' Sutton says that comic-book lettering is wonderfully organic, 'In this computer age where fonts seem to come a dime a dozen, handlettering is what stands out to me.' His rock concert poster for Tales from the Phish (see p. 187) is the perfect send-up of the old EC Comics series 'Tales from the Crypt', which arguably helped make comics lettering an art back in the 1950s. Also, his comic *Wicked* draws from the same well as Crumb's Devil Girl chocolate bar. Being rough and flawed is what makes Sutton's letters compelling.

Not all comic-book lettering is sinuous, metaphorical or even freehand. Some is precisionist and architectonic although unmistakably made by hand, and some display type is produced by a variety of traditional draughtsman's tools to achieve precise geometric effects. Chris Ware's extraordinary typographic homage to turn-of-the-century novelty and mail-order catalogues also falls into the realm of tightly rendered verisimilitude. Ware's *Renaissance Man: Antonio de Bologna* (see p. 189) could fill a veritable catalogue of boisterous display or Sho-card writing. He lovingly re-creates a contemporary world from the visual lexicon of the past through letters that complement his sublime drawing style.

As evidenced here, no absolute paradigm of comics lettering exists today, which means that, even in the computer age, this type of lettering is far from becoming an extinct or even endangered form. As long as graphic novels permeate our culture and comics artists continue to use pen and ink or brush and paint – or as long as expression and emotion are valued in addition to or over modernist objectivity – this kind of lettering will reign. The hand has yet to become a vestigial appendage (we still need fingers to push computer keys after all). Of course, there are scores of 'original' typefaces for comics available as fonts on the web, and even the originators of alphabets have digitized their work for mass consumption. Why spend all the time lettering by hand, goes the logic, when the same result can be achieved with an existing typeface that someone else has drawn. This train of thought is nothing new: in 1936, Howard Trafton designed the once ubiquitous brush letter Cartoon, long accepted as the most common comics typeface. As handlettering continues its unabated comeback, however, comics faces will become increasingly available to those looking for a quirky character. But this quirkiness will never come straight from the box, it has to come from the hand.

Comics lettering, particularly examples from the classic comics splash panel, is perhaps the most vernacular of any commercial art. It began as an unpretentious yet dramatic way of introducing cartoon stories, immediately setting the mood for the reader. In so doing, comic-book lettering signaled (and continues to signal) better than almost any other form of handlettering the purpose for which the letters and ultimately the total design had been created. The benefits of using this type of lettering is that it has no boundaries or rules; in other words, it is extremely versatile. It reflects an early-twentieth-century naivety but has a particular sophistication, too. There is no danger of multiple interpretations, but neither does all comic-style lettering represent the same thing. What is more, comic-book lettering is fun to look at and delightful to render. Who does not enjoy the humour in all the bulbous, shaking and shimmying letterforms that transform words into sounds like 'Ya-hoo', 'Boom', 'Whack' and 'Crunch'?

pp 180–83 **R. Crumb is the undisputed master** of 1930s-style classic cartoon and comic-book lettering. As shown in these magazine illustrations for *The New York Times*, called 'An Eye for the Ladies', words flow from him with the command of a calligrapher and the precision of a computer expert.
Letterer, illustrator: R. Crumb Client: *The New York Times*

This page of Charles Crumb's childhood comic [left] has been copied virtually panel for panel decades later in the comic-book story 'The Adventures of Fuzzy the Bunny'. The only differences are that the drawing is slightly more refined and the lettering slightly more sophisticated in the later version.
Illustrators: R. Crumb, Charles Crumb Letterer: R. Crumb Client: *Zap Comix*

Crumb borrowed his signature lettering technique from an earlier generation of comic-strip artists who could almost render perfect letters with their eyes closed. A good example of Crumb's approach is shown in the story 'A Bitchin' Bod!'.
Illustrator, letterer: R. Crumb Client: *Zap Comics*

185

A perfect blend of sarcasm and suggestiveness, the lettering for Devil Girl ingeniously complements the licentious image of Crumb's sexy she-devil on the packaging for the chocolate bar.
Designer, illustrator, letterer: R. Crumb Client: The Kitchen Sink

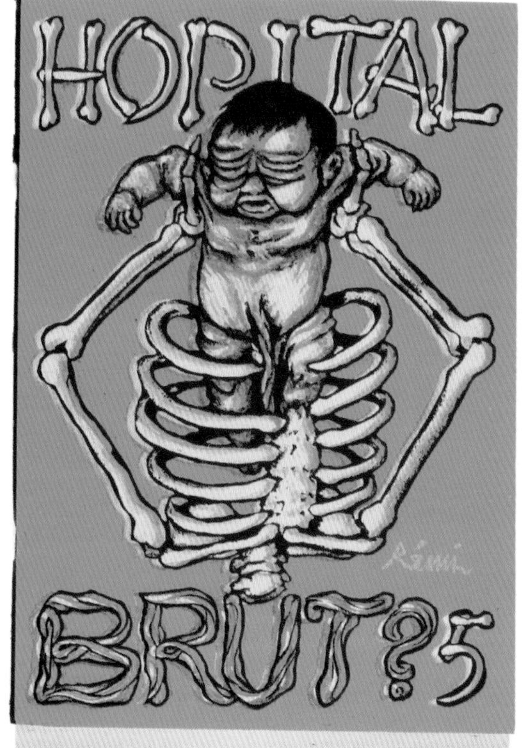

ABOVE **Comic-book lettering is ostensibly found in cartoons as well.** These words, on two book covers for *Vagina Mushroom,* illustrate in a symbolic and realistic manner both the message and the joke.
Designer, letterer, illustrator: Caroline Sury Client: Le Dernier Cri

LEFT **This is a case of lettering as illustration as manuscript illumination.** The book's title, *Hopital Brut?*, is cleverly rendered as a skeleton with umbilical cord and baby – it is unpleasant but should still be admired.
Designer, letterer, illustrator: Rémi Client: Le Dernier Cri

OPPOSITE **The presentation of the titles for these quirky comic books** adhere to the classic comics tradition. The shadowed and suggestive letters on the posters for [top left] *The Ex* and [bottom left] *Darkwood Dub* are consistent with the silent-movie title card lettering that was also used in the splash panels of comic strips and books.
Designer: [top left] Ivica Barichevich [bottom left] Tomislav Turkovich
Letterer, illustrator: Igor Hofbauer Client: KSET, Zagreb

OPPOSITE **A direct tribute to the EC Comics series 'Tales from the Crypt'**, the lettering is used in this instance on rock concert posters for [top right] Tales from the Phish and [bottom right] Bighead Todd.
Designer, letterer, illustrator: Ward Sutton Clients: Phish, Program Council at the University of Colorado

THE EX
HOLLAND
AND
ZU
ITALY
TOUCH AND GO records
WIDE records
KSET
27.
10.
PETAK
20h
Znata li zašto Sonic Youth,
Steve Albini, John Zorn i Fugazi proglašavalu
The Ex svojim velikim utjecajem, ili zašto
John Zorn kaže "ZU blows away what most bands
do these days." Prilika da provjerite zašto vam je pod nosom!!!
ULAZNICA 35 kn

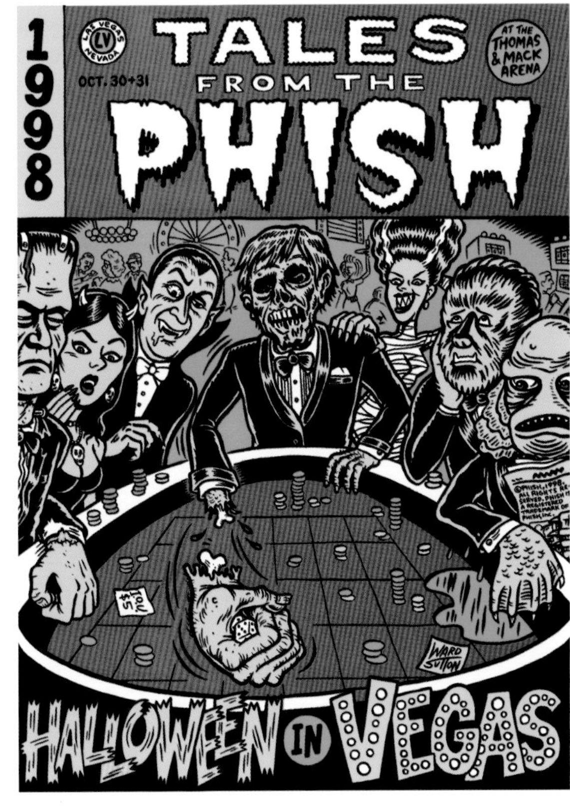
1998
LAS VEGAS NEVADA
OCT. 30+31
TALES FROM THE
PHISH
AT THE THOMAS & MACK ARENA
WARD SUTTON
HALLOWEEN IN VEGAS

DARKWOOD DUB
NAJBOLJI BEOGRADSKI BAND
35 KUNA
bTS
Canon
Slušaona
groove exploitation
MOĆVARA 5.5. PETAK
www.urk.hr

BILL GRAHAM PRESENTS / CHUCK MORRIS PRESENTS
CU PROGRAM COUNCIL
AND
KBCO
PRESENT
BIG HEAD TODD AND THE MONSTERS
TIX $25
RETURN TO CAMPUS!
FRIDAY SEPTEMBER 4TH, 1998
DOORS 6PM @ SHOW 7PM
FRANKLIN FIELD

BELOW **Comics lettering is not exclusive to comic books** and can add an element of wit or irony to any graphic design, as on this application kit for Brightest Young Minds.
Designer: Brandt Botes Letterer, illustrator: Conrad Botes Client: BYM (Brightest Young Minds)

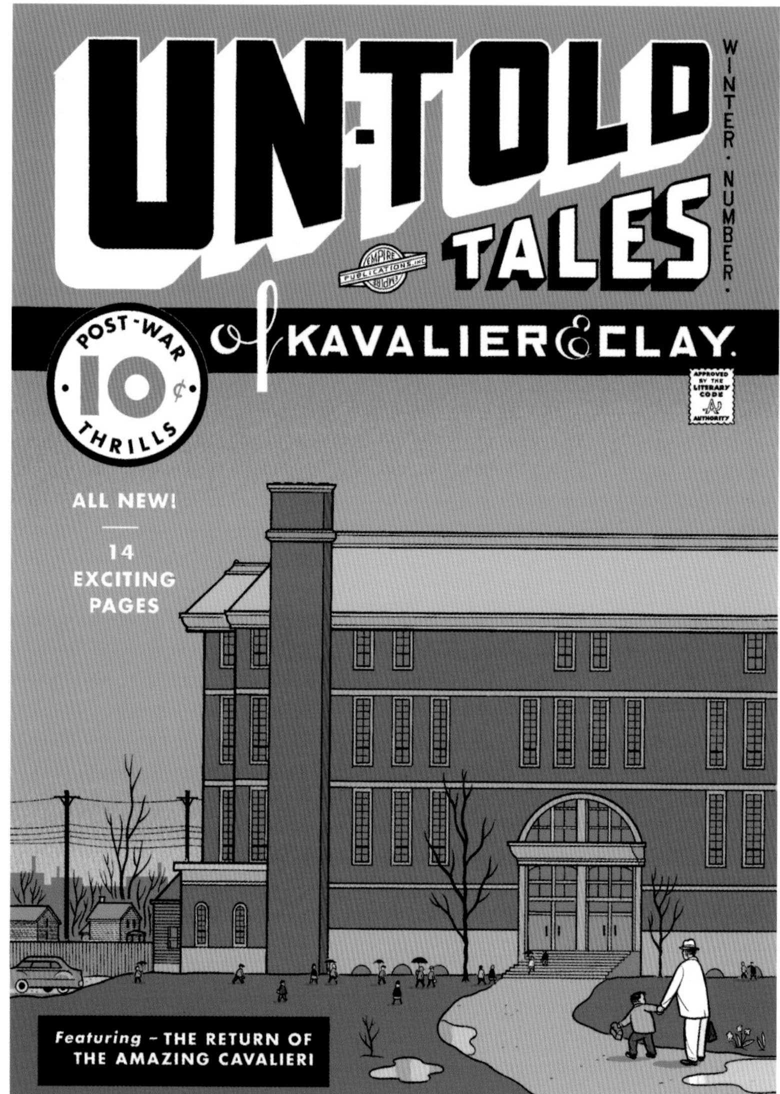

ABOVE **There is nothing more satisfying for an artist** than to create a perfectly composed comics page with precisely rendered lettering, as seen on these pages from *BitterKomix* (no. 13).
Designer, letterer, illustrator: Anton Kannemeyer Client: Orange Juice Design

NOBODY WILL EVER LIKE ME

EVEN THE ROSY-FINGER'D DAWN SEEMS TO MOCK MY VERY CORPUS...

ANOTHER ORGY LAST NIGHT... WAS **I** INVITED? **NO!** PERHAPS I SHOULD DRINK HEMLOCK...

AH WELL... AT LEAST I STILL HAVE **YOU**, MY ONLY LOVE...

ANTONIO de BOLOGNA.

DIO MIA...MY **BACK!** I CURSE MY FATE. ALL ALONE AM I. THE BIRDS HAVE YET TO BREAKFAST, MY GUILDSMEN ARE STILL ASLUMBER, AND I AM FORCED TO TOIL! THE DEADLINE LOOMS, AND MY POCKET IS EMPTY.

IN MY LIFE, I SHALL REMAIN ALWAYS ALONE, WITHOUT SOLACE OF LOVE, OR FAMILY.

ACH! IN MY WEARINESS, I HAVE RELIED TOO MUCH ON LINE, AND SPOILT THE LUMINOSITY OF THE FORM. FIE. **FIE!**

ANGUISH HAS DESCENDED. I AM FLESH, YET I SEEK TO LIMN THE LIKENESS OF ANGELS...SUCH FOLLY! I AM NO BETTER THAN A FOOL IN A PRINTED BROADSHEET...

snif

OH, GOD! SHOW ME! **SHOW** ME HOW I MAY RISE, CLOSER TO THEE!

RENAISSANCE MAN

Morning, at the Painter's Studio.

And suddenly, a revelation as to the nature of flesh.

HENCE.

The science of verisimilitude is advanced

and the artist is hanged for his insolence.

NEXT: LOCATING THE SEAT OF THE SOUL.

CITY of GOLD

AND.

LATER.

MY FELLOW COUNTRYMEN, NOW THAT OUR NATION IS ESTABLISHED, WE MUST SEEK TO CREATE A CULTURE WHICH IS NATIVE TO ITS SOIL.

JOHANN GUTENBURG, JR.

FUCK BOOKS & BIBLES... FUCK BOOKS & BIBLES... THAT'S ALL I EVER PRINT...

JEEZUZ, YOU'D THINK THERE'D BE MORE TO THIS RACKET...

I GUESS THOSE PUBLIC EXECUTION SOUVENIRS MOVED OKAY... NOT NEARLY AS WELL AS I'D HOPED, THOUGH...

MAYBE IT WAS THE HALF-ASSED ENGRAVING... WE DID KINDA RUSH IT...

BUT THOSE "FOLIOS OF FAMOUS PAINTINGS"... FOR-**GET** IT! I'LL BE **BURIED** WITH THE GODDAMN THINGS...

sigh

IS THERE NOT **SOME** MEANS BY WHICH TO FORGE THE SOLACE OF GREAT ART VIA **REPRODUCTION**... WHICH IS, AFTER ALL, A MIRROR OF THE VERY ACT FOR WHICH **GOD HIMSELF** HAS PLACED US ON THIS EARTH?

EH... PROBABLY NOT...

Mr. Mannerism

THIS WEEK: LATE MORNING REVIEW of FIRST PRINCIPLES.

1. "MAN IS THE MEASURE OF ALL THINGS"

2. "THE EYES MUST BE KEPT OPEN TO THE WORLD... esp. VIA RATIONAL INQUIRY (*but ONLY in so far as such inquiry celebrates MAN*)"

3. "THE GREEKS & THE ROMANS... ...THE GREEKS... & THE ROMANS..."

OH, **DARN** IT!... I ALWAYS FORGET THAT ONE!

AND · SO

AH, WHO CARES? BESIDES, WHAT DIFFERENCE MAKES IT, IF, FOR MY UGLINESS, I SHALL NEVER LIE WITH A WOMAN?

BAROQUE SHIPWRECK.

CONSEQUENTLY.

1.

2.

3.

ROCOCCO DEJEUNER

HA HA HA

LATER

STILL, NOBODY LIKES ME

THAT **GOETHE**--HE'S A FAMOUS HUMANIST! I'VE GOT TO DO SOMETHING TO **IMPRESS** HIM!

PERHAPS I'LL COMBINE TWO DISPARATE FIELDS OF CIVILIZATION INTO ONE... THAT SORT OF TRICK IS ALL THE RAGE AT THE MOMENT... *LESSEE NOW...*

AHA! **I** KNOW... I'LL MIX UP ART AND LITERATURE... **THAT'LL** GET HIS GOAT!

THUS.

NICE WORK, M'BOY... BUT I AM DYING...

HE LIKES IT!

CITY of GOLD. PART TWO: ORIGINS of CULTURE.

HAHAHAHAHA!

OPPOSITE, RIGHT **Chris Ware's meticulous re-creation of** 1930s-style comic-book covers and pages are alluring. His skill at cartoon lettering that hits exactly the right note adds a level of virtuosity to this cover for *Un-told Tales of Kavalier & Clay*.
Letterer, illustrator: Chris Ware
Clients: Michael Chabon, McSweeney's Quarterly Concern

LEFT **Precisely planned on complex grids**, Chris Ware's comics work uses clear lettering as a navigational device in this page from *Renaissance Man: Antonio de Bologna*.
Letterer, illustrator: Chris Ware
Client: The Whitney Museum of American Art

bibliography

antique type and lettering specimen books produced by foundries

Album d'alphabets pour la pratique du croquis-calque (Paris: Fonderies Deberny & Peignot, c. 1920).

Petzendorfer, Ludwig. *Schriften Atlas* (H. Berthold, Vienna, 1914).

S.A. Fabrique de Caractères en Bois (Roman Scherer, Lucerne, c. 1920).

Schriften un Zierat für Anschläge, Große Druck-Arbeiten (J. G. Schelter & Giesecke, Leipzig, 1909).

Schriftproben. Verlagsgesellschaft Deutscher Konsumvereine mit Beschränkter Haftung (Hamburg).

Spécimen-album (La Fonderie Gve. Mayeur, Paris, c. 1899).

Specimen Book of Bauer Types (New York City, NY: Bauer Type Foundry, Inc., 1934).

Specimen Book of Type Faces (Western Typesetting Co. Ltd., Bristol, 1923).

Spécimen Général (Paris, France: Fonderies Deberny & Peignot, 1926).

Type (Catalog 25-A) (Chicago, IL: Barnhart Brothers & Spindler, c. 1915).

Type Faces (New York City, NY: Frederic Nelson Phillips, Inc., 1929).

Wood Letter (Sheffield, UK: Stephenson, Blake & Co., 1939).

books on design and type

Ackland-Snow, Nicola, et al. *Fly: The Art of the Club Flyer* (London: Thames & Hudson, 1996).

Adams, Steven. *The Arts & Crafts Movement* (Secaucus, NJ: Chartwell Books, 1987).

Becker, Stephen. *Comic Art in America: A Social History of the Funnies, the Political Cartoons, Magazine Humor, Sporting Cartoons and Animated Cartoons* (New York City, NY: Simon and Schuster, 1959).

Blackwell, Lewis. *The End of Print: The Grafik Design of David Carson* (San Francisco, CA: Chronicle Books and London: Laurence King Publishing, 1996).

———. *20th Century Type* (New York City, NY: Rizzoli and London: Calmann & King, 1992).

Cabarga, Leslie. *Progressive German Graphics 1900–1937* (San Francisco, CA: Chronicle Books, 1994).

Carter, Rob. *American Typography Today*

(New York City, NY: Van Nostrand Reinhold, 1989).

Chernevich, Elena and Mikhail Anikst, eds. *Soviet Commercial Design of the Twenties* (New York City, NY: Abbeville Press, 1987).

Couperie, Pierre, et al. *A History of the Comic Strip* (New York City, NY: Crown Publishers, 1968).

DeNoon, Christopher. *Posters of the WPA, 1935–1943* (Los Angeles, CA: The Wheatley Press, 1987).

Friedman, Mildred S. with Steven Heller, ed. and Walker Art Center. *Graphic Design in America: A Visual Language History* (New York City, NY: Harry N. Abrams, Inc., 1989).

Glauber, Barbara, ed. *Lift and Separate: Graphic Design and the Vernacular* (New York City, NY: The Herb Lubalin Study Center of Design and Typography, 1993).

Greiman, April. *Hybrid Imagery: The Fusion of Technology and Graphic Design* (New York City, NY: Watson-Guptill Publications, 1990).

Gottschall, Edward M. *Typographic Communications Today* (Cambridge, MA and London: The MIT Press, 1989).

Heller, Steven. *Design Literacy (continued): Understanding Graphic Design* (New York City, NY: Allworth Press, 1999).

Heller, Steven and Gail Anderson. *American Typeplay* (New York City, NY: PBC International, Inc., 1994).

Heller, Steven, and Seymour Chwast. *Graphic Style: From Victorian to Postmodern* (New York City, NY: Harry N. Abrams, Inc. and London: Thames & Hudson, 1988).

Heller, Steven and Louise Fili. *Typology: Type Design from the Victorian Era to the Digital Age* (San Francisco, CA: Chronicle Books, 1999).

Heller, Steven and Anne Fink. *Faces on the Edge: Type in the Digital Age* (New York City, NY: John Wiley & Sons, 1997).

Heller, Steven and Julie Lasky. *Borrowed Design: Use and Abuse of Historical Form* (New York City, NY: John Wiley & Sons, 1992).

Heller, Steven and Karen Pomeroy. *Design Literacy: Understanding Graphic Design* (New York City, NY: Allworth Press, 1997).

Heller, Steven and Christine Thompson. *Letterforms: Bawdy, Bad and Beautiful* (New York City, NY: Watson-Guptill Publications, 2000).

Hiesinger, Kathryn B. and George H. Marcus. *Landmarks of Twentieth-Century Design: An Illustrated Handbook* (New York City, NY: Abbeville Press, 1993).

Hollis, Richard. *Graphic Design: A Concise History* (London: Thames & Hudson, 1994).

Horsham, Michael. *20s & 30s Style* (London: Chartwell Books, Inc., 1989).

Julier, Guy. *The Thames & Hudson Dictionary of 20th-Century Design and Designers* (London: Thames & Hudson, 1993).

Kinross, Robin. *Modern Typography: An Essay in Critical History* (London: Hyphen Press, 1992).

Lesser, Robert. *Pulp Art* (New York City, NY: Gramercy Books, 1997).

Lewis, John. *The Twentieth Century Book: Its Illustration and Design* (London: Studio Vista Limited, 1967).

Lista, Giovanni. *Le Livre Futuriste* (Paris: Editions Panini, 1984).

Lupton, Ellen. *Mixing Messages: Graphic Design in Contemporary Culture* (New York City, NY: Princeton Architectural Press and San Francisco, CA: Chronicle Books, 1996).

McAlhone, Beryl, et al. *A Smile in the Mind: Witty Thinking in Graphic Design* (London: Phaidon Press, 1998).

McDermott, Catherine. *The Design Museum Book of 20th Century Design* (Woodstock, NY: Overlook Press, 1998).

Meggs, Philip B. *A History of Graphic Design* (New York City, NY: John Wiley & Sons, 3rd ed., 1998).

———. *6 Chapters in Design: Saul Bass, Ivan Chermayeff, Milton Glaser, Paul Rand, Ikko Tanaka, Henryk Tomaszewski* (San Francisco, CA: Chronicle Books, 1997).

———. *A History of Graphic Design* (New York City, NY: Van Nostrand Reinhold, 2nd ed., 1992).

———. *Type and Image: The Language of Graphic Design* (New York City, NY: Van Nostrand Reinhold, 1989).

———. *A History of Graphic Design* (New York City, NY: Van Nostrand Reinhold, 1st ed., 1983).

Miller, J. Abbott. *Dimensional Typography: Case Studies on the Shape of Letters in Virtual Environments* (A Kiosk Report) (New York City, NY: Princeton Architectural Press, 1996).

Minick, Scott and Jiao Ping. *Chinese Graphic Design in the Twentieth Century, 1870–1920* (New York City, NY: Van Nostrand Reinhold, 1990).

Müller-Brockmann, Josef. *A History of Visual Communications* (Teufen, Switzerland: Verlag Arthur Niggli and New York City, NY: Visual Communication Books, Hastings House, 1971).

Naumann, Francis M. et al. *Making Mischief: Dada Invades New York* (New York City, NY: Whitney Museum of American Art, 1996).

Remington, R. Roger and Barbara J. Hodik. *Nine Pioneers in American Graphic Design* (Cambridge, MA and London: The MIT Press, 1989).

Selz, Peter, and Mildred Constantine, eds. *Art Nouveau: Art and Design at the Turn of the Century* (New York City, NY: Museum of Modern Art, 1959).

Spencer, Herbert, ed. *The Liberated Page* (San Francisco, CA: Bedford Press, 1987).

Spiegelman, Art. *Comix, Essays, Graphics and Scraps*. Designed by Raw Books (Sellario Editore/La Centrale dell'Arte, 1998).

Steranko, James. *The Steranko History of Comics* (Reading, PA: Supergraphics, 1972).

Thomson, Ellen M. *The Origins of Graphic Design in America, 1870–1920* (New Haven, CT and London: Yale University Press, 1997).

Thorgerson, Storm and Aubrey Powell. *100 Best Album Covers: The Stories Behind the Sleeves* (London, New York City, Sydney: DK Publishing, Inc., 1999).

VanderLans, Rudy and Zuzana Licko, with Mary E. Gray. *Emigre: Graphic Design into the Digital Realm* (New York City, NY: Van Nostrand Reinhold, 1993).

Wozencroft, Jon. *The Graphic Language of Neville Brody* (London: Thames & Hudson and New York City, NY: Rizzoli, 1988).

Wrede, Stuart. *The Modern Poster* (New York City, NY: The Museum of Modern Art, 1988).

articles

Heller, Steven. 'Introducing the First Digital Lettering Tool'. *Baseline* (no. 38, 2002).

———. 'More than Wham Bang Boom'. *Baseline* (no. 35, 2001).

———. 'Do It Yourself: The Graphic Design of Punk Zines'. *Baseline* (no. 34, 2001).

———. 'Sho-Cards'. *Baseline* (no. 30, 2000).

———. 'Mapbacks: High End of a Low Art'. *Print* (XLVIII:III, 1994).

———. 'Alex Steinweiss: For the Record'. *Print* (XLVI:II, 1992).

Heller, Steven, and Barbara Kruger. 'Smashing the Myths'. *AIGA Journal of Graphic Design* (vol. 9, no. 1, 1991).

Lupton, Ellen. 'The Academy of Deconstructed Design'. *Eye* (vol. 1, no. 3, 1991).

Lupton, Ellen, and J. Abbott Miller. 'Deconstruction and Graphic Design: History Meets Theory'. *Visible Language* (28.4, 1994).

McCoy, Katherine. 'The Evolution of American Typography'. *Design Quarterly* (no. 148, Walker Art Center and MIT: 1990).

Poynor, Rick. 'Jon Barnbrook'. *Eye* (vol. 4, no. 15, 1994).

———. 'Pierre Bernard'. *Eye* (vol. 1, no. 3, 1991).

Rock, Michael. 'Fuse: Beyond Typography'. *Eye* (vol. 4, no. 15, 1994).

Spiegelman, Art. 'Comix 101: Forms Stretched to Their Limits'. *The New Yorker* (April 19, 1999): 77–85.

VanderLans, Rudy. 'Second Wind'. *Emigre* (no. 24, 1992).

websites and web articles

Brown, David E. Brown. 'Punk is Not Dead'. Metropolis Insites, July 1998. www.metropolis-mag.com

Communication Arts, www.commarts.com

Cooper-Hewitt, National Design Museum, www.si.edu/ndm

Emigre, www.emigre.com

Graphis, www.graphis.com/main.EN.html

The Herb Lubalin Study Center of Design and Typography, www.cooper.edu/art/lubalin

The Museum of Modern Art, www.moma.org

National Cartoonists Society, www.reuben.org

Print magazine, www.printmag.com

Rochester Institute of Technology Design Archive, http://wally.rit.edu/depts/ref/speccoll/#design

Society of Illustrators, www.societyillustrators.org

Scudiero, Maurizio, 'The Italian Futurist Book', www.colophon.com/gallery/futurism/index.html

Typographic, www.TYPOgraphic.com